CONFLICT AND VIOLENCE IN LEBANON:
Confrontation in the Middle East

HARVARD STUDIES
IN INTERNATIONAL AFFAIRS
Number 38

CONFLICT AND VIOLENCE IN LEBANON:

Confrontation in the Middle East

by Walid Khalidi

Published by the
Center for International Affairs
Harvard University

Copyright © 1979 by the President and Fellows of Harvard College
Library of Congress Catalog Card Number 77-89806 3/16/82
ISBN 0-87674-037-9 (Cloth)
ISBN 0-87674-038-7 (Paper)
Printed in the United States of America

The Center for International Affairs is happy to provide a forum for the expression of responsible views. It does not, however, necessarily agree with them.

085409

Harvard University
Center for International Affairs

Executive Committee

Created in 1958, the Center for International Affairs fosters advanced study of basic world problems by scholars from various disciplines and senior officials from many countries. The research of the Center focuses on economic, social, and political development; the management of force in the modern world; the problems and relations of advanced industrial societies; transnational processes and international order; and technology and international affairs.

The Harvard Studies in International Affairs, which are listed at the back of this book, may be ordered from the Publications Office, Center for International Affairs, 1737 Cambridge Street, Cambridge, Mass. 02138. Recent books written under the auspices of the Center, listed on the last pages, may be obtained from bookstores or ordered directly from the publishers.

About the Author _____

Walid Khalidi, a Palestinian professor of Political Studies at the American University of Beirut, is a graduate of the University of London and Oxford University. He has taught at Oxford and Harvard, and has been a Research Associate at Princeton University as well as at the Center for International Affairs and the Center for Middle Eastern Studies, Harvard University.

CONTENTS

ACKNOWLEDGEMENTS

I am grateful to many people for their help. It was Benjamin H. Brown, Adviser to the Fellows of the Center for International Affairs and its Acting Director during the first half of 1978, who first suggested to me the idea of writing on the Lebanese Civil War. Eric Nordlinger suggested the organization of the first four chapters and read an early draft of them. Early drafts of the same chapters were also read by Kamal Salibi, Tarif Khalidi, Michael Simpson, Ahmed Khalidi, and Rashid Khalidi. I benefited greatly from their comments. Mary Neznek, Nawwaf Salaam, Riyad Ashkar, and May Kadi gave valuable assistance with the gathering of data and documents. Eva Morvay and Deb Forrester stoically typed endless versions of the manuscript.

Maury Feld and Peter Berry were ever ready to assist at the Center's Library. Sally Cox and Jean Allison briskly solved every problem of life brought to their doorsteps during my two years (1976-78) of residence in Cambridge. The first year I was a Fellow of the Center for International Affairs and Visiting Lecturer in Government; the second, Research Associate at both the Center for International Affairs and the Center for Middle Eastern Studies. To Raymond Vernon, Director of the former, and Benjamin Brown, as well as to Muhsin Mahdi and A. J. Meyer of the latter my heartfelt thanks for their hospitality, help, and encouragement. A very special debt of gratitude I owe to Peter Jacobsohn, the Center for International Affairs' Editor of Publications, not only for his painstaking work on the manuscript but also for the warmth of his companionship during many hours of discussion and joint revision of the text.

TANTUM RELIGIO POTUIT
SUADERE MALORUM

This is neither a socio-political study nor a diplomatic or military history. It is partly a narrative and partly an interpretive political essay. Its subject is the genesis, development, and aftermath of the Lebanese Civil War of 1975-1976. Its cutoff point is 13 June 1978, the date of the final Israeli withdrawal from southern Lebanon. Although its focus is on developments inside Lebanon, one of the main themes I have tried to develop is that the Civil War and the subsequent prolonged crisis leading to the Israeli invasion in March 1978 were the result of the interplay between internal Lebanese developments and external ones. Chief among the external developments were the Arab-Israeli conflict and inter-Arab tensions that were themselves exacerbated by this conflict.

I was in Beirut during most of the period of the Civil War, having left it for Cambridge in September 1976. Since my arrival in the U.S. I have been back in Lebanon three times: in January and July 1977 and again in January 1978, spending on each occasion some three to four weeks there. Throughout the period of the Civil War and since then I have had access and have been on friendly terms with leading protagonists on all sides. I have naturally made use of data and insights thus gained, but because of the proximity to the events described I have not been able to use all the information at my disposal. For the same reason I have not always identified (whether in the text or the notes) the individuals whom I met or interviewed, or the sources of documents in my possession.

This work suffers from all the drawbacks of instant history. Its saving grace, if any, may lie in its very nature as instant history. Although writing under the immediate impact of terrible events, I have had an opportunity to observe many of these events and the actors involved at close range. I have written as a Palestinian and a student of the Arab-Israeli conflict, to whom Lebanon has been a second home, and the Lebanese tragedy the greatest catastrophe to befall the Middle East since the 1948 Palestine War.

A word about my concentration on the Maronites when dealing with the Christians of Lebanon. I do this for two main reasons. Firstly, I do not see the internal conflict in Lebanon as one fundamentally between the Christians as such and the Moslems as such. The conflict's sectarian dimension involves rather the Maronites on the one hand and the non-Maronite Lebanese on the other. To be sure, the antithesis is greatest between the Maronite Lebanese and the Moslem Lebanese, but the tension, for example, between the Maronites and the Greek Orthodox Lebanese (the second largest Christian community in the country), has been traditionally very great and indeed precedes Maronite-Moslem

13

tension. Secondly, the Maronites are the largest single Lebanese Christian community, constituting about one half the number of Lebanon's Christians (and about one third of its total population). There are more than twice as many Maronites as there are Greek Orthodox. They have held the reins of political and economic power since the establishment of modern Lebanon in 1920. Of all the Christian communities in the country they are the most conscious of their group identity, the best organized politically and militarily, and the most articulate and militant. They are the pace-setters for all non-Maronite Lebanese Christians who sympathize with them. Of course, a fuller and more detailed study would have to take into account the attitudes and perspectives of each Christian sect, viz., the Greek Orthodox, the Greek Catholics, the Armenian Orthodox and Catholics, the Protestants, etc. But this seemed unwarranted given the nature and scope of this book.

GLOSSARY

ADF	See Arab Deterrent Force.
Ahdab, Aziz, Brigadier	Lebanese Sunnite (see Sunnite) army officer, commander of the Beirut garrison. On 11 March 1976, he declared a *coup d'état* against President Suleiman Franjieh (see Franjieh).
Ain Rummaneh	Christian suburb of Beirut, scene of massacre on 13 April 1975 of 28 Palestinians—the Sarajevo of the Civil War.
Alawites	A Syrian Shiite (see Shiite) schismatic sect to which President Asad of Syria belongs.
ANM	See Arab Nationalist Movement.
Arab Army of Lebanon/ Army of Arab Lebanon	Name given to rebel units of Lebanese Army after their mutiny under Lieutenant Ahmed Khatib (see Khatib) in January 1976. Khatib's forces joined the National Movement (see National Movement).
Arab Deterrent Force (ADF)	The Inter-Arab Force (30,000 strong) agreed upon at the Riyad and Cairo summits in October 1976 to enforce the cease-fire ordered by these summits. The Syrian contingents formed the bulk of the Force. (See Riyad Summit and Cairo Summit).
Arab Nationalist Movement	Pan-Arab party founded in late 1940s by Palestinian Christian leader Dr. George Habash (see Habash).
Arafat, Yasir	Leader of the Palestinian Fath (see Fath) movement and Chairman

since February 1969 of the Executive of the Palestine Liberation Organization (PLO).

Asad, Hafez

Baathist (see Baath) President of Syria since November 1970.

As'ad, Kamel

Lebanese Shiite (see Shiite) traditional leader and Speaker of Parliament.

Baath (Party)

Literally "Resurrection," the name of the Pan-Arab socialist party founded in the early fifties by the Syrian Christian leader Michel Aflak. Different factions of the party currently rule in both Syria and Iraq.

Bekaa Valley

The fertile plain in eastern Lebanon lying between Mount Lebanon and the Anti-Lebanon mountain ranges bordering Syria.

Brown, Dean

U.S. diplomat and Washington's special envoy to Lebanon during the Civil War.

Cairo Agreement

Signed in Cairo on 3 November 1969 by Lebanese army commander and Yasir Arafat, chief of the PLO. It aimed at the regulation and control of Palestinian armed presence and activity in Lebanon.

Cairo Summit

A plenary summit of the heads of Arab states held on 25-26 October 1976 following the mini-summit at Riyad (see Riyad Summit). Both aimed at ending the Civil War in Lebanon.

Chamoun, Camille

Veteran Maronite leader, President 1952-58, member of the Lebanese Front (see Lebanese

Front), leading Maronite hawk. His two sons Dory and Dany played active roles during the Civil War.

Chehab, Fuad, General	Leading Maronite figure, commander of the Lebanese army 1943-1958, President 1958-1964. Died in 1975.
Constitutional Document	Name given to reform program announced by President Suleiman Franjieh on 14 February 1976 in an attempt to end the Civil War.
Deuxième Bureau	Military Intelligence Branch of the Lebanese Army, first given significant political role during presidency of Chehab (see Chehab).
Dhur Shuweir (Salient)	Town lying north of the Beirut-Damascus highway at the eastern approaches to Mount Lebanon (see Mount Lebanon)—the Maronite heartland. Together with its neighboring villages it constituted a salient in which heavy fighting took place at the height of the National Movement's (see National Movement) offensive in the spring of 1976.
Druzes	The name of a schismatic Shiite Moslem sect which has followers in Lebanon and Syria and to a lesser extent in Israel—(see Jumblat, Shiites).
Eddé, Emile	Leader of the Francophile Maronite faction in the early forties. During the Civil War his son, Raymond, several times a cabinet minister and member of Parlia-

ment, was critical of President Franjieh and the other Maronite leaders.

Ehden

Mountain stronghold of President Suleiman Franjieh in northern Lebanon. It was the scene of an attack on 13 June 1978 by Phalangist militiamen in which Franjieh's son, Tony, and the latter's wife and daughter were massacred (See Franjieh).

Erskine, Emmanuel, General

Commander of UNIFIL (see UNIFIL).

Fath

An inverted acronym for the "Movement for the Liberation of Palestine." In its inverted form it signifies "victory" in Arabic. The name of the largest Palestinian political and guerrilla organization, led by Yasir Arafat. It is the centrist backbone of the PLO (see Arafat, PLO).

Gemayel, Pierre

Leader of the Phalanges party— the largest political and paramilitary Maronite organization. Pierre is also a member of the Lebanese Front. His son Basheer, a leading hawk, is commander of the paramilitary forces of the Phalanges as well as of the United Forces of all Maronite militias in the country. Amin, Gemayel's younger son, has the reputation of being a moderate. (See Phalanges).

Geneva Conference

Refers to two things: a) The Geneva Middle East Conference held in December 1973 in the wake of the 1973 War. This was attended by Israel, Egypt, Jordan, the U.S., and the Soviet Union under the chairmanship of United Nations Secretary General Kurt Waldheim; b) The future reconvening of this conference with other Arab participants to pursue negotiations for an overall Middle East settlement.

Ghanem, Iskandar, General

Controversial Maronite commander of the Lebanese army and protégé of President Franjieh. Relieved of his duties in September 1975.

Golan I

The Syrian-Israeli disengagement agreement concluded in the wake of the 1973 War. The agreement was reached on 31 May 1974 and is still in effect.

Grand Liban

The name given by the French in 1920 to the modern state of Lebanon which they created in that year. It was "grand" because the new state involved the addition of largely Moslem districts and cities to Mount Lebanon province, the Maronite heartland proper (See Mount Lebanon).

Greek Orthodox

The Eastern (originally Byzantine) Orthodox Church. Most of the Arab Christians of Syria and Jordan belong to this church. In Lebanon they constitute the largest Christian community after the Maronites.

Haddad, Saad, Major

An officer of the regular Lebanese army (before its disintegration), protégé of Israel and commander of Maronite forces in "the 6-mile belt" near Israel's border.

Hafiz, Amin

Sunnite Prime Minister of Lebanon May-July 1973.

Helou, Charles	Maronite President 1964-1970.
Hoss, Salim	Sunnite ex-professor and banker, Prime Minister from 8 December 1976 and during the entire period covered in this book. His cabinet was composed largely of technocrats.
Jalloud, Abdul Salaam	Prime Minister of Libya. Jalloud paid several visits to Lebanon during the Civil War to mediate between Syria and the PLO.
Jumblat, Kamal	Traditional leader of the Lebanese Druze community, head of the Progressive Socialist Party, founder, leader, and main driving force behind the National Movement (see National Movement). He was assassinated in March 1977 and has been succeeded by his son Walid.
Kaddafi, Muammar	President of Libya.
Karami, Rashid	Sunnite traditional leader of Tripoli, several times Prime Minister before the Civil War, occupied this post again as from the summer of 1975, until the appointment of Hoss. (See Hoss). Rashid's father, Abdul Hamid, had also been Prime Minister in the 1950s.
Kassis, Sharbel, Father	Head of the Conference of Maronite Monastic Orders, and member of the Lebanese Front.
Khaddam, Abdul Halim	Deputy Prime Minister and Foreign Minister of Syria.
Khalid, Hassan, Sheikh	Sunnite Mufti (jurisconsult) of Lebanon, technically the head of the Sunnite religious establishment.

Khatib, Ahmad, Lieutenant	Sunnite ex-officer in the regular Lebanese army, Khatib led the mutiny of pro-National Movement units in January 1976, creating the Arab Army of Lebanon. (See Arab Army of Lebanon).
Khoury, Bishara, Sheikh	Leader of the Arabophile Maronite faction in the early 1940s, President 1943-1952.
Lebanese Front	The highest Maronite political and military decision-making body. It is a coalition of the four leading Maronite figures: ex-Presidents Suleiman Franjieh, Camille Chamoun, Pierre Gemayel of the Phalanges, and Father Kassis of the Monastic Orders. The Front was formed in 1976. It maintained its cohesion until early 1978, when Franjieh withdrew from it.
Litani River	It flows southwards in the Bekaa Valley in the east and then westwards into the Mediterranean. For most of its course it runs parallel to the Israeli border at a distance of between 2 and 15 miles in the east and 15 and 17 miles in the center and the west. Somewhere north of it ran the Israeli Red Line (See Red Line). The river was the farthest limit of the Israeli invasion in March 1978.
Mandate	The trusteeship arrangements under the auspices of the League of Nations which enabled Britain and France at the end of World War I to legitimize their occupation of several Middle Eastern countries. The territories of Syria and Lebanon fell under the French Mandate.

Marj Uyun

A town in the eastern sector of the six-mile "security belt" inside Lebanon created by Israel. It is Major Haddad's main base of operations (see Major Saad Haddad).

Maronites

An eastern Catholic community named after their eponymous patron saint Marun (died c. 410 A.D.). They have been in full union with Rome since 1736. The largest and strongest Christian community in Lebanon.

Melkart Understanding

An agreement reached in May 1973 between the Lebanese Government and the PLO elaborating on some provisions of the Cairo Agreement and annulling others. So-called after the Beirut hotel in which it was concluded. (See Cairo Agreements).

Mount Lebanon

The mountainous hinterland of Beirut stretching from Tripoli in the north to Sidon in the south. It is inhabited largely by Maronites, the majority of whom live north of the Beirut-Damascus highway, and by Druzes, the majority of whom live south of it. As a result of inter-communal massacres in 1860 and under pressure from the European powers this area was accorded extensive local autonomy under the Ottomans.

National Movement

The highest political and military decision-making body during the Civil War of the Lebanese leftist-progressivist-radical Moslem alliance. Its leader was Kamal Jumblat. (See Kamal Jumblat).

National Pact (1943)

An unwritten understanding reached between the Christian and Moslem Lebanese in 1943. The Christians renounced their reliance on France, the Moslems their demand for union with neighboring Arab countries. The Pact became the basis of Lebanese independence the same year.

PLA (Palestine Liberation Army)

The regular army of the PLO, to be distinguished from the Palestinian guerrilla organizations. Units of this army were stationed in Syria, Jordan, Iraq, and Egypt. They are all technically under the command of Yasir Arafat. Several PLA units took part in the Civil War.

PLO (Palestine Liberation Organization)

Created by the Arab League in 1964, its leadership passed after the June War of 1967 from the hands of civilians into those of the guerrilla organizations, and particularly Fath. Yasir Arafat, leader of Fath, has been the chairman of the PLO's Executive Committee since 1969 (see Fath, and Arafat).

Phalanges Libanaises

A right-wing Maronite party (originally a Youth movement) formed by Pierre Gemayel in the mid-1930s. It has become the largest Maronite political and paramilitary organization (See Gemayel, and Lebanese Front).

Qabadai

Neighborhood strongman. In pre-Civil War days the power of traditional leaders, especially among the Sunnites, rested to a large extent on qabadais.

Red Line

A putative line visualized by the Israelis somewhere north of the Litani and possibly along it, beyond which the troops of the Arab Deterrent Force were not to cross southwards in the direction of the Israeli border. (See ADF).

Rejectionists/Rejection Front

A general designation given to Palestinian groups and organizations as well as to certain Arab parties and Arab countries (e.g. Libya, Iraq, and South Yemen). These reject a Middle East settlement that involves recognition of Israel. The Palestinian rejectionists favor the establishment of a democratic secular state in all Palestine including Israel, in which Jews and Arabs (whether Christian or Moslem) would be equal citizens.

Riyad Summit

A mini-summit called by Saudi Arabia in October 1976. It was attended by Lebanon, Syria, Egypt, the PLO, and Kuwait. It brought about an end to general hostilities in Lebanon and created the Arab Deterrent Force (see ADF).

Sadat, Anwar

President of Egypt since 1970.

Sadr, Musa, Imam

Populist head of the Shiite religious hierarchy. Founded the Shiite Movement of the Disinherited.

Saiqa

Literally "lightning." The name given to a Palestinian guerrilla group organized under the auspices of Damascus from Palestinian residents in Syria. The Saiqa is a member of the PLO.

Salaam, Saeb

Veteran Sunnite traditional leader, several times Prime Minister—the last time under the Franjieh administration from 1970 to 1973.

Sarkis, Elias

Elected President of Lebanon on 8 May 1976, he assumed his office on 23 September 1976, the day Franjieh's term as President ended (see Franjieh).

Security Council Resolutions 425 and 426

Both resolutions were adopted on 19 March 1978 after the Israeli invasion of Lebanon. The first called for total Israeli withdrawal and the creation of a UN interim force. The second spelled out the force's terms of reference.

Shiites

The second largest sect in Islam after the Sunnites. Called thus because Shiites were originally *Shiah* or partisans of Ali (d. 661 A.D.), first cousin of the Prophet Muhammad and husband of his only surviving daughter, Fatimah. The Shiites are probably the single most numerous sect in Lebanon—they are also the underdogs of the country. (See Sunnites, Druzes, Alawites).

Shtaura Accord

An accord reached in July 1977 at Shtaura, a town in the Bekaa Valley, between the Lebanese Government, the PLO, and Syria. The accord involved a timetable for the implementation of the Cairo Agreement in the light of the Riyad and Cairo summits. (See Cairo Agreement, Riyad Summit, Cairo Summit, and Melkart Agreement).

The Shuf

The Druze heartland lying south of the Beirut-Damascus highway in the central mountain area.

Sinai II

The second Egyptian-Israeli disengagement agreement after the 1973 War. The agreement was reached on 4 September 1975.

Solh

A prestigious Sunnite family. Its most distinguished member was Riyad Solh, co-architect with Bishara Khoury of the National Pact (1943). Two other members, Taqiyuddin and Rashid, served as Prime Ministers in succession on the eve of the Civil War (see Bishara Khoury, and National Pact 1943).

Sunnites

The "orthodox" sect in Islam, so-called after the "sunna" or lifestyle and rules of conduct of the Prophet Mohammad. The Sunnites were politically the most powerful of the Moslem sects in Lebanon (See Shiites, Druzes, Alawites).

Tel Zaatar

Palestinian refugee camp in the suburbs of Beirut. After a siege lasting 53 days, the camp was overrun by Maronite militiamen on 12 August 1976, with a heavy loss of Palestinian lives.

Tyre Salient

The city of Tyre and a coastal corridor linking it to the Litani river and the north was not occupied during the Israeli invasion in March 1978—hence the name.

UNIFIL

The United Nations Interim Force in Lebanon created by Security Council Resolutions 425 and 426 of 19 March 1978, immediately after the Israeli invasion of Lebanon.

MAPS

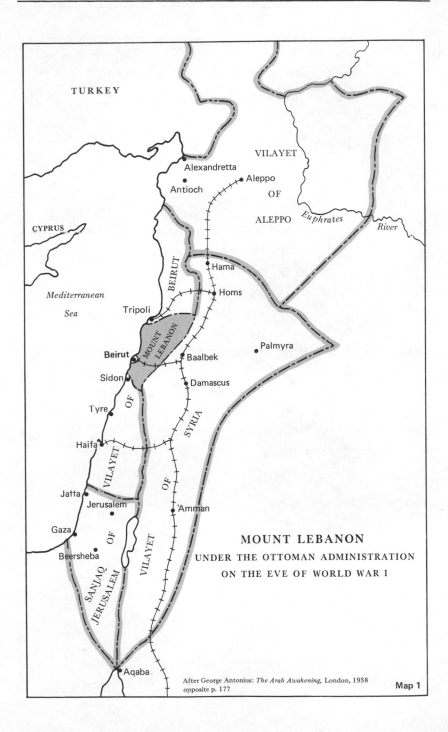

TURKEY

VILAYET

Alexandretta

Aleppo

Antioch

OF

ALEPPO

Euphrates

CYPRUS

River

BEIRUT

Hama

Homs

Mediterranean

Sea

Tripoli

MOUNT LEBANON

Beirut

Palmyra

Sidon

Baalbek

OF

Damascus

Tyre

SYRIA

Haifa

VILAYET

Jaffa

OF

Jerusalem

'Amman

Gaza

MOUNT LEBANON

Beersheba

UNDER THE OTTOMAN ADMINISTRATION

SANJAQ

VILAYET

ON THE EVE OF WORLD WAR I

JERUSALEM

OF

Aqaba

After George Antonius: *The Arab Awakening,* London, 1938
opposite p. 177

Map 1

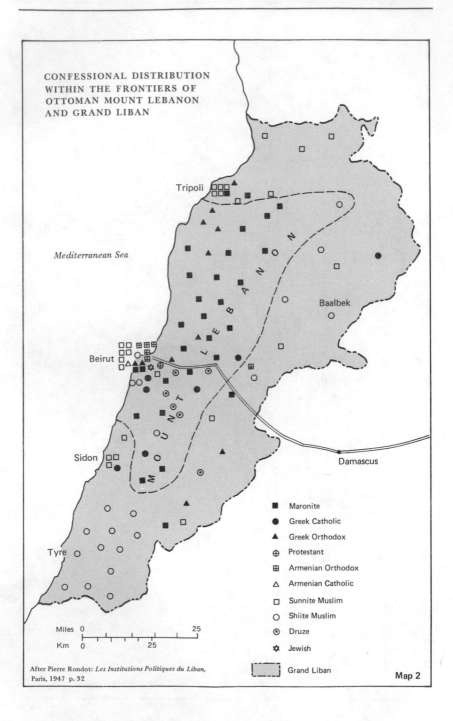

CONFESSIONAL DISTRIBUTION
WITHIN THE FRONTIERS OF
OTTOMAN MOUNT LEBANON
AND GRAND LIBAN

Tripoli

Mediterranean Sea

Baalbek

Beirut

Damascus

Sidon

Tyre

Miles 0 _____ 25
Km 0 _____ 25

After Pierre Rondot: *Les Institutions Politiques du Liban,*
Paris, 1947 p. 32

■ Maronite
● Greek Catholic
▲ Greek Orthodox
⊕ Protestant
⊞ Armenian Orthodox
△ Armenian Catholic
□ Sunnite Muslim
○ Shiite Muslim
◉ Druze
✿ Jewish

Grand Liban

Map 2

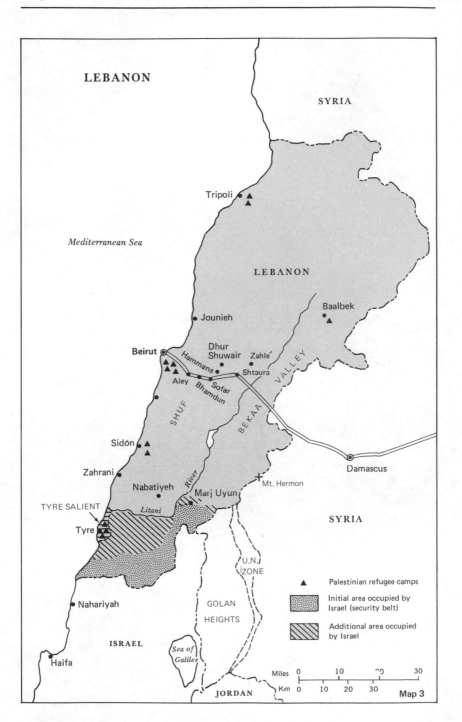

LEBANON

SYRIA

Tripoli ▲

Mediterranean Sea

LEBANON

Baalbek ▲

Jounieh

Beirut

Dhur Shuwair

Zahle

Hammana

Shtaura

Aley   Sofar

Bhamdun

BEKAA VALLEY

SHUF

Sidon ▲

Zahrani

Damascus

Nabatiyeh

Mt. Hermon

Marj Uyun

SYRIA

TYRE SALIENT

Litani   River

Tyre ▲

U.N. ZONE

Nahariyah

GOLAN

HEIGHTS

ISRAEL

Sea of Galilee

Haifa

JORDAN

▲ Palestinian refugee camps

Initial area occupied by Israel (security belt)

Additional area occupied by Israel

Miles   0   10   ~0   30

Km   0   10   20   30

Map 3

THE HISTORICAL
BACKGROUND

1. From the French Occupation to Independence: 1920-1943

At the end of World War I, present-day Lebanon and Syria fell to the French, just as Palestine, Transjordan, and Iraq fell to the British. This was part of the horsetrading between the victorious Western allies for the division of the Arab provinces of the vanquished Ottoman Empire that had fought on the German side during the war.[1] This division of the spoils was presently consecrated by the League of Nations under a new trusteeship system known as the Mandate, ostensibly deriving from the principle of self-determination enshrined in Article 22 of the Covenant of the League. France's status in international law, in both Lebanon and Syria, was therefore that of a mandatory power, although the wishes of the local population were not consulted in the choice.[2]

In the summer of 1920 the French had marched on Damascus, ousted Feisal, the son of Sherif Hussein of Mecca and military leader of the Arab Revolt, and imposed themselves by force of arms. Feisal had just been declared by an all-Arab congress King of a united Syria, Lebanon, Palestine, and Transjordan.[3]

The present states of Lebanon and Syria (as indeed the other Arab countries mentioned above) were post-World War I creations, having formerly been—though not within their present borders—only provinces or sub-provinces of the Ottoman Empire.[4] The vast majority of the inhabitants of these provinces were Arabs, the bulk of whom belonged to the two major sects of Islam, the Sunnites and the Shiites. The former predominated in the Western Arab provinces, the latter in the Eastern ones, particularly in those that became Iraq.[5] A small schismatic Moslem sect—the Druzes—were concentrated largely in Mount Lebanon as well as in the Syrian interior.[6] There were also Christian Arab minorities scattered throughout the region. These belonged mostly to the Maronite or the Greek Orthodox sects.[7] The Maronites, like the Druzes, were concentrated in Mount Lebanon. The Greek Orthodox were more evenly distributed in the Arab provinces.

Mount Lebanon was the ancestral home of both the Druzes and the Maronites.[8] As a political entity it included the mountainous hinterland of Beirut lying west of the Bekaa Valley, to the north and south of the main Beirut-Damascus highway. Northwards, Mount Lebanon reached the environs of Sunnite Tripoli and southwards those of Sunnite Sidon. As a result of inter-communal massacres between the Maronites and Druzes in 1860,[9] the Ottoman Empire, under pressure from the European powers, reorganized the administration of Mount Lebanon. The Mountain was accorded greater local autonomy and linked directly to Constantinople rather than to a regional provincial capital.

✓In 1920, the French, following their imperial instincts, decided to divide the Ottoman Arab provinces that had fallen to them into several mini-states, including present-day Lebanon. Modern Lebanon was built around Mount Lebanon, the autonomous province of 1860. To this were now attached the three principal Sunnite coastal cities of Beirut (formerly the capital of the Ottoman province of Beirut), Tripoli, and Sidon, the hinterlands of the two latter cities, as well as the entire Bekaa Valley. The population of the Tripoli hinterland was largely Sunnite Moslem or Greek Orthodox, that of the Sidon hinterland and the Bekaa Valley largely Shiite.[10] All these components were now to constitute "Grand Liban," as the new state was called. The French expectation was that this new state (Grand Liban—present-day Lebanon) would be Maronite-dominated and would thus become a permanent French dependency in the Moslem Arab Near East.

The more "conservative" Maronites considered themselves *from*, but not *of*, the Near East. Their spiritual and cultural Meccas were Rome and Paris,[11] respectively. Their mythology stressed their non-Arab or pre-Arab ancestry.[12] To these Maronites, the French-protected Grand Liban of which they were at once the core, linchpin, raison d'être, and chief beneficiary, was an act of historic justice. It was tantamount to the lifting of a putative Moslem siege laid as early as the 7th century with the advent of Islam. But many Maronites had more complex attitudes towards their Moslem environment and Arab antecedents. These were a composite of pride, fascination, and awe. Also involved was a yearning to be accepted for what they were and a craving to put their talents and access to the West to use for the benefit of the Arab World.[13]

To the Moslems, particularly the Sunnites, the French were latter-day

Crusaders bent on avenging the defeat of Latin Christendom at the hands of Saladin. They had torn them away from Mother Syria. They had crushed their hopes for postwar independence. The Moslems were all the more disoriented because they had taken literally the Western commitment to Woodrow Wilson's principle of self-determination and had placed their naive trust in the secret promises of their British wartime "allies."[14] Nor were the Moslems alone in these feelings of rejection and betrayal. Most Greek Orthodox Arabs as well as Christian Arabs of other denominations, including many Maronites, shared these sentiments and traumas. To the Moslems, again, the French posed the threat of cultural annihilation already meted out to their coreligionists in Algeria. To incorporate them into Grand Liban was to add insult to injury: it had turned them overnight from a millennium-old ruling majority into a "minority." They had become subject not only to the French themselves but to France's client, the Maronites.[15] Thus the Christian-Moslem cleavage predating Grand Liban was exacerbated by its establishment. It became the cornerstone of the new state—a perhaps not undesirable effect from the perspective of its French architects.

In 1926, the French-controlled Lebanese administration promulgated a constitution for Grand Liban. This perpetuated the customary system of confessional representation that had prevailed in Mount Lebanon. Seats in the executive and legislative branches of government as well as appointments in the civil service were to be "equitably" distributed among the sects, though no specific ratios were explicitly provided for. But because the Moslem population included in Grand Liban was greater than the French cared to admit, and their natural growth rate higher than that of the Christians, the French were careful not to allow demographic reality to be accurately reflected in the actual distribution of seats and political posts between the two major religions. They also avoided the holding of a regular census, the only occasions when they conducted one being in 1922 and 1932. In these censuses (which left much to be desired in matters of procedure), the Christians were officially declared to be the majority, which they may indeed have been at the time.[16]

The Maronites as well as the other Christian sects (the Greek Orthodox, the Greek Catholic, etc.) participated in the French Lebanese system, although the Greek Orthodox were somewhat lukewarm in their attitude because of their closer historical identification with the Arabs and their traditional alienation from the "Latin" Maronites.[17] The French also succeeded in inducing the participation of the bulk of the Moslem Shiite and Druze communities because of the traditional alienation of these two sects from the Sunnite Moslem majority during centuries of Sunnite dominance in Ottoman and pre-Ottoman times.[18] The Sunnites, on the other hand, with few exceptions, were adamant in their boycott of the French mandate and their espousal of the cause of independence and union with Syria. But even among the Maronites, the struggle for power as well as French high-handedness produced in time a divergence of attitudes vis-à-vis the French which centered around two Maronite leaders: Emile Eddé, a Francophile, and Bishara Koury, who was more Arab-oriented.[19]

The fall of France during World War II sealed the fate of the French in the Levant. Under British tutorship,[20] Bishara Khoury and the Lebanese Sunnite pan-Arab leader Riyad Solh[21] hammered out an unwritten agreement known as the National Pact which provided the basis for Lebanon's independence from the French in 1943.[22]

The essence of this agreement was Moslem renunciation of the aim of Arab union (their *enosis* complex) in return for Christian renunciation of Western (French) protection (their metropolitan complex). Corollary to this was a reinterpretation of the constitutional provisions for the "equit- able" distribution of seats in the executive and legislative branches of government in such a way as to approximate more closely to proportional representation. The ratio agreed upon was 6:5 in favor of the Christians. This may or may not have reflected the actual distribution of the population between Christians and Moslems. But it was based on the assumption that the Moslems had acquiesced in this weighting of the system in favor of the Christians, irrespective of demo- graphic realities, in order to allay Christian minoritarian fears of engulfment by the overall regional Moslem majority.[23] The implied reason for this Moslem "concession" was that the relatively large Christian community of Lebanon made it *sui generis* among the predominantly Moslem Arab countries, requiring the adoption of a "noblesse oblige" attitude towards Lebanese Christian and particularly Maronite susceptibilities.[24]

Shortly thereafter, however, in 1945, Lebanon joined the Arab League.[25] This did not signify Maronite acceptance of either "union" with the other Arab countries or of the Arab identity of Lebanon. The Arab League was, in fact, loosely confederal in structure and based on the principle of unanimity in decision-making.[26] What it did signify was a ceremonial bow in the direction of Pan-Arab Lebanese Moslem sentiment. The specific issue of the identity of Lebanon was ingeniously skirted in the National Pact by declaring that the country had an Arab "face."[27] It was presumably hoped that with time the Moslems and Christians would both acquire the taste of being *Lebanese*—no more, no less.

2. From Independence to the Civil War: 1943-1975

The Khoury Administration: 1943-1952

Under the administration of President Bishara Khoury the rules of the game of the confessional system were applied and developed in the new circumstances of independence. The leaders of the various sects were clearly the principal players and beneficiaries of the system. The three highest posts, in order of precedence according to protocol, of President, Speaker of the House, and Prime Minister went respectively to the Christian Maronites, Moslem Shiites, and Moslem Sunnites.[28] (The Speaker's role was more ceremonial than political.) It also became clear that none of the sects was monolithic and that intense rivalries existed among the leaders of each sect, generating cross-cutting influences which bolstered the system. The crucial role of the President[29] emerged, as well as the importance of a working rapport between Maronite President and Sunnite Prime Minister.[30] The President was faced with the challenge of preserving the privileged position of the Christians while appearing to transcend his loyalties to them. The Prime Minister had to reconcile his position as Number Two with his role as an equal partner to the President in his capacity as the representative of the Moslem party to the National Pact of 1943.

Khoury's foreign policy balanced moves popular in Moslem circles with moves popular with the Christians. His involvement in the Palestine War of 1948 and his admission of some 150,000 Palestinian refugees was of the first kind,[31] although many Christians also approved these policies. The termination of the economic union with Syria in 1950 (a relic of the French joint mandate over both countries) was of the second kind.

With the end of economic union with Syria the laissez-faire and service-oriented trend in the Lebanese economy became firmly entrenched. The 1948 Palestine War brought with it a considerable influx of the talent and wealth of the Palestinian bourgeoisie, as well as the diversion of the regional transit traffic (because of the establishment of the state of Israel) from Haifa to Beirut. But Khoury's Achilles heel was his nepotism and the growing corruption of his administration. These, and his decision to amend the Constitution to secure his reelection, eventually rallied a powerful coalition of sectarian leaders, both Christian and Moslem, against him. When a national strike was declared demanding his resignation, Khoury called on the Maronite Army Commander General Fuad Chehab to break it. In a coup d'état by omission, Chehab demurred and Khoury resigned. His successor was Camille Chamoun, a former supporter of Khoury under the French Mandate.

The Chamoun Administration: 1952-1958

The interaction between domestic and foreign policy issues during Chamoun's administration revealed the country's high permeability to regional developments and influences. By 1956 the population had almost doubled as compared to 1932.[32] The disparity of living conditions between Christians and Moslems was reflected in mounting Moslem grievances against the socio-economic order. These were exacerbated by inadequate governmental social services, administrative corruption, and the Maronite-dominated political system. Nasser's charismatic spell enabled him to establish direct "plebiscitary" links with the Moslem Lebanese urban masses, raising their level of expectations, and activating their feelings of pride and defiance. Nasser thus undercut the authority of the traditional Moslem leaders who hastened to pay their "homage" to Cairo, to the growing distaste and consternation of the Maronites.

Chamoun fell out with his Moslem Sunnite Prime Minister over the issue of the diplomatic action to be taken in support of Nasser during the 1956 Suez War. By pushing on with an anti-Nasser foreign policy, exemplified by his endorsement of the Eisenhower Doctrine propounded in early 1957 to contain both communism *and* radicalism in the Middle East, Chamoun only aggravated the Christian-Moslem cleavage.[33] Inspired by his own boldness, as much, perhaps, as by the promptings of anti-Nasser capitals both Arab (Baghdad and Riyad) and non-Arab (Washington, London, and Paris),[34] Chamoun proceeded with an electoral "reform" calculated to reduce the influence of the pro-Nasser Moslem sectarian oligarchy. As the result of the parliamentary elections of 1957 showed, he was only too successful. The elections eliminated leading pro-Nasser Moslem leaders (the Sunnite Saeb Salaam, the Shiite Ahmad Asad, and the Druze Kamal Jumblat) and returned pro-Chamoun Moslem deputies with no power base of their own. This seemed only to undermine still further the legitimacy of Chamoun's regime in the eyes of the Moslem masses. The ensuing civil war took a toll of some 2000 lives. But by the time the U.S. Marines had landed in July 1958 (in the aftermath of the anti-monarchical and anti-Western revolution in Iraq), a stalemate had already been reached. The country had been saved from an open religious conflict by Chamoun's genius for antagonizing Christian[35] as well as Moslem members of the establishment.

Another contributory factor was the Moslem leadership's fundamental commitment to the Lebanese political *status quo*, notwithstanding the general Moslem infatuation with Nasser.

But the title of savior of the republic must be awarded to the Maronite Army Commander, General Fuad Chehab. He now repeated his coup d'état by omission of 1952 by refusing to obey Chamoun's order to pit the army against the predominantly Moslem rebels. Chehab's policy greatly strengthened the trans-sectarian centripetal influences resulting from Christian opposition to Chamoun and paved the way for his own Presidency.

The Chehab Administration: 1958-1964

Chehab's refusal to use the army in a repressive role endeared him to the Moslem if not the Maronite masses. But this welcome Christian-Moslem symbiosis through Chehab was tempered by a growing estrangement between the senior leader of the Moslem Beirut rebels, Saeb Salaam, and Chehab himself. This development was partly the result of idiosyncratic factors; it was also due to their differing conceptions of the relationship that should obtain between Maronite President and Sunnite Prime Minister. For the greater part of his term, Chehab relied for Moslem oligarchic support on Rashid Karami as his Prime Minister, as well as on the dynamic Druze leader Kamal Jumblat. (Karami had been the more pliant Sunnite rebel leader during the Civil War of 1958.)

Chehab conceived of a grand strategy for the invigoration and consolidation of the system. In foreign affairs he followed an avowed policy of détente with Nasser. Domestically, he aimed at a *para-étatisme* paternalistically centered on his person. In this way he hoped to bypass the bulk of the oligarchs both Christian and Moslem, whom he contemptuously dubbed "fromagistes"—cheese-eaters. He concentrated power in a kitchen cabinet led by a trusted Maronite technocrat, Elias Sarkis. Sarkis was to oversee a series of ambitious socio-economic reforms designed to improve the conditions of the deprived Moslem areas. The ultimate objective was to win over the Moslem population to the concept of Lebanese (as opposed to Pan-Arab) nationalism.

But the seemingly inherent immobilism of the system and the extent of administrative corruption soon caught up with Chehab. He sought to cut the Gordian knot by increasing resort to the Deuxième Bureau (Military Intelligence Branch of the Army) which was effectively under his command. The proliferation of Deuxième Bureau personnel into

ubiquitous mini-ombudsmen operating with less than maximum tact of-
fended the susceptibilities of the Maronite oligarchs. These had been
already piqued by Chehab's pro-Nasser bias and were harboring
mounting fears of his Caesarean ambitions.[36] An additional cause of their
displeasure was Chehab's sponsorship of the Phalanges Party, an
expanding countrywide Maronite "rational" political organization which
was rapidly supplanting the more traditional patron-client relationship
of the Maronite oligarchs based on clan or village loyalties.[37] Meanwhile
an activity of the Deuxième Bureau which was to have future relevance
was its systematic wooing of the network of Moslem neighborhood
strongmen (qabadais) on which Sunnite urban leadership was heavily
dependent.

Small wonder that a grand Moslem-Christian coalition was eventually
formed whose aim was to block Chehab's alleged intent (by now a
customary charge against an incumbent president) to seek reelection.
Too fastidious or weary to make a bid for himself, Chehab succeeded in
having his nominee, Charles Helou, elected as the next president.

The Helou Administration: 1964-1970

With no power base of his own, Helou became the hostage of the
Deuxième Bureau whose activities continued unabated. The rapport
between the Presidency on the one hand and Karami, Jumblat, and the
Phalanges Party on the other was maintained, as was the "ostracism" of
Saeb Salaam. Helou ran up against the same forces of political immobilism and administrative corruption that had frustrated his formidable
predecessor. Except that with the slowing down of the pace of reform
during the Helou administration, little hope was entertained for the
future in this respect.[38]

A series of momentous regional developments was to absorb Helou's
time and energies (such as they were). These developments began with
Israel's diversion of the River Jordan in 1964 and climaxed in the 1967
War. The political fallout of this war in Lebanon took the form of the
abrupt intensification of the process of radicalization among the Moslem
intelligentsia (particularly the student body) and the urban and rural
masses. Soon after the 1967 War, Palestinian commandos began to
infiltrate Lebanon from Syria with the encouragement of Damascus. This
resulted in the steady polarization of Maronite and Moslem opinion
about the commandos' presence and activities. The vehemence of the
opposition to the Palestinian presence of certain Maronite oligarchs (e.g.,
Raymond Eddé and ex-President Camille Chamoun) was partly aimed

at Chehab, perceived to be the "efficient" power—through the loyalist Deuxième Bureau—behind the "dignified" facade of Helou. The Deuxième Bureau was seen as playing a subtle game of frightening the Maronite oligarchs and even President Helou himself (because of the latter's presumed attempt to shake off the Deuxième Bureau's tutelage) with the Palestinian bogey, by turning a blind eye to Palestinian commando infiltration into the country in the service of some ulterior purpose of Chehab.[39]

As Israeli retaliatory raids in response to Palestinian operations from Lebanese soil extended their area of devastation, matters came to a head between President Helou and his Prime Minister Karami.[40] Rather than sanction army containment of the Palestinian commandos (whose presence and activities were passionately supported by his Sunnite constituency), Karami tendered his resignation in May 1969 while accepting to continue to serve *ad interim*. When the Lebanese army, stung by Maronite charges of collusion with the Palestinians, exploited this hiatus in government and started a series of vigorous operations against the Palestinian commandos, the indignation of Moslem and radical opinion, now led by Jumblat, mounted ominously. Karami, characteristically clinging to both his resignation and his premiership, appealed in desperation to Nasser. On 3 November 1969 Nasser successfully mediated the so-called Cairo Agreement between the PLO and the Lebanese army.[41] The essence of the agreement was the legitimization and control of the commando presence and of operations against Israel. Palestinian armed presence was henceforth to be restricted to certain localities while operations against Israel were to be secretly "coordinated" with the Lebanese army.

There was an immediate Maronite outcry. The anti-Chehabist Maronite oligarchs saw this as still very much in line with Chehab's old policy of détente with Nasser in order to curry favor with the Moslems. But the more important effect was that it strengthened the trend towards the organization of militias by the Maronites. The Phalanges had already had a militia of their own for many years but now the infection spread to ex-President Camille Chamoun, Suleiman Franjieh (the Maronite leader in northern Lebanon), and others. The Maronites' militia fever in turn confirmed the worst suspicions of the Lebanese Moslems and radicals, as well as those of the PLO.

At the presidential elections of 1970, a coalition of Maronite leaders and the Sunnite Saeb Salaam again concentrated on preventing the dreaded prophesied return of Chehab. In fact, Chehab again had a nominee—his old aide, Elias Sarkis. Sarkis was defeated by this coalition and, paradoxically, by the Chehabist Jumblat, whose bloc split its votes. Suleiman Franjieh, the mountain chieftain from the north, was elected President by a majority of one vote.

The Franjieh Administration: 1970 to the Beginning of the Civil War, April 1975

Franjieh called on the veteran Sunnite leader Saeb Salaam, an old friend and political ally, to form the cabinet. Their first move was to dismantle the Chehabist Deuxième Bureau. Salaam's cabinet of young, politically "untainted" but inexperienced technocrats soon lost its reformist zeal. After some 18 months of the experiment and with little to show for it, a new cabinet was formed based on the traditional oligarchical recipe (minus Jumblat, a veteran rival of Salaam). This, together with mounting rumors about Franjieh's favoritism towards his clansmen and their transgressions, snuffed out any residual illusions about possible reform. The outcome of the parliamentary elections of 1972 demonstrated how weighted the electoral system was in favor of the oligarchs. But the overwhelming victory of a young, altogether unknown neo-Nasserist candidate against an established conservative rival in Beirut was an index of the crystallizing Moslem and radical mood.[42] This mood, however, was best exemplified by the vigor and intensity with which the National Movement (a coalition of radical and leftist parties organized by Jumblat in 1969) pressed during the elections for the deconfessionalization of the system—a frontal assault on the 1943 National Pact.

After the 1970-71 Civil War in Jordan, the PLO virtually transferred its center of activities to Lebanon. Israeli retaliatory raids against Lebanese border villages gave new momentum to the steady exodus of Moslem Shiite peasants towards the shantytowns and Palestinian refugee camps ringing Beirut in the east and to the consolidation of a "comradeship in misery" between the two communities.[43] The disillusionment of the Shiite intelligentsia (particularly the students) and rural masses with their traditional leaders paralleled the Sunnite disillusionment with their own leadership. The Shiite phenomenon was best reflected in the deep penetration of Shiite areas by radical, and particularly the Marxist, political organizations. It was also reflected in the increasing militancy of Musa Sadr, the populist head of the Shiite religious hierarchy, against the regime.

The appointment of Maronite General Iskandar Ghanem, a noted disciplinarian and close friend of Franjieh, as army commander, against a background of potential friction between the Lebanese army and the Palestinian commandos, heightened the suspicions of the National Movement and the PLO. Thus, when the Israelis carried out their raid of April 1973 into the heart of Beirut, assassinating three top leaders of the Palestinian *Fath* organization, monster anti-government demonstrations were staged by the National Movement. Prime Minister Salaam demanded the resignation of General Iskandar Ghanem and, when Franjieh refused, himself resigned. This was the watershed of the Franjieh administration, as the Maronites asked themselves: If Salaam cannot control the Moslem "Street," who can? And if Franjieh and Salaam, the old-time friends, cannot establish a working rapport between themselves as President and Prime Minister, who can?

The spiraling tension between the Lebanese army and the PLO erupted in May 1973 in the most serious confrontation between them since 1969. The Lebanese Air Force was brought into action for the first time against Palestinian positions inside refugee camps. But the new Prime Minister, Amin Hafiz, Salaam's successor, mediated a new accord with the PLO (the so-called Melkart Understanding)[44] which partly reaffirmed and partly circumscribed the provisions of the 1969 Cairo Agreement.

In spite of Hafiz's success, he was unacceptable to the Sunnite oligarchs because he had been Franjieh's nominee and was considered a "second-tier" Sunnite (i.e., ineligible to membership in the Sunnite Prime Ministerial "club").[45] The Sunnite establishment was engaged in a rearguard action, ostensibly against the Maronite establishment, but in fact in an outbidding game with the National Movement in an attempt to rehabilitate itself with its Moslem constituency that was now falling increasingly under Jumblat's sway.

Franjieh bowed before unprecedentedly solid ranks of the Moslem oligarchs demanding Hafiz's resignation. But he quickly turned the tables against them by asking Jumblat to bless Hafiz's successor. Two members of the politically respected Solh family, but themselves politically powerless, succeeded each other as Prime Minister: Taqiyuddin Solh (July 8, 1973, to October 31, 1974) and Rashid Solh (October 31, 1974, to May 23, 1975). The nominees of Jumblat and the National Movement participated in their cabinets alongside the Phalanges. This was an ironically anachronistic resurrection of the old Chehabist formula.

But it was also a dangerous ploy on the part of Franjieh. The arrangement served only to deepen the cleavage between the strategic allies of the system, the Maronite and Sunnite establishments. It also accelerated the outbidding game between the Sunnite establishment and the National Movement. It was at this point, for example, that Karami, a phlegmatically self-composed master of the Lebanese political ring, first declared that he himself would run for President. His ostensible ground for doing so was that the allocation of the Presidency to the Maronites was only customary and not ordained by the Constitution. Likewise, the Moslem establishment raised the shrill cry of "musharaka," i.e., equal distribution of power between the President and Prime Minister, thus fanning the flames of intersectarian hatred. Not to be outdone, the Shiite Musa Sadr, himself now fighting a rearguard action against his own radicals, announced in March 1974 the establishment of the Shiite Movement of the Disinherited. He threatened to march on the capital at the head of his army of underdogs, there to squat in the palaces of the affluent, both Christian and Moslem.

The 1973 October War produced a temporary lull. But Kissinger's step-by-step diplomacy activated the Palestinian and Arab rejection fronts.[46] Meanwhile, continuing Israeli retaliatory raids against Palestinian incursions and clashes between the Lebanese military and the Palestinian commandos prompted Phalangist leader Pierre Gemayel to demand a national referendum to "revise" the 1969 Cairo Agreement, which he had earlier endorsed.

It was in this atmosphere that Maaruf Saad, the Sunnite leader of the Popular Nasserist Organization of Sidon, was shot when a demonstration he was leading in support of a strike by local fishermen confronted army units. The strike had been called in protest against the extraordinarily ill-timed formation of an offshore fishing monopoly sponsored by, of all people, ex-President Camille Chamoun. Maaruf Saad's death from his wounds on 6 March 1975 touched off a violent populist uprising in Sidon. Palestinian commandos joined radical Lebanese militiamen to thwart Lebanese Army attempts to control the city. The episode epitomized the dynamics of interaction between the various local factors that constituted the Lebanese crisis. From the National Movement perspective, the "Maronite" army was seen as acting on behalf of Maronite big business. From the Maronite perspective, Palestinian participation in the Sidon fighting was but a taste of what was to come and incontestable proof of Palestinian commitment to a Lebanese social and political revolution. At the governmental level the uneasy alliance between the National Movement cabinet members and their Phalangist colleagues reached the breaking point. The National Movement was now blamed by its own constituency as well as by the rival Moslem establishment for army brutality in Sidon. It tried to recover the initiative by calling for the immediate resignation of the Maronite Army Commander, General Iskandar Ghanem. Massive counter-demonstrations in favor of the army commander were promptly organized by the Maronites. The polarization of the country now engulfed the army—the one institution that had saved it in the earlier crises of 1952 and 1958.

2

THE CIVIL WAR

1. From Ain Rummaneh, April 1975, to the Franjieh-Karami Accord, November 1975

The Sarajevo of the Lebanese Civil War occurred at Ain Rummaneh, a Christian suburb of Beirut, on 13 April 1975. Unknown assailants fired at a Sunday church gathering attended by Pierre Gemayel, leader of the Maronite Phalanges, killing his bodyguard and two others. Maronite militiamen in blind retaliation ambushed a bus passing through the neighborhood a short while later, massacring the 28 passengers (mostly Palestinians) on board.

Widespread clashes immediately erupted in the country between Maronite militiamen on the one hand and National Movement and Palestinian militiamen on the other. But the political reaction of the National Movement came in the form of a declaration proscribing the Phalanges, with whom henceforth no political dealings would be countenanced.[17] As Maronite opinion instinctively rallied round the Phalanges, the latter threw down the gauntlet to the National Movement by withdrawing from Rashid Solh's National Movement-sponsored cabinet, thus forcing its resignation.

His lines of communication now broken with both the Sunnite establishment and the National Movement, Franjieh called on a retired gendarmerie brigadier, Nureddin Rifai (a third-tier Sunnite on the political scale), to form the new cabinet which also included a majority of military officers. Instantly, if momentarily, closing their ranks, the National Movement and the Moslem establishment demanded Rifai's resignation and nominated Karami as the sole candidate for successor. Franjieh had no option but to comply.

Meanwhile, PLO leader Yasir Arafat, who under the immediate

impact of Ain Rummaneh had precipitately endorsed the proscription of the Phalanges, met with Franjieh. At the latter's request he made a public statement to the effect that the PLO was not a party in Lebanese domestic politics and would abide by the 1969 Cairo Agreement.[48] But the meeting, the last to take place between them, failed to produce the expected rapport.

With such a powerful mandate, Karami seemed in a position to establish a working relationship with Franjieh. But he had been nominated by the Moslem-National Movement consensus as sole Sunnite candidate for the premiership precisely because his relations with Franjieh were known to be severely strained. Matters were further complicated by the fact that the proscription of the Phalanges had somehow to be bypassed in the formation of the new cabinet. The only Maronite leader other than Pierre Gemayel acceptable to Maronite opinion as a member of Karami's forthcoming cabinet was ex-President Camille Chamoun, with whom Karami had literally not been on speaking terms since the 1958 Civil War. But Chamoun it was.

For several weeks between July and August a truce of sorts prevailed. On 22 August Franjieh declared in a speech that the Constitution "was not sacred," thus hinting at a preparedness for wide-ranging reform. Meanwhile, however, the National Movement had announced its own reform program on 18 August whose principal plank was the deconfessionalization of the system.[49]

With the security situation again deteriorating daily, the most pressing issue was whether or not to use the army to maintain law and order. This was vehemently advocated by Chamoun, the Interior Minister, and just as vehemently opposed by Karami in his capacity as both Prime Minister and Defense Minister.

The security and reform issues became interlocked: No reform before security, the Maronites maintained, and they meant the curtailment through army action of Palestinian transgressions in support of the National Movement as a preliminary to the subjugation of the latter. No security before reform, maintained the National Movement, and they meant the use of the Palestinians as leverage to secure a revolutionary change in the status quo.

Incidents of appalling savagery flared up, partly as the result of the operation of the *lex talionis* in a society based on the clan and extended family now armed to the teeth and caught in the grip of sectarian hysteria. In late August large-scale fighting spread from Zahle in the Bekaa Valley to Tripoli in the north. As a conciliatory gesture, Franjieh replaced General Ghanem as army commander with a more palatable Maronite. But apparently reacting to this concession, the Phalanges launched a full-scale attack on downtown Beirut on 17 September. Karami came under mounting National Movement and Moslem establishment pressure to "explode" the situation in the face of "the real culprit"—the President. The resignation of Franjieh was now openly demanded by Salaam and the Maronite "dissident" Raymond Eddé[50] as the only solution to the crisis.

On 20 September Syrian Foreign Minister Abdul Halim Khaddam opened his country's diplomatic offensive by arranging for a cease-fire. He also prevailed upon the Maronite Patriarch[51] to declare himself opposed to the partition of the country—the implicit Maronite Sword of Damocles over the Moslem head.

This paved the way for Karami to call for a Committee of National Dialogue to include the principal oligarchs and leaders. The meetings were held in the eerie surroundings of the beleaguered former Ottoman Grand Serail where the Prime Minister's office was located. Chamoun attended the first session or two, only to boycott the proceedings on the grounds that the Committee was a tactic to dodge the issue of army intervention. Jumblat attended under Syrian and Palestinian pressure but would not address Pierre Gemayel of the Phalanges. The mere formation of the Committee was a tribute to the oligarchs' lingering sense of political upmanship just as it was a pathetic exercise in nostalgia for consensual politics. Soon enough, however, the meetings degenerated into a dialogue of the deaf.[52] The assembled oligarchs may not have heard one another but they could not have failed to hear the rising din of bursting mortar shells and machine-gun fire outside.

As violent fighting broke out in the suburbs of Beirut and Maronite villages were overrun in the north, the Phalanges (probably with Egyptian support) called for the intervention of the Arab League. Israel warned against Syrian intervention in Lebanon, and Jumblat declared the Maronite objective to be the creation of a "second Israel" in Lebanon. On 24 October a fierce battle began between the Phalanges and the National Movement for the control of the Beirut hotel area. On 27 October fighting broke out again in Zahle in the Bekaa Valley, and at Damour, south of Beirut.

By late October Karami was at the end of his tether and in an "explosive" mood. He suspected Franjieh of sabotaging him and colluding with Chamoun and Gemayel to force him out of office because he had been imposed upon Franjieh by the Moslem-National Movement consensus. The combined efforts of a Vatican emissary, Cardinal Paolo Bertoli (November 9-16), and the former French Prime Minister Maurice Couve de Murville (November 19-30), as well as Syrian and Palestinian mediation, deflected Karami from his collision course with Franjieh.[53] By

14 November the two had reached a decision to cooperate more closely with each other.

2. From the Franjieh-Karami Accord to Franjieh's Constitutional Document, February 1976

The first fruits of the Franjieh-Karami rapport were concurrent public statements by the two leaders on 29 November. These implied agreement on tackling the reform issue as a priority (a concession to the National Movement), and, with this in mind, inclusion in the cabinet of the National Movement nominees. But the latter, spurning "tribal reconciliations," insisted on prior acceptance of their reform program (i.e., deconfessionalism) as the essential prerequisite for participation in the Cabinet.

On 6 December the Syrians boldly tried to break the deadlock by inviting Phalangist leader Pierre Gemayel (who had been proscribed by the National Movement) to Damascus. On the same day the Unforeseen (that great protagonist of History) stepped on to the stage: Four Phalanges company commanders were ambushed and murdered inside Maronite-held territory, even while Gemayel was in the Syrian capital.[54] In a mad spasm of vengeance, 200 Moslem civilians were seized within hours by Maronite militiamen and butchered. In retaliation, National Movement forces reinforced by Palestinian militiamen launched a major successful offensive against Phalangist positions in the hotel and downtown areas of Beirut. To compensate for their defeat in these two areas, the Phalanges overran a Moslem hamlet in the suburbs of Beirut, while a Christian village was simultaneously being overrun by pro-National Movement forces in the Bekaa Valley. Meanwhile, Palestinian mediatory efforts to maintain lines of communication between Yasir Arafat and ex-President Camille Chamoun (now Minister of Interior) floundered when another Moslem village in the Beirut suburbs was seized by Christian militiamen.

It was at this point, on 16 December, that Franjieh, bitterly denouncing the Palestinians, decided to turn in earnest to Damascus. This was a fateful decision, inasmuch as the earlier Syrian interventions had been initiated by Damascus. Now the Lebanese President was calculatingly inviting Syria into Lebanon to redress the balance in favor of the Maronites.

The essence of Franjieh's strategy at this stage seemed to be to concede the principle of reforming the status quo, to circumscribe the reforms, to bargain from a position of military strength, and to prevail on Syria to contain the National Movement and the Palestinians.

The Maronites thus held a carrot and a stick. Their stick was two-forked. Between 31 December 1975 and 13 January 1976, Maronite leaders issued strong hints of partition and "federal" formulas, both anathema to the Moslems and the National Movement. This prompted even the Syrian Foreign Minister to warn that Syria would "reunite" Lebanon with itself rather than see it partitioned. Militarily, a major Maronite offensive was launched in early January with the siege of the Palestinian Tel Zaatar refugee camp in the eastern suburbs of Beirut. It continued with the overrunning by 12 January of the Dbaiyeh refugee camp north of the city, which, ironically enough, was inhabited by Maronite Palestinians. By 19 January the Karantina slum area (inhabited by Moslem Lebanese and Palestinian-protected) had been stormed and bulldozed. The Palestinian and Moslem Lebanese death toll from these operations was about 1000, with the expellees numbering about 20,000. In a counter-offensive, the National Movement and Palestinian forces found themselves engaged in trading territory with Maronite militiamen in the eastern suburbs of Beirut. But the major thrust of the National Movement was directed against Chamoun's fief south of Beirut: the Maronite town of Damour, its neighboring village of Jiyeh, and the adjoining suburbs of Saadiyat where Chamoun's residence was located.[55]

The National Movement and the Palestinians were caught off guard by the force of the Maronite offensive. Yasir Arafat, who was still hoping to avoid an all-out confrontation with the Maronites, had kept the bulk of his forces deployed in the south near Israel's borders. The National Movement offensive at Damour bogged down, causing great anxiety to Jumblat because of the town's proximity to the Shuf, his Druze home base. An SOS by the Moslem and National Movement leadership to Damascus resulted in the dispatch by Syria of Palestine Liberation Army contingents (regular PLO units stationed in Syria and technically under Arafat's control). The arrival of these reinforcements allowed Arafat to withdraw some of his troops from the south for use against Damour. It was only with the help of these troops, and in spite of Lebanese Air Force strikes, that on 20 January Damour, Jiyeh, and Saadiyat were overwhelmed, with Chamoun's son Dany barely escaping with his life. The Maronite death toll was 500, the Maronite expellees numbered some 7000. On the same day Jumblat, on a visit to Damascus, reportedly indicated his readiness for a political solution. The use of the Lebanese Air Force at Damour triggered the first overt signs of sectarian mutiny in the army. A certain Lieutenant Ahmed Khatib (a Sunnite), with a few score of his fellow soldiers, announced their break with the Lebanese Army to form the *Arab* Army of Lebanon with its headquarters in the Bekaa Valley.

As the Karantina was falling, Karami felt obliged to submit his resignation. Franjieh suavely refused to accept it.[56] On 21 January Syrian Foreign Minister Khaddam reappeared on the scene. By the end of the following day a cease-fire had been arranged, and a Presidential communiqué issued. It announced agreement on the outlines of an overall solution and the formation of a Syrian-Lebanese-Palestinian Higher Military Committee to enforce the cease-fire. Presently Karami withdrew his resignation.

On 30 January a meeting of Moslem leaders was held at the house of the Lebanese Mufti (the country's highest Sunnite Moslem religious dignitary). It was attended by Salaam, Karami, Jumblat, Musa Sadr, and the Syrian Foreign Minister Khaddam. Khaddam described the outlines of a reform program to be shortly endorsed in public by Franjieh. This was to include 1) a 50-50 Christian/Moslem representation in Parliament (instead of the 6:5 ratio in favor of the Christians); 2) the election of the Prime Minister by Parliament (instead of his appointment by the President); 3) the three highest posts to remain, according to custom, respectively in the hands of the Maronites (President), Shiites (Speaker of the House), and the Sunnites (Prime Minister); 4) a new special High Court with the powers to try the President, Prime Minister, and other ministers; 5) the formation of a new High Economic Council; 6) naturalization for those eligible (mostly old Moslem residents of Lebanon hitherto denied Lebanese citizenship); and 7) a 50-50 division between Christians and Moslems of the top-category Civil Service posts, with the lesser posts, *including* military appointments, to be based exclusively on merit. (The last provision was clearly a concession to the demand for deconfessionalization.)

There was no opposition at this meeting to the suggested reforms. The main request of the Moslem leaders present was that the allocation of the Presidency to the Maronites (which they conceded) should not be embodied in a specific constitutional amendment but should remain a matter of custom. Another was that Lebanon should be specifically declared an Arab country—a demand which Khaddam (tactically, as it turned out) rejected. There was some disagreement as to what the new document announcing the reform program should be called and Jumblat's suggestion of "National Document" was accepted by all. This contribution by Jumblat seemed to indicate his willingness to go along with the proposed reforms. Towards the end of the meeting, however, Jumblat raised the issue of general deconfessionalization. It was vaguely agreed by some of those present (but neither by Khaddam nor by the majority) that the matter should be pursued further.[57]

On 7 February Franjieh visited Damascus. During this visit the Syrians officially "guaranteed" that the Palestinians would strictly implement "in letter and spirit" the 1969 Cairo Agreement. This seemed to have been Franjieh's precondition for the announcement of the reforms and it did not augur too well for the Palestinians. On 14 February a 17-point reform program (subsequently known as the "Constitutional Document") was announced by Franjieh in Beirut. This incorporated the seven points mentioned above as well as others, e.g., a 55 percent instead of an absolute parliamentary majority for the election of a President. A bonus for the Moslems (undoubtedly the result of Syrian persuasion) was the declaration that Lebanon was "a sovereign *Arab* state."[58] This was about as large a carrot as Franjieh could offer the Moslems and the National Movement without irretrievably alienating his own constituency.

3. From the Constitutional Document to the Election of President Sarkis, May 1976

The next step in the envisaged settlement was the formation of a cabinet of national union, including the National Movement, to implement the reform program. Meanwhile, Khaddam, the Syrian Foreign Minister, had left the meeting at the Mufti's house with the impression that he had won over the Moslem leaders to the proposed reforms. He now reportedly exchanged cabinet "lists" with Jumblat and others until a tentatively final one seemed to be under consideration.[59] But was a cabinet of national union a realistic possibility when the National Movement saw in Franjieh's 14 February Constitutional Document no more than a travesty of their hopes? The answer came in the form of the sudden enactment of a long-dreaded nightmare: the Lebanese Army began to fall to pieces. Early in March dissident Moslem troops seized their barracks, declaring their allegiance to the *Arab* Army of Lebanon led by Ahmed Khatib. It is common knowledge that neither the National Movement nor the Palestinians had been altogether innocent of this development. It is more than likely that Jumblat's apparent vacillation over the cabinet issue since 14 February was in anticipation of the army mutiny.

The disintegration of the Lebanese Army posed the most serious challenge to date both to Franjieh and the Syrians.

The High Command of the Lebanese Army was divided in its opinion on what to do to halt the process of disintegration. Some senior officers favored pressing Franjieh for action but could not agree on what specifically he should be asked to do. Others advised caution in the handling of their willful President. The senior officers were increasingly isolated in the Ministry of Defense from the Maronite middle and junior

officer ranks. The latter clamored for drastic measures against the army
rebels and particularly Lt. Khatib. In some instances they physically
threatened their superiors in their offices. In this atmosphere several
meetings took place between the members of the High Command and
Franjieh. These degenerated into bitter personal and political recrimi-
nations. On more than one occasion, Franjieh himself came under verbal
attack. After one such meeting Franjieh was rumored to have been so
angered as to have decided to dismiss the entire Army Command. Meanwhile, the Syrians, too, grew increasingly impatient with the dithering
of the High Command. They strongly urged it to move against Khatib,
suggesting a three-pronged approach to save the army from total collapse. A general amnesty was to be declared for the entire rebel rank
and file. These would be rounded up and reindoctrinated. The Syrians
themselves would dispatch a special task force for this purpose and
would also arrest Khatib and his principal aides. Although Franjieh
rejected the amnesty idea, the Lebanese High Command seemed, for a
while, to rally around the Syrian plan.[60] On 11 March, however, the
High Command was forestalled by the Sunnite Moslem commander of
the Beirut garrison, Brigadier Aziz Ahdab, himself somewhat of an *opera
bouffe* character. Ahdab, though troopless, proclaimed his own coup
d'état. His move most probably had Egyptian support and was carried
out with at least the foreknowledge of both the National Movement and
the PLO. Ahdab called upon both Franjieh and Karami to resign
forthwith and upon Parliament to meet within seven days to elect a
successor President. The brashness of Ahdab's action had a remarkable
impact. For one thing, the Syrian political offensive that had culminated
in the 14 February Constitutional Document had at least for the time
being ground to a halt.

Presently a Battle of the Barracks developed between Maronite and
Moslem soldiers. Each side tried to take control of garrison towns and
the army's heavy equipment. On 13 March, Parliament met in an
emergency session and by a two-thirds majority passed a petition asking
for Franjieh's resignation. Franjieh refused to comply. Thereupon,
Jumblat warned that the National Movement would take over the country and "change the system in the framework of a total revolution."
Simultaneously, two columns of Khatib's dissident army forces, backed
by Jumblat's Druze followers, converged on the Presidential Palace.

By now the Syrians had become convinced that there was no alternative to Franjieh's resignation, but were determined to bring this about
without "coercion." When Franjieh therefore appealed to the Syrians to
resume their mediation, an agreement was reached between the two
sides. The Syrians would use such troops as they had deployed in Beirut

to prevent the storming of the Presidential Palace. (These Syrian-controlled troops included PLA—regular Palestinian Liberation Army units stationed in Syria—and *Saiqa*—a Palestinian commando organization recruited by the Syrian ruling Baath party from Palestinian residents in Syria but often used as a front for Syrian regulars.) In return Franjieh would accept a constitutional amendment providing for Presidential elections six months (rather than the prescribed two) before the end of the Presidential term in September 1976, thus paving the way for the early election of his successor.[61]

Political developments were overtaken by military developments. On 21 March, upon Jumblat's announcement that a "total and irreversible"[62] military campaign would be waged, the National Movement (now backed by Khatib's armor and artillery as well as by Palestinian militiamen) opened a major offensive in the Beirut hotel area and penetrated deep into Phalangist-held territory. On 25 March the Presidential Palace (its approaches blocked by Syrian regulars masquerading as *Saiqa*) was shelled by Khatib's long-range artillery. Forced to abandon the palace, Franjieh fled to the sanctuary of the Maronite area of Mount Lebanon northeast of Beirut.[63] Panic seized sections of the Maronite community. An exodus to Cyprus began via Jounieh harbor.

Syria's top priority now was a cease-fire. At a meeting with Syrian President Asad on 21 March, Yasir Arafat had agreed to a cease-fire but urged Asad to receive Jumblat. While Pierre Gemayel, leader of the Maronite Phalanges, called upon "all able-bodied Christian men and women" to join the nearest militia posts, Jumblat reaffirmed on 26 March, the eve of his scheduled meeting with Asad, his determination to achieve "full military victory." Simultaneously, the National Movement, Khatib, and Palestinian troops converged in two columns on the Dhour Shuwair area. This was the gateway from the south-east to the Maronite heartland of Mount Lebanon north of the Damascus-Beirut highway.

A seven-hour meeting between Asad and Jumblat on 27 March ended in complete deadlock. This was perhaps the real turning point in the Civil War.[64] The disagreement seemed to spring from intriguingly deep idiosyncratic considerations resulting from the minoritarian backgrounds of the two men, as well as from Jumblat's adamant insistence on a military "solution." But under intense and mounting Syrian pressure, backed on 9 April by the penetration of Syrian armor some three miles into Lebanese territory as well as by the beginning of a Syrian naval blockade of National Movement ports (Tyre, Sidon, Tripoli), a cease-fire was declared. This allowed the Parliament to meet the same day (April 9). By the end of the session it had unanimously approved a constitutional amendment providing for the early election of a successor to Franjieh. But it was not until 24 April that Franjieh reluctantly added his signature to the amendment.

Meanwhile, Yasir Arafat and Syrian President Asad met in Damascus on 16 April and agreed to take a united stand against any resumption of the fighting. Partition was rejected as well as the "Arabization" of the conflict (i.e., calling in the Arab League—the Egyptian ploy) or its "internationalization" (i.e., calling in the UN or soliciting intervention by the Western powers—the Maronite ploy). Moreover, the Syrian-Lebanese-Palestinian Higher Military Committee, dismantled after the March 11 coup by Brigadier Ahdab, was to be reinstated. The National Movement ostensibly acquiesced and the Syrians pulled their armor back from Lebanese territory. Fighting, however, persisted in many parts of the country (e.g., 360 were killed on April 22 and 23 alone), though the National Movement offensive in the Dhour Shuwair area seemed to lose its momentum.

The next immediate political hurdle was the choice of the new President. There were two leading candidates: the "dissident" and courageously outspoken Maronite leader Raymond Eddé, favored by the National Movement; and the old Chehabist Elias Sarkis, considered by many to be Syria's "nominee." The elections scheduled for 1 May were postponed because of National Movement charges of Syrian bulldozing and worse.[65] But following Palestinian and Syrian pressure, elections were held on 8 May under the protection of Syrian-sponsored PLA and *Saiqa* troops. Sarkis received 66 votes out of a total of 69 deputies present, the pro-Eddé deputies having absented themselves. Jumblat and Salaam boycotted the elections, while Karami, Chamoun, Gemayel, and the Franjieh bloc voted for Sarkis.

4. From the Election of Sarkis to the Syrian Entry into Lebanon, June 1976

Sarkis' election did not prove to be the hoped-for psychological turning point, nor did Franjieh's obdurate resolve to stay on until the end of his term on 23 September help to make it so.

Even as Sarkis was being elected, the Lebanese crisis was entering a new phase. The protagonists in this phase were the Syrians on the one hand and the Palestinians on the other. The strain in Syro-Palestinian relations predated the Lebanese Civil War. It basically stemmed from the same cause as the tension between the Palestinians and the Lebanese authorities. This was the claim by the PLO of extraterritorial rights within the frontiers of a sovereign state, except that in the Syrian, as compared to the Lebanese, case the regime was in addition a military authoritarian one. Syria's creation of her own Palestinian militia, the *Saiqa,* and her *de facto* logistical leverage over PLA (Palestine Liberation Army-PLO) units stationed in Syria further heightened the tension. Relations were still further exacerbated by the increasing role given to *Saiqa* and Syrian-sponsored PLA units inside Lebanon—the Palestinians' last "sanctuary" after the expulsion of the PLO from Jordan in 1970/71. Another bone of contention was Syria's growing distaste for the alignment between the National Movement and the Palestinians. The air had not been altogether cleared at the summit meetings between Syrian President Asad and Arafat on 21 March and 17 April.

Yet another dimension of this nagging Palestinian-Syrian tension related to the prospects of an overall Arab-Israeli settlement. Kissinger's latest achievement in his step-by-step diplomacy had been Sinai II, the second Egyptian-Israeli withdrawal agreement concluded in September 1975. To be sure, Asad had violently reacted to this agreement because it seemed to herald Egypt's withdrawal from the field in the face of Israel. Arafat, of course, had no quarrel with this reaction by Asad to Sinai II. But to compensate for the "loss" of Egypt, Asad had drawn closer to Hussein. This was a suspect alignment to Arafat because of the liquidation by Hussein of the PLO in Jordan in 1970-1971 and because of Hussein's ambitions in the West Bank of Jordan. The steady "encroachment" of Asad in Lebanon in conjunction with the developing Damascus-Amman axis raised the specter of a Syrian-Jordanian formula for the West Bank within an overall settlement of the Arab-Israeli conflict at the expense of the PLO. Hence Arafat's paradoxical move early in 1976 to reopen his lines of communication with Sadat of Egypt, ostracized since Sinai II. It was not so much that Sadat was now forgiven. It was rather that Arafat needed Egypt as an immediate counter to Syria and the Maronites in Lebanon. He may also have hoped to renew Sadat's endorsement of the PLO's position on the West Bank to neutralize any potential Syrian-Jordanian coalition on the subject.

The first fruit of the new détente with Cairo was the all-too-eager dispatch by Sadat of PLA units stationed in Egypt to bolster Arafat, ostensibly against the Maronites, but equally against the Syrians—bitter critics of Sinai II.[66]

The Palestinian Rejection Front militias operating in Lebanon and backed by Iraq (the Syrian regime's mortal foe) jumped into the fray against the Syrian PLA and *Saiqa* units. The grand strategy of the National Movement-Palestinian alliance at this stage was to turn the Shuf, Jumblat's largely Druze-inhabited area south of the Beirut-Damascus highway, into a fortified base of operations against the Maronite heartland north of it. Meanwhile, Syria tried to maintain control over events by infiltrating additional PLA units into the country, to the mounting anger of Arafat. The quarrel burst into the open on 14 May when Arafat publicly but unsuccessfully ordered the Syrian-sponsored PLA units (technically under his command in his capacity as chief of the PLO executive and commander of the Palestinian revolutionary forces) to return to Damascus.

On 17 May Prime Minister Abdul Salaam Jalloud of Libya arrived in Beirut while the fighting between Maronite and National Movement militiamen continued apace, claiming 1000 casualties between 16 and 18 May alone. But Jalloud's purpose was to mediate between the Syrians and the Palestinians. Libya's direct cause of alarm at the Lebanese situation was the growing entente between Arafat and Sadat (of whose Sinai II the Libyans, to put it mildly, thoroughly disapproved). Thus Jalloud's instructions were to remove the cause of this entente—Arafat's disagreements with Syrian President Asad. On 21 May French President Valéry Giscard d'Estaing, while on a visit to the United States, announced his readiness to send "several regiments" to Lebanon if requested.[67] This idea had obviously been cleared with Washington and most probably represented Syria's latest version of "internationalization." This would permit French military presence in Maronite areas as a cover for an envisaged overt Syrian military intervention in the Moslem areas. The National Movement rejected the proposal while the Maronites welcomed it. Egypt, sniffing the Syrian hand in the formula, was critical. Presently, Palestinian-Syrian relations reached breaking point on 26 May when Arafat was allegedly denied transit through Syria on his way to Libya. As Arafat reached his destination by an alternative route to rally the Arab countries to his cause, the Syrians pondered their next move.

Late in May, apparently unauthorized units of the Arab Army of Lebanon went into action against isolated Maronite villages in the north. According to rumor, the commander of these units was orchestrating his moves with Syria. When the inhabitants of these villages "appealed" to Damascus, the PLO and National Movement leaders were convinced that these "appeals" were a prelude to a major Syrian move. And, in fact, on 1 June large Syrian forces with armor crossed the Lebanese frontier, even while, interestingly enough, Soviet Prime Minister Kosygin was visiting Damascus.

5. From the Syrian Entry to the Beginning of the Sarkis Administration, September 1976

By 5 June, some 6000 Syrian troops were streaming into Lebanon along three axes of approach: towards Tripoli in the north, along the main highway from Damascus to Beirut in the center, and towards Sidon via Jezzine in the south. Operating from Algiers and Tripoli, Arafat denounced the Syrian intervention as an attempt to liquidate the Palestinian Resistance. An emergency meeting of the Arab foreign ministers was scheduled for 6 June at Egypt's request. Simultaneously, Iraq sent troops to the Syrian border as a warning to Asad. On 6 June Libyan Prime Minister Jalloud arrived in Damascus to reactivate mediation between Arafat and the Syrian government.

As Jalloud began his talks, a skirmish took place between the Syrians and the National Movement-Palestinian militiamen in the foothills of the western Bekaa Valley. Syrian planes were wrongly reported to have gone into action. This touched off violent clashes in Beirut between National Movement and Palestinian militiamen on the one hand, and Syrian-sponsored *Saiqa* and PLA units on the other. The latter were surrounded and disarmed with remarkable speed, although they had been the first to go into action in many localities, suggesting some degree of coordination with the main advancing Syrian forces.[68] Many of the PLA troops went over to the PLO. Doubling their expeditionary force to 12,000, the Syrians on 7 June fought their way over the mountains to Sofar in the central sector and reached the environs of Sidon the same day in the south. A large Syrian armored reconnaissance squadron that tried to probe into the city had several of its tanks knocked out in an ambush by Palestinian and Lebanese Arab Army troops. The disabled hulks (and, the Syrians claim, their captured crews) were displayed in public to the great wrath of Damascus.[69]

Meanwhile, at their meeting on 6 June, the Arab foreign ministers had called for a cease-fire and the formation of an inter-Arab peace-keeping force to replace the Syrians and separate the combatants. On 10 June, Franjieh declared these resolutions null and void on the grounds that Lebanon had not been properly represented at the ministers' meeting.[70] With Franjieh subsequently mollified, advance Sudanese units of the 2300-strong peace-keeping force began arriving at Beirut airport while Syria declared its acceptance of the cease-fire. On the face of it, the Arab ministers' meeting was a defeat for the Syrians. But the small size of the force, the vagueness concerning its Syrian "component," as well as the absence of a timetable for Syrian withdrawal left the initiative in the hands of Damascus. This ended the first stage of this period.

On 16 June, the American ambassador, his aide, and his Lebanese driver were murdered in National Movement territory in Beirut, apparently at the hands of dissident elements on the extreme Left.[71] On 22 June Libyan units of the peace-keeping force began to arrive. The same day the Maronites launched their most ambitious offensive of the Civil War. Its objective was to overrun the Palestinian refugee camps and the National Movement-controlled slums separating Maronite-controlled East Beirut from Maronite territory farther east and north. The offensive started with concerted attacks on the twin camps of Jisr al-Basha and Tel Zaatar (ca. 4000 and 30,000 inhabitants, respectively).[72] As the former was stormed on 1 July, Arafat denounced Syria of complicity, and on 5 July returned to Beirut after an absence of over a month. On 8 July the National Movement-Palestinian forces launched a counter-offensive in the north near Tripoli to relieve the mounting pressure on Tel Zaatar. In a counter counter-offensive in the north the Maronites reached the gates of Tripoli, wreaking terrible vengeance on the Greek Orthodox and Moslem villages in the area sympathetic to the National Movement.[73] Meanwhile the Phalanges declared that there would be no cease-fire unless the Palestinians were disarmed, while Jumblat declared that Syrian withdrawal was the National Movement's condition for any cease-fire.

The Maronite militiamen tightened their grip on Tel Zaatar. On 11 July, Arafat appealed to all Arab capitals, and Libyan Prime Minister Jalloud returned to Damascus for another attempt at mediation while his President, Kaddafi, openly denounced the Syrians. On 12 July, Basheer Gemayel, son of Pierre and military commander of the Phalanges, exhilarated by the successes at Jisr al-Basha and in the north, annouced the aim of "liberating" all Lebanese territory from the National Movement-Palestinian alliance. On the same day, the Syrians pulled back from Sidon to Jezzine as a conciliatory gesture at Jalloud's request. Simultaneously, Jumblat announced the establishment of an *ad hoc* central administration throughout National Movement territory in belated response to a similar earlier move by the Maronites in Maronite-held territory.

On 22 July, two days after the Syrians had begun closing in on National Movement-Palestinian positions in the Dhour Shuwair area in the mountains east of Beirut, the PLO Executive opened negotiations in Damascus. Perturbed by signs of burgeoning Syrian-Palestinian détente, the Maronites intensified their pressure against Tel Zaatar. They also mounted a new offensive against the adjacent National Movement-controlled Shiite-inhabited shantytown of Nabaa.

On 29 July a joint Syrian-Palestinian communiqué, partly the result of Libyan mediation, announced agreement on the termination of the fighting and "non-interference" in Lebanon's internal affairs. The use of this last expression was the result of a compromise. Thus, "non-interference" was tacitly construed by the Palestinian party to the communiqué to mean Syrian withdrawal. But to the Syrians it meant Palestinian disengagement from the National Movement. The Palestinians also undertook to adhere to the 1969 Cairo Agreement and even commended the Syrian role "in defense of the Palestinian cause."

The phraseology of the communiqué provoked an immediate furor among the National Movement and the Palestinian Rejection Front. Their chagrin was due to the fact that the communiqué did not explicitly call for Syrian withdrawal, but, on the contrary, gave Damascus high marks for its defense of the Palestinians. Another phrase in the communiqué, to the effect that the Lebanese crisis "followed" Sinai II, prompted Cairo to describe the agreement as a "document of submission" of the PLO to Syria. Cairo's chagrin was aroused by the implication, however delicate, that there was a cause and effect sequence between its second disengagement agreement with Israel (Sinai II) and the Lebanese crisis. But the word "followed" had been included in partial absolution of Damascus for its anti-PLO role in Lebanon and as a bonus to the anti-Sinai II Libyans for their mediation efforts.

Nevertheless, a Lebanese-Syrian-Palestinian committee to implement the agreement met on 30 July. But developments in the field presented insurmountable obstacles to further progress. On 6 August the Shiite-inhabited Beirut shanty suburb of Nabaa fell to Maronite militiamen. On 12 August the Palestinian refugee camp of Tel Zaatar was subdued and stormed after a siege and bombardment lasting 53 days. Palestinian losses at Tel Zaatar were estimated at 3000 (mostly civilians) killed and at least as many wounded. Already on 5 August, Tony Franjieh (son of the President and commander of the Maronite militiamen in the north) had declared "full liberation" to be the Maronite aim, while Jumblat (in an attempt to escape isolation by a resumption of the Palestinian-Syrian détente) announced "all doors to an agreement" closed and all-out war against Syria as the only option. The breakdown of the latest Syrian-Palestinian agreement marked the end of the second stage of this period.

The third stage started with the "Battle of the Mountain." This revolved around the salient held by National Movement-Palestinian forces in Maronite territory (the Dhour Shuwair area) north of the Beirut-Damascus highway. The issue of this salient compounded the difficulty in arriving at a politico-military truce to pave the way for the formal investiture of Elias Sarkis. A special session of the Parliament was due to be held for this purpose on 23 September, the last day of Franjieh's term. The Maronites insisted on unconditional National Movement-Palestinian withdrawal from the salient, as did the Syrians. The National Movement-Palestinian alliance expected the Syrians to withdraw from Sofar in the central sector into the Bekaa Valley on a *quid pro quo* basis for their own withdrawal from the salient. The fighting in the salient meshed with the fighting in Beirut, where utterly indiscriminate shelling and counter-shelling of residential areas and civilian institutions had been going on unabated for weeks. Now the use by both sides of howitzers and rockets in addition to heavy mortars brought the violence to a new climax of savagery. This paralyzed all movement in the capital and threatened to make it physically impossible for Parliament to meet for the inauguration of President-elect Elias Sarkis.

On 13 August Syrian troops moved into Hammana, which straddled the main line of communications between the National Movement-Palestinian-held salient at the edge of the Maronite heartland and the Druze-National Movement sanctuary—the Shuf region south of the main Damascus-Beirut highway. Three days later Maronite militiamen opened their assault on their side of the salient in the area of Dhour Shuwair against the National Movement-Palestinian positions. On 19 August, Libyan Prime Minister Jalloud proposed the withdrawal of "all" combatants from the battle zone (i.e., Maronites, National Movement-Palestinian forces, *as well as* Syrians) to be replaced by troops of the Arab League peace-keeping force.

The first two weeks of September witnessed intensive secret but inconclusive talks between Damascus and the hawkish Palestinian leader Salah Khalaf (better known as Abu Iyad), the Number Two man in *Fath*. The PLO was apparently willing to consider unilateral withdrawal from the salient against binding guarantees that Syria would refrain from further moves against National Movement-Palestinian forces in Lebanon.[75] With five days to go before President-elect Sarkis' investiture, talks held on 17 September between Sarkis and Arafat on the same issue were likewise inconclusive. As the fighting in the salient between the Maronite militiamen and the National Movement-Palestinian forces intensified, the deadlock over the Libyan joint withdrawal proposal deepened. This was reflected in the continued escalation of the artillery and rocket barrages in Beirut uninhibitedly aimed by both sides against exclusively civilian targets. The entire constitutional transition from Franjieh to Sarkis was in jeopardy.

But in a lightning turn of events between 17 and 19 September President-elect Sarkis paid unannounced visits to Damascus and Cairo. During these visits he seems to have succeeded in reaching a compromise agreement with the two capitals: the site of the Parliamentary investiture meeting was resourcefully changed from Beirut to Shtaura, a honeymooners' hideaway in the Syrian-controlled Bekaa Valley. And it was there that on 23 September Elias Sarkis finally and formally succeeded Suleiman Franjieh as President of the Republic. The ceremony was boycotted by the Sunnite Saeb Salaam and the Druze Kamal Jumblat, but attended by a total of 67 deputies out of 99.

6. From the Inauguration of Sarkis to the End of General Hostilities

It will be recalled that Sarkis was elected President on 8 May. That event did not constitute the hoped-for psychological turning point in the Civil War, largely because of Franjieh's insistence on remaining in office until the end of his term on 23 September. Sarkis' inauguration on that day was the last remaining hope for such a psychological turning point, if indeed there still could be one. His inaugural address to the nation was both firm and conciliatory.[76] There would be no partition of the country. Its sovereignty was sacred. Lebanon supported the Palestinian cause, but the Palestinians should adhere to the 1969 Cairo Agreement. Addressing the National Movement, he expressed his determination "to champion any changes which . . . may contribute to national welfare." Syrian military presence in Lebanon was formally declared to be at the invitation of the Lebanese government.

Yasir Arafat responded immediately by declaring a cease-fire. But Syrian-Palestinian relations underwent a dramatic deterioration when on 26 September dissident anti-*Fath* Palestinian commandos stormed a Damascus hotel. The Syrians recaptured it and summarily hanged three of the captive assailants in public. But in their anger the Syrians directly accused the Palestinian organization *Fath* and peremptorily demanded the replacement of Arafat in the leadership of the PLO.

On 28 September the Syrians, complementing their political offensive with a military one, assaulted and dislodged the National Movement-Palestinian forces from the Dhour Shuwair salient in Maronite territory in a brisk battle, driving them southward towards the main Damascus-Beirut highway. The National Movement-Palestinian forces now regrouped at Bhamdun and Aley, below the Syrian armor massed at the mountain resort of Sofar. The Syrians paused at Sofar while contemplating their next move.

Meanwhile, National Movement-Palestinian hopes were pinned on an Arab League foreign ministers' conference scheduled for 15 October in Cairo, to be followed by a plenary summit of the Arab heads of state on 18 October. But the Syrian mood was reflected in demands made to the Palestinians between 4 and 11 October to retreat forthwith to their camps and disengage from the National Movement. The Palestinians, still hoping to buy time until the plenary summit convened, demanded the interposition of the Arab League peace-keeping force between themselves and their National Movement allies on the one hand and the Syrians on the other. While these talks were in progress, or rather foundering, the Syrian embassies in Rome, London, and Islamabad were attacked by motley groups of enraged pro-PLO Arab students.

On 13 October, five days before the scheduled plenary summit of the heads of Arab states, the Syrians made their next military move. They stormed Bhamdun, dislodging the Palestinian and National Movement forces in costly hand-to-hand combat. The Syrians took somewhat longer than they had expected—72 hours—to clear the town, and this seems to have had a sobering effect both on them and on the Arab capitals watching from the sidelines. Simultaneously, Damascus announced that President Asad would not be attending the Cairo plenary summit.

Syrian armor was now poised for the advance downhill against Aley. This was the regional headquarters of the National Movement and the Palestinians. Arafat appealed to the Arab heads of state and to Soviet leader Brezhnev. As Syrian columns tentatively edged their way towards Aley, Saudi Arabia at long last took its courage in both hands and declared that enough was enough. On 15 October, it called for a mini-summit to be held the very next day in its capital, preliminary to the Cairo plenary session which in the meantime had been postponed. Kuwait, Lebanon (Sarkis), the PLO, Egypt, and Syria were invited to attend. Miraculously, President Asad assented and Arafat was whisked off in a special Saudi plane to Riyad, while a de facto cease-fire between the Syrians and Palestinians came into effect as of 16 October.

The Riyad summit announced its resolutions on 18 October.[77] These included an immediate general cease-fire to be supervised by an inter-Arab force of 30,000 men under Lebanese President Sarkis. The force was empowered to confiscate heavy weapons and arrest violators. The combatants were to disengage within 10 days as of 21 October (the date when the cease-fire was to take effect in all areas of confrontation.) The Palestinians were to withdraw to areas in the south assigned to them by the 1969 Cairo Agreement. They were to adhere strictly to this Agreement. And a political dialogue for national reconciliation was to start forthwith in Lebanon. By avoiding to spell out the detailed composition of the new Arab Deterrent Force (ADF), the summit tacitly recognized the Syrian forces in Lebanon (declared at the summit meeting to be 30,000) as the main component of this Force. Concurrent meetings between Asad and Sadat cleared the air between them for the first time since Sinai II. A meeting between Arafat and Asad in Damascus on 20 October was tantamount to a new recognition by the latter of the former's status as leader of the PLO. On 25 October, 19 out of 21 heads of Arab states meeting in Cairo in the first plenary summit since October 1974 approved the resolutions of the Riyad mini-summit.[78] The only dissenters were Iraq and Libya.

Painting their helmets green—the color of the "Arab League" peace-keeping forces—the Syrians prepared to move into new positions. The major remaining obstacle was the Maronite refusal to accept the Syrian presence in Maronite territory. Sarkis' intensive talks with the Maronite quadripartite leadership in the Lebanese Front (ex-Presidents Franjieh and Chamoun, Pierre Gemayel of the Phalanges, and Father Sharbel Kassis of the Maronite Monastic Orders), supplemented by the persuasive reassurances of King Hussein of Jordan (an intimate friend of Chamoun's), overcame their opposition. The Syrians took their time before moving in, so as to allow the Palestinian moderate organization *Fath* to tighten its grip on dissident National Movement and Palestinian elements who might otherwise have resisted Syrian entry. As Palestinian troops began pulling out from Aley and surrounding areas and moved south, Lebanese President Sarkis appealed for an end to the bloodshed. He called upon all to greet the Syrians "in love and brotherhood." The 56th cease-fire since April 1975 came into effect.

But tension loomed on the horizon in the south, the new area of Palestinian concentration. For some time the Israelis had been warning that they would not tolerate the resumption of commando activities from southern Lebanon. Early in the Civil War they had started a "good neighbor" policy (medical aid, fuel, food, employment) to woo the Maronite border villages in anticipation of the return of the Palestinians. In recent weeks they had actively encouraged these villages through the supply of arms and logistical support to fill the vacuum created by the collapse of the central government. Emboldened, the Maronites had clashed with the local National Movement, the Palestinian and the Arab Army of Lebanon units, and had extended their control over a considerable part of the border with the exception of the central area around Bint Jubail, where the Palestinians were now concentrating.

On 14 November, some 6000 Syrian troops and 200 tanks moved into and occupied the entire city of Beirut, while other Syrian columns advanced into Maronite and National Movement territory in other parts of the country. The National Movement declared the very entry of "Arab" troops into Maronite territory a victory for themselves. If there was no great jubilation at the entry of the Syrians, there was no resistance to them either.

3

THE ACTORS

1. The Lebanese

The Lebanese Armed Forces

Long before the Ain Rummaneh massacre of April 1975 which triggered the Lebanese Civil War, the army had become controversial. It is a moot point, therefore, whether it could long have survived an attempt to use it to restore law and order after the Ain Rummaneh massacre. What is certain is that by the late autumn of 1975 it had become so polarized that even its Christian-dominated high command accepted its political unreliability and cautioned against its use in a security role.[79]

On the eve of its disintegration in January-February 1976, the Lebanese army was 19,000 strong.[80] Contrary to widespread belief, the Moslems had a slight edge over the Christians among the rank and file (53 percent: 47 percent), but the composition of the officer class was 65:35 percent in favor of the Christians, even though 18 of the 37 top posts were in Moslem hands.[81] The Christians, however, predominated at the operational and particularly the battalion commander level (there were 24 battalions in all), in addition to occupying the key posts of Commander of the Armed Forces and Chief of Military Intelligence.[82] The predominance of the Christians at the battalion commander level was not altogether the result of a sinister Maronite plot to retain effective control over the army. To some extent, at least, it was due to the logic of the promotion ladder and seniority considerations, because the Moslems, and particularly the Sunnites, had boycotted the Lebanese army when it was first organized under the French Mandate. Ironically, it was Franjieh who soon after he assumed the presidency had tried to rectify this state of affairs by insisting that the battalion commands be equally divided between Moslems and Christians. Franjieh's reorganization plan foundered, partly on the unavailability of suitable Moslem commanders, and partly, it is alleged, on the coyness of eligible but comfortable Moslem officers to assume combat responsibilities.[83]

In early 1976 the army had about 100 tanks and an equal number of armored cars and armored personnel carriers. It had about 75 artillery pieces as well as an equal number of self-propelled anti-aircraft guns. There were also some anti-tank missiles.[84]

The army split four ways. One section constituted itself the Arab Army of Lebanon under the Sunnite Lieutenant Ahmed Khatib and his fellow rebel officers. Another joined the right-wing Christian militias under the Maronite Colonels Antoine Barakat and Fuad Malik. A third, comprising perhaps the bulk of the officers, remained, at least until the autumn of 1976, "neutral" under the High Command and the Maronite army commander Hanna Saeed. A fourth section went home. In general, about half the rank and file joined one side or the other. The Sunnite Brigadier Ahdab, who declared the coup d'état of 11 March 1976, demanding the resignation of the President and Prime Minister, had more officers than privates, and most of his followers eventually joined Saeed or went home.

It is impossible to ascertain with exactitude the quantities of equipment that went to the various contestants, but a rough guess is that they went almost equally to Khatib, Barakat-Malik, and Saeed.[85] In calculating the clout of the Maronite and National Movement militiamen, one must therefore consider the proportion of the Lebanese army that joined either side as a crucial added component. The bulk of the Maronite army rebels seem to have joined Chamoun rather than Gemayel, while some of Khatib's heavy weapons were transferred to the Palestinian Resistance. The "navy" (five patrol boats) were largely under Maronite control, while, mercifully, the air force—some 24 combat aircraft—remained neutral.[86]

The Maronites

Until early February 1976, the principal objective of the Maronite establishment had been to maintain intact the *status quo* created by the National Pact of 1943. Until the late sixties, barring the panic of the early weeks of the 1958 Civil War, the Maronites had not perceived a serious challenge to this *status quo*. They had, of course, always been disenchanted with the Sunnite Moslem tendency to look for help across the Lebanese borders to the Arab capitals and also with the activities of the Pan-Arab and the radical and Marxist parties on Lebanese soil. But they were convinced that all these trends and events could be contained thanks to their control of the levers of power.

Developments in the period 1967-69 made the first serious dent in Maronite self-confidence. The 1969 Cairo Agreement indicated the extent to which the Palestinians, hitherto largely passive, had become a major defiant actor on the Lebanese scene under the dynamic leadership of the PLO—an actor who, moreover, had not been a party to the National Pact of 1943. Particularly galling to the Maronites was the manner in which the traditional Moslem élite and masses were seen to be "siding" with the Palestinians against their own country. But most alarming, perhaps, was the developing symbiosis between the Palestinians and avowedly anti-*status quo* radical and/or Marxist Lebanese and Pan-Arab groups and organizations (increasingly supported by revolutionary Arab groups and countries) under the leadership of the Druze Kamal Jumblat. Jumblat's role had a particularly traumatic effect on the Maronite mind because deep in their hearts the Maronites had counted on Lebanese Druze solidarity with them (on account of traditional Sunnite-Druze tensions) as a strategic reserve to counter Lebanese Sunnite Pan-Arab waywardness.

Jumblat's "defection" aroused feelings of atavistic insecurity in the Maronites: they perceived the shifting balance of power resulting from the developing alliance between Jumblat and Arafat as a threat to their identity and survival. When Jumblat fastened on deconfessionalism as the main axis of attack for the National Movement, the Maronites could see nothing but a Leftist-Palestinian conspiracy to dislodge them from their position guaranteed under the 1943 National Pact and reduce them to a Christian minority living on Moslem-Arab sufferance. The ghost of Coptification (reduction to the status of the powerless ancient Christian Coptic minority in overwhelmingly Moslem Egypt) seemed to be knocking at their front door.

The reason why deconfessionalization had such sinister implications to the Maronites is not difficult to discern. When Jumblat and the National Movement spoke of deconfessionalism, they fundamentally meant *political* deconfessionalism, i.e., doing away altogether with the distribution of *political* power between the Christian and Moslem "confessions" or sects *per se* upon which the National Pact of 1943 had been established. The National Pact had not only divided parliamentary power among the sects but had done so according to a fixed 6:5 ratio between Christians and Moslems. The implicit Christian-Moslem understanding at the time of the National Pact in 1943 (or such at least was the Maronite perception of it) was that this ratio would not be tampered with by the Moslems. This symbolized as much as it guaranteed Christian predominance in the country in perpetuity irrespective of demographic realities, i.e., the current or future numerical strengths of the Christian and Moslem populations in Lebanon.

The Moslems made this concession at the time (if indeed they made it) in order to wean the Maronites from dependence on their traditional foreign protector, France, which had been in actual occupation of the country since the end of World War I. What Jumblat and the National Movement in effect were now saying was that the Lebanese Moslems had meanwhile become such an overwhelming majority of the total population in comparison to the Christian Lebanese that the 6:5 ratio in favor of the Christians was obsolete and no longer tolerable. Jumblat and the National Movement appealed to the majoritarian principles: let political power in the country be distributed according to the demographic realities. Although no one knows what these realities are (since no official census has been undertaken in the country since 1932, precisely because of its explosive political implications), a fair guess would be that the Moslem Lebanese are today in a 55:45 majority compared to the Christian Lebanese.[87] The cry of political deconfessionalism raised by Jumblat and the National Movement was therefore seen by the Maronites as an attempt to establish Moslem majority rule, albeit under the guise of secularization, at the expense of the predominant Christian status guaranteed by the 1943 National Pact.

The concessions, such as they were, made by President Suleiman Franjieh in his Constitutional Document of 14 February 1976, had strained the limits of Maronite tolerance.[88] The Maronites had offered them in desperation partly as the price for Syrian support and partly as a tactic to drive a wedge between the Moslem moderates and the radicals. The rejection of these concessions by the National Movement only confirmed in Maronite eyes their initial conviction that to concede the principle of change in the *status quo* of the 1943 National Pact was to embark on the slippery slope towards a bottomless pit. Their mood drew them increasingly closer to saying to the Moslems: You take your majority, and we will take our Mountain, i.e., retreat into their Maronite heartland (Mount Lebanon proper) and partition the country rather than live under radical Moslem rule.

The Maronites were led by a loose quadripartite coalition known as the Lebanese Front. The leaders were: Suleiman Franjieh, Camille Chamoun, Pierre Gemayel, and Father Sharbel Kassis, Head of the Conference of Maronite Monastic Orders. If two of these leaders (Chamoun and Gemayel) agreed on a course of action they could swing the other two, as well as the bulk of the Maronites along with them. The record indicates that these four leaders were capable of cooperating effectively with one another in spite of the tensions between them. The greatest tension existed between Chamoun, the charismatic leader in his own right, and Gemayel, the leader of the charismatic institution, the Phalanges. Chamoun[89] tended to take the hardest line among the four, followed by Kassis, Franjieh, and Gemayel, in that order. Three of them directly controlled militias: the largest was Gemayel's Phalanges (about 15,000 militiamen) followed by the "Tigers" of Chamoun's National Liberal Party (about 3500 militiamen), and Franjieh's private army (about 1500 militiamen), while Kassis was believed to sponsor "The Organization" (about 1500 militiamen). One other relatively large Christian militia existed: the Guardians of the Cedars (1000 militiamen), while some 20 other smaller militias operated within limited areas in Beirut or in different parts of the country.[90]

Some of these militias often seemed to act in defiance of the quadripartite leadership, by either refusing to acquiesce to agreed-upon cease-fires, or going completely berserk, as happened to the Phalanges after 6 December 1975 (the massacre of 200 Moslems in Beirut in "retaliation" for the killing of four Phalangists). Nevertheless, the general impression is that "insubordination" was as often as not a function of outbidding within the quadripartite coalition. But it was also a deliberate escalation-by-proxy strategy: the task of escalation would be assigned by tacit or explicit agreement among the quadripartite leadership to one of the four principal militias or a minor one, depending on the political implications.

The larger militias were heavily armed. In addition to automatic rifles, machine guns, anti-tank guns and missiles, and mortars of all calibers, they also had some field artillery, rockets, armored personnel carriers, and armored cars and tanks.[91] This list does not, of course, include the equipment of the Maronite contingents in the fragmented Lebanese army, which joined the Maronite camp, nor that supplied by Israel.

A word is in order here about the political role of the Maronite religious hierarchy. Historically, the leader of the Maronite community in the spiritual and (very often) political fields has been the Maronite Patriarch, who to all intents and purposes has traditionally represented the Maronite ethos. The French mandatory authorities, in line with their heavy dependence on the Maronites in Lebanon, paid particular deference to the Patriarch throughout the period of their administration of the country. Because the real center of power under the Mandate was the French High Commissioner rather than the incumbent Lebanese President, the Patriarch tended to maintain his pre-eminence over the latter. However, with the coming of independence in 1943 and the succession of the President to the supreme powers formerly wielded by the French High Commissioner, the seeds of tension were perhaps inevitably sown between President and Patriarch. The relations between these two

depended to a large extent on personal idiosyncrasies and their images of
their respective roles. The reigning Patriarch at the time of independence
was Antun Arida, a Maronite "hawk" whose political forthrightness (to
put it mildly) on such subjects as the relationship of the Lebanese to the
Arab World was a cause of acute embarrassment not only to President
Bishara Khoury (co-author of the 1943 National Pact with the Sunnite
leader Riyad Solh) but also to the Vatican. Since Patriarch Arida, in his
old age seemed reluctant to acknowledge the passage of the years, the
Vatican was finally obliged to intervene and "retire" him in 1954 in favor
of Paul Meouchy, Bishop of Tyre. Meouchy's appointment was made
directly by Rome to forestall the election of a less moderate Patriarch by
the Lebanese synod of Maronite bishops.[92]

Meouchy and President Camille Chamoun (1952-1958) did not quite
see eye to eye, partly because tact to Chamoun was often a matter of
mood. Nor was Meouchy particularly enamored of Chamoun's domestic
and foreign policies. Indeed, Meouchy's vigorous opposition to
Chamoun was one of the most important single factors in preventing the
1958 Civil War from degenerating into the inter-sectarian conflict of
1975-76.[93] Meouchy, however, subsequently fell out with both Presidents Chehab (1958-1964) and Helou (1964-1970), indicating perhaps
a continuing ineluctable "debate" between the Maronite "State" and the
Maronite Church. When Meouchy died in 1975 on the eve of the Civil
War, he was succeeded by Antoine Khraish, an uncharacteristically self-
effacing, low-keyed Patriarch. Throughout the fighting, Khraish seemed
visibly affected by what was befalling the country and exerted himself
tirelessly but ineffectively in behind-the-scenes attempts at sectarian
reconciliation. On the other hand, the main Maronite monastic orders—
the grassroots institutions on which the Maronite Patriarchate and to
some extent the Maronite community are based—became unprecedentedly prominent at both the political and military levels. Their Superior,
Father Sharbel Kassis, a member of the quadripartite Lebanese Front,
was no dove. This salience of the monastic orders may reflect a shift
between its base and top in the internal balance of power within the
Maronite religious hierarchy. This shift could perhaps itself have been a
function of the personality of the incumbent Patriarch or it could indicate
a subtly prudential division of labor between the two. But it could also
reflect the "last ditch" Maronite mood and be yet another manisfestation
of the intensity of the sectarian character that the conflict had assumed.

The Moslem Establishment

The basic grievances of the Moslem establishment had been the
preponderant power enjoyed (not without some hauteur) by the

Maronite President as opposed to the Sunnite Prime Minister, as well as the general socio-economic and political imbalance in the system in favor of the Maronites and at the expense of the Moslems. Before the outbreak of the Civil War the Moslem establishment had generally concentrated on two major demands: *musharaka* (a balanced distribution of power between the Maronite President and the Sunnite Prime Minister) and fairer access for the Moslems in general to the senior civil service and military posts. Much effort was also spent on "politics of the gesture," or histrionic reactions to real or perceived slights to the dignity of the Moslem sects by the Maronite authorities in matters of precedence and protocol.

The major socio-economic grievances of the Moslem communities based on discrimination in education, social services, and regional economic development were given only verbal attention by the Moslem establishment: an alibi for lack of progress in their redress was readily found in the Maronite "monopoly" of power. This, in addition to Sunnite thirst for the Prime Ministerial office (parallelled only by the intra-Maronite race for the Presidency), gradually alienated increasing sections of the status-starved, disillusioned, morally enraged, often remorselessly idealistic Moslem intelligentsia and the rapidly proliferating student population from the Sunnite leaders.

Fundamentally, of course, the Moslem oligarchs were at peace with the status quo of 1943, which explains their general approval (except for Jumblat) of Franjieh's Constitutional Document of 14 February 1976. On the Palestinian issue, they consistently came out in favor of the commandos, but after the outbreak of the Civil War major differences of opinion developed among these oligarchs with regard to the strategy to be pursued vis-à-vis the Maronites as well as Syrian intervention. Ex-Premier and pre-eminent Sunnite leader Saeb Salaam reached an early decision that President Suleiman Franjieh was the root of all evil and should resign forthwith, whereas after much hesitation the incumbent Sunnite Premier Rashid Karami decided, at least until March 1976, to explore the possibility of cooperating with him. Salaam was at first vehemently opposed to the Syrian intervention, whereas Karami's lines of communication with Damascus seemed to remain open.

Kamel As'ad, the pre-eminent secular Shiite leader and Speaker of the Parliament, was on the defensive both against the populist religious Shiite leader Musa Sadr and the leftist and radical Shiite forces. These forces were in physical control of As'ad's political constituency and base in southern Lebanon from which he was in effect "exiled." As'ad belatedly threw his energies into an attempt to revive parliamentary life in order to seize the initiative from the combatants. He was active in organizing the legislative moves that gave a semblance of constitutional-

ity to the transition from Franjieh to Sarkis. Of all Moslem leaders he
was the closest to the Maronites and resided during most of the fighting
in Maronite-controlled territory. Of these Moslem leaders, only Jumblat
had a militia comparable to those at the command of the Maronite
leaders of the Lebanese Front.

A word about the political role of the Moslem religious hierarchy. By
and large the secular leadership (the traditional oligarchs) has tended to
overshadow its strictly religious counterpart. This applies to Sunnites,
Shiites, and Druzes. In the case of the last two the position of the secular
leadership vis-à-vis the religious leadership has been enhanced by two
considerations. First, the secular leaders themselves (unlike their Sunnite
fellow oligarchs) have been traditionally endowed with some religious
attributes in the eyes of their largely rural, tribal, and conservative
followers. Secondly, again unlike the Sunnite constituency, the Druze
and Shiite constituencies have been rigidly hierarchical, with the secular
leadership concentrated over the last decades in two families for each sect
(the Jumblats and Arslans for the Druzes and the As'ads and Himadehs
for the Shiites).

While this has been the general pattern, at least since independence in
1943, some variations have occurred in more recent times, especially
among the Sunnites and Shiites. Among the Sunnites the most
prestigious religious post is that of Mufti (or jurisconsult) of Lebanon.
This has usually been occupied by pious and elderly dignitaries enjoying
vastly varying degrees of learning and grasp of Islamic jurisprudence.
They acted more or less as decorative umpires to the contending
members of their community under the conspicuous wings of such
powerful secular leaders as Riyad Solh, Abdulhamid Karami (father of
Rashid), and Saeb Salaam. In 1967, however, a relatively young Islamic
scholar, Sheikh Hassan Khalid, was appointed Mufti. The appointment
seemed to have the blessing of Presidents Chehab and Nasser and reflected the entente between Cairo and Beirut under Chehab. Khalid's
sponsorship by the two capitals was designed to create a malleable
Sunnite counterpoint to the Sunnite oligarchs. The Mufti's curiosity, in
the circumstances, was not confined to things ecclesiastical, prompting
him to explore the leeway that he could exercise at the expense of the
secular leadership. Needless to say, this brought him into conflict with
the Sunnite oligarchs who were indefatigable in reminding him of the
transcendent functions of his office.

Given the Mufti's propensities and backing and the eroded prestige of
the secular traditional leadership, it was inevitable that disaffected
Sunnite Moslems, unwilling to follow Jumblat or join the radical and
Marxist parties, should gravitate towards Sheikh Hassan Khalid and try

to get the most out of him in their fight against the Sunnite secular establishment, as well as against the Maronites. Thus, a new behind-the-scenes power center was created within the general Sunnite establishment which during the Civil War generated much of the out-bidding climate of opinion both inside the Sunnite fold and between the Sunnite establishment and the National Movement.

A similar phenomenon occurred at about the same time in the Shiite community. There, the leaders of the religious hierarchy have usually been characterized by formidable erudition and have led the lives of anchorites, leaving things mundane to the traditional leading houses of the As'ads and Himadehs. In the early sixties, however, a Shiite religious dignitary, Musa Sadr, appeared on the scene. Sadr was in his thirties, and of literally heroic physical proportions. Unlike the Mufti, he was a determined activist and agitated openly on behalf of his crushed but awakened community, the most deprived of all Lebanese sects. This brought Sadr into increasing conflict, not only with the Shiite traditional secular leaders but also with the Marxist and radical parties who were canvassing in the same constituency. Initially a member of the National Movement, Sadr inclined to the Syrian side after the Syrian confronta-tion with the Movement. There is no doubt that Sadr played a leading role in the mobilization of Shiite mass opinion on the eve of the Civil War, in the course of which he organized and commanded a somewhat ramshackle militia called AMAL, numbering several hundreds.

The Druze religious leadership was kept well in line by Kamal Jumblat throughout the Civil War, although he was outwardly as deferential to it as it was to him.

The National Movement

Before the schism over Syrian intervention the National Movement was a broad coalition embracing the entire activist Moslem-Leftist opposition. The Leftist components included substantial numbers of Christians, particularly from the Greek Orthodox sect.[94] The National Movement included established Lebanese parties and more recently formed ones, Lebanese branches of Pan-Arab parties, popular action-oriented *ad hoc* groups and student organizations. All these differed in size, structure, strength, purpose, affiliation, as well as in political phil-osophies and programs (if any). Many engaged in intense rivalry and competition among themselves.

Nevertheless, they did share certain general common characteristics and immediate objectives. All were at least left of Center. Most were undeflectedly confrontational. Their overriding target was a revolution in the *status quo*. Their battering ram: deconfessionalism. Their enemy: both the Maronite *and* the Moslem establishments. Their strategic ally: the Palestinian commandos. Their patron saint and mentor: Kamal Jumblat.

For all of them, deconfessionalism was not an ideal laid up in Heaven, the Vision of the Good Life about which one daydreamed,[95] but a concrete program instantly realizable by storming the Bastille of the 1943 National Pact.

Paradoxically, even after the Ain Rummaneh massacre in April 1975, the National Movement was not self-consciously committed to "armed struggle" as a means of achieving its ends. An index of this was the utter military unpreparedness of its members, well into the spring of 1976, as compared to the Maronite militants. This was partly due to their tacit reliance on Palestinian military prowess—hence, partly at least, their embrace of the cause of the Palestinian commandos. But it was also a tribute to their amateur status as "revolutionaries" too dazzled by their own enunciation of grandiose ends to give much thought to the mechanics of their realization.

The National Pact was perceived to be a conspiratorial covenant between a small band of oligarchs both Christian and Moslem whose purpose was to perpetuate, in the name of obsolete and irrelevant criteria of sectarian equilibrium, the socio-economic dominance of some four percent of the upper crust of society[96] at the expense of the vast downtrodden majority of the population. The concessions in Franjieh's Constitutional Document of 14 February 1976 were a cynical exercise in "cosmetic" reform in the tradition of the tribal nose-rubbing reconciliation ritual between bedouin chieftains after a vendetta. What was needed was a clean break with the past on the basis of truly democratic participation which alone could guarantee social justice for the greatest number, irrespective of sectarian affiliation. The Syrian intervention was seen as having snatched victory from their grasp under the hypocritical cover of concern for the prevention of the partition of the country by the Maronites. In fact, it was motivated by the desire to subjugate the Palestinian commandos in preparation for Syrian surrender at the Geneva Peace Conference in the service of Washington and Tel Aviv. Syria was also acting in a Metternichian role on behalf of the conservative Arab regimes who quaked at the idea of the triumph of democracy and socialism in Lebanon. The threat of partition by the Maronite right was seen as a bluff that could and should be called once and for all.

At the center of the National Movement was Kamal Jumblat's Progressive Socialist Party, composed largely of intellectuals and students. Its base, however, was Jumblat's Druze clansmen organized in a militia about 3000 strong. Around this party was gathered a hard core of four principal groups:

1) The Communists. These were organized in two parties: the old Moscow-oriented Lebanese Communist Party (C.P.) and the Organization for Lebanese Communist Action (O.L.C.A.). The latter was formed in the 1960s around a splinter group from the C.P. and another such group from the Arab Nationalist Movement (A.N.M.). As for the C.P., the leadership had been wrested from old party veterans by young militants, largely from the Lebanese University. Relations between this leadership, on the one hand, and the party veterans and Moscow, on the other, had become increasingly strained as a result of the leadership's passionate espousal of a brand of Marxist Arab nationalism, to which O.L.C.A. also subscribed. The Lebanese crisis brought the C.P. and O.L.C.A. so closely together that communiqués were issued by them in the name of "communists in the C.P. and O.L.C.A."[97]

2) The Syrian Social Nationalist Party (formerly the Parti Populaire Syrien - P.P.S.). This was the most genuinely, if fanatically, secular of all nationalist political parties in the Arab world, containing in its ranks as many Christians as Moslems. Of all the members of the National Movement coalition, the Syrian Social Nationalist Party was again the most genuinely "rejectionist" with regard to an Arab-Israeli settlement involving acceptance of Israel as a state. The Syrian Social Nationalist Party as well as the C.P. and O.L.C.A. were country-wide organizations. Between them they exercised the greatest intellectual and tactical leverage over Jumblat and often were the pace-setters of the National Movement coalition.

3) The Lebanese branch of the Iraqi Baath Party, largely based in Tripoli.[98]

4) The Nasserists and neo-Nasserists whose principal organizations were: the Independent Nasserists and their militia, the *Murabitun*; the Union of the Forces of the Working People-The Corrective Movement (one group); the Socialist Arab Union-The Nasserite Organization (another single group), all three being based in Beirut; the 24 October Movement of Tripoli; and the Popular Nasserist Organization of Sidon.[99]

All these groups enjoyed the support of radical Arab regimes, particularly Iraq and Libya, as well as that of the PLO. The Independent Nasserists of Beirut had the largest militia force—the *Murabitun*, which was about 500 strong. The militia forces of the others varied between 200-400 each.

Until the confrontation with Syria, the National Movement also included the Lebanese branch of the Baath Party of Syria, the Shiite

Movement of the Disinherited under the Shiite religious leader Musa Sadr, and the Union of the Forces of the Working People of Beirut. These organizations each had a militia of about 200 and enjoyed Syrian support.

In addition, the National Movement included some half dozen Lebanese student and youth militias and organizations, each 100-200 strong, directly affiliated to the Palestinian Resistance, particularly to *Fath*.

The larger militias, like their Maronite counterparts, had access to the armaments of the dissident Lebanese Army contingents which had joined forces with them. Given their differing political philosophies and external affiliations, coordination between the members of the Movement was more difficult than within the Maronite coalition, while outbidding and escalation by proxy were a matter of routine in their decision-making.

Kamal Jumblat

Paradoxically, Jumblat was the most secure of all Lebanese traditional political leaders in his own Druze constituency, where he had little cause to look over his shoulder. He had been one of the principal props and beneficiaries of the Lebanese system, and had served in various ministerial posts for at least as long as any other Moslem or Christian oligarch since the mid-forties. As a Druze aristocrat whose family had been involved in the politics of Mount Lebanon for centuries, he was the repository of a rich heritage of insights into the psychology and phobias of his traditional neighbors, the Maronites.

On the other hand, Jumblat had always been a critic of the Lebanese system and since the early fifties had intermittently tried his hand at forging an oppositional coalition dedicated to its reform. Probably one of the earliest influences on him was British welfare socialism of World War II vintage.[100]

Jumblat's deconfessionalist program was not on the face of it unreasonable. The principle of one-man-one-vote, which is its practical application, was hardly revolutionary by Western liberal democratic standards. In the Lebanese context, however, it was just that, as Jumblat knew only too well. The question remains as to why he took up this principle as a matter of supreme urgency and pursued it so relentlessly.

One could assume that several considerations played a role: the failure of Chehabist reform, the actual or perceived deterioration of living conditions for the Moslem masses, the general indifference of the Moslem and Maronite establishments, and the hopes pinned on him by the Lebanese Moslem intelligentsia and students as a fellow intellectual and a leader. All of these finally reached saturation point and he underwent a

Pauline conversion stemming from his sense of accumulated moral anger.

A less charitable though still respectable explanation is that, observing the erosion of the sectarian hierarchical system among the Sunnites and Shiites and the gravitation towards himself of the younger generation of radicals away from their Moslem sects, he had the shrewdness to realize that a historic opportunity beckoned to make a qualitative political jump from his Druze sectarian straitjacket (where the blind loyalty of his kinsmen may have occasioned some feelings of ennui) into the wider pastures of secular national leadership. Elaborating on this hypothesis, his critics maintain that Jumblat's main objection to the concessions of Franjieh's Constitutional Document of 14 February 1976 was that they still blocked the avenues for him not only of the Presidency but also of the Premiership. This document, it will be recalled, preserved the *status quo* with regard to the distribution of the three highest posts of the state—the President, the Speaker of the House, and the Prime Minister among the Maronites, the Shiites, and the Sunnites respectively—thus perpetuating the exclusion of the Druzes from these posts.

Yet another, more Machiavellian, hypothesis is that Jumblat, ahead of all the other oligarchs, whether Christian or Moslem, saw only too clearly the writing on the wall. A bloody social revolution was in the offing which could sweep away everything before it, Jumblat and all. Better to ride the tiger of a bloody political and constitutional reform (1789) than drift into the inferno of an October (1917) Revolution. The hypothesis is not altogether implausible. Although a holder of the Order of Lenin, Jumblat was wont to mutter dire warnings in tête-à-têtes with fellow oligarchs about a possible Communist takeover. Moreover, he was one of very few populist leaders in the Arab World who did not lash out against Sadat's Sinai II.

Whatever the truth, there is no doubt that some of Jumblat's pronouncements give the impression that his self-image was of someone not only leading the downtrodden of Lebanon into the millennium but also initiating a new revolutionary surge in the entire Arab world based on a genuine grass-roots phenomenon, rather than the adventurism of a man on horseback or in a tank turret.

2. The Palestinians

The backbone of the Palestinian Revolution was the centrist *Fath* organization led by Yasir Arafat, a Sunnite Moslem.[101] Next in political importance came the Marxist PFLP (Popular Front for the Liberation of Palestine) of George Habash (a Greek Orthodox Christian), followed by the Marxist DFLP (Democratic Front for the Liberation of Palestine) of

Naif Hawatmeh (a Greek Orthodox Christian from the *East* Bank of the Jordan). *Saiqa,* recruited from Palestinian residents in Syria under the aegis of the Syrian Baath Party, and the Arab Liberation Front, organized under the sponsorship of the Iraqi Baath Party, cannot be said to be completely autonomous Palestinian organizations. The PFLP-General Command, a breakaway group from Habash's PFLP under Ahmed Jibril, was more of a para-military than a political entity, as indeed were both the *Saiqa* and the Arab Liberation Front. Jibril was said to have been close to Libya, while also having good lines of communication to Damascus.

The Palestinian Rejection Front was led by Habash. It was unswervingly opposed to any settlement with Israel except on the basis of a reconstituted democratic secular state of all Palestine to include Arabs, Jews, and Christians. It included Jibril's organization as well as the Arab Liberation Front.

Before the Syrian intervention which polarized relations between the *Saiqa* and all the other organizations (except Jibril's PFLP-General Command), the Palestinian commando organizations—in spite of the rivalries and differences among them—had the same perception of Lebanon, a perception fundamentally conditioned by their common Jordanian experience during 1970-71.

Yet even before the tragic events in Jordan the Palestinian commando organizations tended to start from the premise that all Arab countries, but particularly those adjacent to Israel, were duty-bound in the name of Pan-Arabism and the sacrosanctity of the Palestinian cause to proffer assistance and sanctuary to the Palestinian revolution. The price for these services had to be paid, however costly it might be, in the form of the Israeli strategy of retaliation and deterrence through punishment.

Given this premise, the argument of Lebanon being *sui generis* among the Arab countries because of its delicate sectarian equilibrium, possessed at best only limited plausibility. Priority was given to the need to maintain military pressure against Israel. This more often than not was difficult if not impossible to do across the main confrontation lines in the Syrian Golan and Egyptian Sinai because of the differing priorities of the regular Syrian and Egyptian armed forces. Hence the temptation of construing the very fragility of the sectarian equilibrium in Lebanon as a potential asset to be turned, if necessary, to the advantage of the Palestinian revolution. The Cairo Agreement of 1969 tended to be looked upon as an acquired extraterritorial right never to be abandoned but rather to be consolidated and expanded where possible. The concurrent halos of martyrdom and championship surrounding the Palestinian revolution exerted a powerful fascination over the Moslem masses and radicals of Lebanon. And the almost mystical bond that sprang up between them and the Palestinian leadership confirmed the latter's already foreshadowed reading of the Lebanese political and sectarian map.

All this was reinforced by the Jordanian experience. Never again would the Palestinian revolution face a regular army on its own. The Jordanian catastrophe had occurred precisely because the revolution had abided by constraining principles of behavior vis-à-vis the Jordanian masses which had merely played into the hands of the Jordanian authorities, thus facilitating the latter's liquidation task. If the Lebanese Moslem and leftist waters were crying for the Palestinian fish to jump into them, the Palestinian fish were not going to play coy.

To be sure, there were differences of emphasis. Arafat's centrist *Fath,* while imbued with these sentiments, tended also to be aware of their pitfalls. Hence Arafat's predisposition to keep his options open with all Lebanese parties. If he was not successful in this endeavor, it was due as much to his misreading of the Lebanese political-sectarian map as to the pressures of the Palestine Rejection Front and the Lebanese National Movement itself. Unlike *Fath,* the Palestine Rejection Front, and particularly the PFLP, were further propelled by their secular or Marxist ideology into symbiosis with the Lebanese underdog and into championship of the cause of deconfessionalism.

From Ain Rummaneh (April 1975) onwards the Conspiracy Theory dominated Palestinian analysis—as it colored the perceptions of all the other protagonists, local as well as regional. The massacre of the busload of Palestinians by Maronite right-wing militiamen was seen as the opening move in a deliberate strategy directed by hidden players whose primary purpose was to bleed the Palestinians to death in a conflict with the Maronite establishment. The objective of this strategy was to deflect their attention from Kissinger's step-by-step diplomacy whose cornerstone was deliberate purblindness to the centrality of the Palestinian issue in the Arab-Israeli conflict.

The same theory was later drawn upon to explain Syrian intervention on the side of the Maronites. The Syrians, anxious to curry favor with Washington, were seizing the opportunity of the Lebanese crisis to cut the Palestinians down to size. This was to be preliminary to their sacrifice at the conference table in collusion with the Jordanians and the conservative oil-rich Arab regimes frightened by dark American warnings about the consequences of oil price increases. But even if the Syrian army were powerful, the Palestinian Movement in alliance with the Lebanese National Movement and the Lebanese masses would put up such a heroic fight that the very pathos of their resistance would rally popular support not only in Damascus but in other Arab capitals as well. This would surely turn the tables against the "conspirators."

Arafat's position within the *Fath* leadership was that of *primus inter pares*, with a somewhat long lead in his primacy. In theory, he coordinated overall Palestinian policy with regard to the Lebanese National Movement. In practice, however, the members of the Palestinian Rejection Front had direct links with members of the National Movement, and vice versa. In moments of extreme crisis, Arafat had the power and prestige to impose his will on the Palestinian Rejection Front and the Lebanese National Movement. That he was sometimes averse to exercising this leverage was as much a reflection of his innate propensity to temporize as of his tactical perceptions of the moment.

Unquestionably, *Fath* had the largest military and militia forces in the field on the Palestinian and Lebanese Moslem-Leftist side. Its front-line troops numbered 8,000-10,000, with as many militiamen. In addition, *Fath* called on Palestine Liberation Army units (the regular army units of the PLO) loyal to Arafat and stationed in Syria and Egypt[102] (about 4000 strong) as well as on Palestinians trained in Iraq. Some 3000-4000 troops were dispatched from Iraq to reinforce *Fath* via Egypt.[103] The Syrian-sponsored *Saiqa* Palestinian units and the Syrian-based Palestine Liberation Army (PLA) units dispatched by Damascus to Lebanon were the second most important "Palestinian" forces.[104] They numbered some 3000 each. Both these forces had proved unreliable from the Syrian point of view during the height of their confrontation with Arafat.[105] Many of the PLA units rebelled against their senior pro-Syrian officers and went over to Arafat. In comparison with *Fath*, *Saiqa*, and the PLA, the combatant strength of the other Palestinian organizations did not amount to much. The PFLP-The Popular Front for the Liberation of Palestine (Habash), the DFLP-The Democratic Front for the Liberation of Palestine (Hawatmeh), the Popular Front for the Liberation of Palestine-General Command (Jibril), and the Arab Liberation Front (Iraqi-sponsored) were militarily insignificant. Perhaps the largest of these was Jibril's (ca. 800 men) before it split in two halves as a result of Jibril's pro-Syrian policy. In the early stages of the Civil War the armament of *Fath* easily compared to that of the principal Maronite militia, the Phalanges.[106]

3. The Arab Countries

Syria

Until well into the autumn of 1975 the Syrians were strongly backing the National Movement and *Fath*. They relied for control, first, on the Syrian-sponsored Palestinian *Saiqa* militia; second, on the Lebanese branch of the Syrian Baath Party; and third, on their protégés inside the National Movement: the Union of the Forces of the Working People and Musa Sadr's Shiite Movement of the Disinherited. As the National Movement gathered momentum and its alliance with the Palestinian Resistance took on firmer contours, the Syrians began a process of reappraisal, though they maintained their support of the National Movement and *Fath* with diminishing enthusiasm until the middle of March 1976. An early harbinger of the change in Syria's attitudes was its termination of the political proscription of the Phalanges (announced by the National Movement after the Ain Rummaneh massacre in April 1975). This they did by inviting Pierre Gemayel, leader of the Phalanges, to Damascus on 6 December 1975.

Two nightmares began to haunt the Syrians about this time: that the Maronites would decide on partition, or that the National Movement would, with Palestinian help, rout the Maronites and establish a radical regime in Lebanon. There was little to choose between the two scenarios. The first promised to create a permanent thorn in Syria's side through the establishment of a new Maronite "Israel." It would encourage schism and centrifugal minoritarian tendencies in Syria itself and throughout the region. The second, if successful, would create a beachhead against Syria for regimes hostile to it (e.g., Iraq), while at the same time serving as an alternative repository for Soviet favors. A radical Lebanese regime would by its very nature have imponderable results on the internal Syrian scene. It would be tempted to pursue a precipitatedly escalatory policy against Israel. It could drag Syria into a war at a time and place not of its choosing. Either process—a Maronite movement towards partition, or a radical movement to topple the existing Lebanese regime—might at any moment provide Israel with a credible pretext for intervention, and so trigger a premature confrontation with it. And even if the leftist forces succeeded in gaining control in a swift *coup de main*, the Israelis were bound to claim "compensation" by annexing southern Lebanon in anticipation of the forthcoming militancy of the new radical regime.

On the other hand, the cost of Syrian intervention would be high. It was bound to raise the cry of a conspiracy to liquidate the Palestinians as part of some shabby horse-trading over the occupied Syrian Golan. It would project an image of revolutionary Syria as the enemy of the Moslem underdogs of Lebanon and the champion of a corrupt Christian upper bourgeoisie in league with Moslem feudal overlords. The Syrian regime would be particularly vulnerable to such propaganda in the vast world of Sunnite Arabdom because its ruling military group itself belonged to a small minority, the Alawites (a schismatic offshoot of

Shiism).[107] But the cost of non-intervention, as the Syrians perceived it, would be even higher.

It was this Syrian awareness of the delicate cost-benefit calculus which caused them to move in a methodically graduated manner, partly to scrutinize the political fallout after every move, and partly in the hope that the next turning of the screw against the National Movement and the Palestinians would be unnecessary. And it is in this context that their political offensive, culminating in Franjieh's concessions in the Constitutional Document of 14 February 1976, must be seen. But the Syrian strategy of Push-and-Pause largely foundered on the Come-and-Get-Us-if-You-Can counter-strategy of the National Movement and the Palestinians.

Egypt

At the time when Syria was backing the National Movement and *Fath*, the Egyptians were discreetly backing the Maronites. As the Syrians began to change course, the Palestinians began to thrash around for help and suppressed their nausea at Sadat's Sinai II in the interest of what they saw as their survival against Syria. Early in 1976, Sadat's political periscope discerned the possibilities of a veritable windfall. For months he had been taking his punishment for Sinai II from a vast orchestra of abuse conducted by Asad of Syria and Arafat of the PLO, with the supporting choruses of the Palestinian Rejection Front and the radical Arab countries associated with it, Iraq and Libya. So, in a moment of inspiration, he ditched the Maronites. Now he could appear in the new shining armor of champion of the Palestinians and the Moslem underdogs and stretch the Syrians on the rack he had but recently inhabited. Palestine Liberation Army contingents stationed in Egypt and loyal to Arafat were rushed to Lebanon together with ordnance in defiance of the "Syrian-Israeli blockade" of Sidon and Tyre to bolster the military position of the National Movement and the Palestinians. A bonus for Sadat was the service he could render Iraq, one of his sharpest critics for Sinai II. Iraq had been at a loss as to how to transport reinforcements to the Palestinians in Lebanon, to which it had no direct land access. Sadat obliged by providing an air-bridge with Baghdad and shipping the Iraqi volunteers to Lebanon via Egypt. Meanwhile Sadat eluded the pressures of Saudi Arabia for a summit by demanding that his price for attendance would be Syrian silence about Sinai II during any forthcoming conference on Lebanon. Only when Damascus and Cairo had had their fill of this game of chicken and it became obvious that no Arab country was willing to send substantial forces to co-police Lebanon with the Syrians, that the Israelis were daily getting bolder in southern

Lebanon, and that the Maronite partition trend was becoming more pronounced—then and only then did Sadat and Asad discover that they had a common interest in cooperating to try to put an end to Lebanon's agonies.

Iraq

Relieved of the Kurdish rebellion[108] after embarking on a policy of détente with Iran (which had been the principal sponsor of this rebellion), Iraq was anxious to resume its Pan-Arab role. Iraq considered itself entitled to this role on two grounds: by virtue of its resources and Arab nationalist tradition, but also in its capacity as host to the headquarters of the "legitimate" Pan-Arab leadership of the Baath Party (the wing of the Greek Orthodox founding father Michel Aflak).[109] This leadership had originally been based in Damascus but had been ousted in the early sixties by a Syrian Baath "dissident" faction which since 1970 had been led by President Asad. With the disintegration in the late sixties of the other principal Pan-Arab Party, the Arab Nationalist Movement (ANM) of Habash, into Lebanese and Palestinian Marxist organizations (the Organization for Lebanese Communist Action, the PFLP and DFLP, etc.), Iraq was in theory the sole remaining guardian of Pan-Arabist ideology as an autonomous (non-Marxist) doctrinaire philosophy. From this perspective (sharpened by geographical distance from the confrontation lines with Israel), Baathist Baghdad was adamantly opposed to any Middle East settlement that implied Arab acceptance in any form of the state of Israel. This attracted to Baghdad not only the Palestinian Rejection Front but also several members of the Lebanese National Movement.

From this perspective, too, Baghdad looked upon the present Syrian regime essentially as a usurper regime within the Baathist fold—hence Syrian nervousness about any Iraqi activity in Lebanon.

Iraq would have liked Syria to turn its back on the pursuit of a peaceful settlement with Israel and form with it the principal axis of an Eastern Front which it hoped would be joined by the other Arab countries. A radicalized Lebanon would fall within this grand strategy of Baathist Baghdad—hence Syria and Iraq found themselves on a collision course in Lebanon.

Libya

Next to Syria and Iraq, Libya was the Arab country that showed the greatest interest in Lebanon. All the antitheses of the Lebanese crisis: Christian vs. Moslem, haves vs. have-nots, Left vs. Right, Pan-Arabism vs. "isolationism," Maronite army vs. Palestinian commandos, status quo forces vs. the winds of change, Moslem counter-elite vs. Moslem feudal barons, were calculated to rivet Kaddafi's attention. They would also pluck at the heartstrings of his Islamic fundamentalism, his pristine Bedouin anger at social injustice, his contempt for the traditional Arab ruling class, and the self-consciousness with which he had donned the late Nasser's mantle. Small wonder that soon after his accession to power in 1969 Kaddafi began a policy of steady encouragement, both moral and material, of the Moslem Lebanese radical forces, inspiring in them a neo-Nasserist renaissance.

There were mundane calculations too. Kaddafi saw himself as countering the support given by the conservative Arab regimes and Iran to the Maronite and Moslem establishments. Moreover, as a result of the widening rift between him and Sadat over what he perceived to be the latter's anti-Nasserist revisionism and his sycophantic courting of Washington, Kaddafi deliberately set out to weaken Sadat's influence in Lebanon by wooing the old Nasserist organizations in the country. Like Iraq, he aspired to the creation of a Rejection Front against Israel to include Syria and a radicalized Lebanon. Hence Kaddafi's mounting anxiety at Syria's intervention in Lebanon (and subsequently at the growing detente between Sadat and Arafat). Hence also the assiduous if fumbling efforts at mediation between Syria on the one hand, and the National Movement and the Palestinians on the other, undertaken by his Prime Minister Jalloud.

The Conservative Arab Regimes

Close coordination existed between Kuwait and Saudi Arabia over the Lebanese crisis. These two countries were appalled by the estrangement between Cairo and Damascus over Sinai II, and the trend of events in Lebanon.

They were also torn in two directions. On the one hand they viewed the Maronite establishment as a bulwark against the forces of radicalism and the Left. On the other, there was the spontaneous sympathy of public opinion in Saudi Arabia and Kuwait and sectors of their ruling élites with the Lebanese Moslems and the Palestinians. Both countries, however, feared a leftist takeover of Lebanon, not only because of its likely impact on the Arab-Israeli conflict, but also because of the "subversive" currents it might generate throughout the region, and particularly among the large Palestinian communities in the Arabian (Persian) Gulf.[110] At the same time, they feared that the continuous confrontation between Syria and the Palestinians might undermine the

Syrian regime. This could pave the way for a monolithic Baathist Damascus-Baghdad axis which, with Libyan support, would alter the balance of power east of Suez and usher in a new uncontrollable phase of escalation of the Arab-Israeli conflict and the inter-Arab Cold War.

Thus Saudi Arabian-Kuwaiti diplomacy oscillated between restraining President Asad of Syria and turning a blind eye to what he was doing in Lebanon. At the same time it tried to bring about a reconciliation between Damascus and Cairo as a *sine qua non* for the containment of the Lebanese crisis and the resumption of efforts for an overall Middle East settlement. Meanwhile, in their agonizingly prolonged quandary they bounteously poured fuel on the raging conflagration in Lebanon by evenhandedly supplying both the Maronite and the Palestinian combatants with the financial and military wherewithal. That the Arab conservative regimes took so long to make up their minds was a function partly of the intensity of the conflict between Sadat and Asad and partly of the absence of the authoritative voice of Faisal of Saudi Arabia.[111]

4. The Non-Arab Countries

The United States

It would be disingenuous to assume that the U.S. was altogether displeased with the course of events in Lebanon since Sinai II. The political pluses from Washington's perspective are not difficult to list: the relaxation of Arab pressure for an overall Middle Eastern settlement during the remainder of the Ford Administration; the disarray in Arab ranks which reduced their diplomatic effectiveness; the breathing space won by Israel from harassment by the Palestinian commandos; the increased military vulnerability of Asad and his consequent automatic acquiescence in the renewal of the mandate of the United Nations Disengagement Observer Force installed after Golan I; the discomfiture of Moscow at the internecine conflict between its Syrian and Palestinian allies; the tarnishing of the PLO's international image and its military domestication; the clobbering of the forces of the Lebanese Left; and last, but not least, the paradoxical strengthening of Egyptian President Sadat's position throughout this process. But it would be equally disingenuous to infer intention from result and *a fortiori* authorship from the latter. This is not to deny that Sinai II was a crucial catalyst in the genesis and escalation of the Lebanese crisis, nor to banish into the realm of the unthinkable that some deft push was given by some deft hand in Washington to events in Lebanon at some moment of particular stagnation.

Likewise it should be borne in mind that not long before the outbreak of the Lebanese Civil War, Henry Kissinger had been infuriated with the decision of the Rabat Arab Summit, in October 1974, to declare the PLO the "sole legitimate representative" of the Palestinians. The PLO was not Kissinger's favorite liberation movement, and his recipe for the solution of the Palestine problem was to sweep its dust under the Hashemite carpet, i.e., restore Hussein's rule in some form or other over at least part of the West Bank. The Rabat decision dramatically enhanced the international status of the PLO. It was, in effect, an implicit collective Arab recognition of a PLO regime on the West Bank and the Gaza Strip, should these two territories ever be recovered from Israel. The Rabat PLO decision therefore threatened to undermine the overall thrust of Kissinger's diplomacy with regard to the solution of the Palestinian component of the Arab-Israeli conflict. In these circumstances it could be expected that Kissinger would be receptive to attempts to cut the PLO down to size in its haven in Lebanon.[112]

There is no evidence, however, that Washington worked for or favored the partition of Lebanon. Such evidence as exists would seem to suggest that Washington disabused the Maronites of any illusions in this regard, as well as of a possible repetition of the 1958 landing of the U.S. Marines. It is not altogether unlikely that Washington supplied the Maronites with financial and other help, directly or by proxy (e.g., through Israel, Jordan, and Iran), as part of its general policy of containing both the PLO and what were perceived to be anti-American forces. But the general tenor of its policy was probably reflected in the encouragement it repeatedly gave to Lebanese Prime Minister Karami to reach an accommodation with President Franjieh.[113] Likewise, the mission of Dean Brown (the casually briefed[114] U.S. emissary dispatched to Lebanon in April 1976) remained mediatory, its content substantively diffuse.[115] Neither was Washington necessarily in favor of the Lebanese 1943 *status quo* in all its details, and such reforms as it may have encouraged the Maronites to concede are probably reflected in Franjieh's Constitutional Document of 14 February 1976.[116]

Again, there is no evidence that Washington prompted Asad to intervene, or, for that matter, that Asad needed to be prompted. It would seem that Asad took care to signal his intentions to Washington, but was not necessarily waiting for its green light, just as he did not wait for Moscow's. It is a fact that Asad was not particularly enchanted by Dean Brown's presence in Lebanon.

After the Syrian intervention, Washington's principal concern was the likely reaction of Israel. Again, it would seem that, faced with the Syrian *fait accompli* (about which it stoically concealed its contentment behind measured officialese), Washington's main purpose was to keep Syrian intervention below the threshold of Israeli tolerance.[117] It is probably in this context also that one should see Asad's strategy of Move and Pause. Also in this context must be seen the exploration by Washington and France of a "consortium" of forces (broached by French President Valéry Giscard d'Estaing during his visit to the U.S. in May 1976) in a peace-keeping role to include Syrian and French contingents. This idea seems to have been vaguely explored by Brown in meetings with Lebanese leaders including Jumblat on the eve of the Syrian intervention, presumably as a means of containing it.[118]

The U.S.S.R.

If many of the results of the Lebanese Civil War have been a cause of satisfaction for the U.S., the same can hardly be said of the U.S.S.R. Moscow was definitely sympathetic to the National Movement, and early in the summer of 1975 it indiscreetly intervened on its behalf with Franjieh, only to receive a dour rebuff.[119] While Moscow was in touch with the National Movement as a whole, and the Russian Ambassador in Beirut openly and frequently held meetings with its leaders, the Soviets' closest links were with the Lebanese Communist Party. The leaders of the Communist Party belonged to the inner decision-making circle of the National Movement. They were particularly close to Jumblat. But given their Arab nationalist orientation, the composition of the National Movement, and the independent posture of the PLO vis-à-vis Moscow, the strategy of the National Movement-Palestinian alliance could hardly be said to have closely reflected the Moscow line.[120]

There is no evidence to suggest either that Moscow encouraged the National Movement in its insistence on deconfessionalism as an immediately realizable target or that it considered the partition of Lebanon a desirable objective. Partition would have created a new area of conflict which, by interacting with the Arab-Israeli conflict, would have multiplied the danger of superpower confrontation. To be sure, a radicalized Soviet-oriented Lebanon would have yielded rich prizes in the form, *inter alia*, of the Mediterranean ports of Tripoli, Beirut, and Sidon, and the airports of Beirut and Riyak (in the Bekaa Valley), not to mention stronger leverage over Israel. But it would have simultaneously complicated relations not only with Syria but also with the U.S., Western Europe, and Israel. On balance, the costs and risks of a radicalized Lebanon—if it was ever seriously contemplated, which is doubtful— were probably conceived as too high by Moscow.

The general impression is that Moscow found itself in quite a predicament over Lebanon. It was powerless to influence the course of events and confused by the conflicting crosscurrents within the National Movement-Palestinian alliance. It was exasperated by the spiraling Syrian-Palestinian dogfight and inundated with the National Movement-Palestinian perceptions of a Western imperialist conspiracy (which it verbally encouraged). Thus, it would seem that Moscow acquiesced by increments in the National Movement-Palestinian strategy while counseling moderation, and hoping perhaps through controlled escalation in Lebanon to check Syria's pro-American proclivites.

The joint Russian-Syrian communiqué[121] issued during Kosygin's visit to Damascus in June 1976—while Syria was actually dispatching its expeditionary force into Lebanon—did not refer to the ongoing intervention. This gave the impression of Russian approval of the Syrian move. But it is not improbable that, faced with the Syrian *fait accompli*, Moscow had only philosophically decided not to give Washington the satisfaction of any public indication of Soviet-Syrian discord on the subject.

As the confrontation between Damascus and the National Movement-Palestinian alliance developed, and as the Maronites, emboldened by the Syrian umbrella, launched their general offensive against the Palestinians in late June, Moscow's verbal disenchantment with Damascus became more pronounced.[122] But there is little evidence of any real pressure (withholding of arms supplies or economic assistance) exerted against the Syrians.[123] Presumably the Russians were not anxious to push Asad farther on the Sadat Trail in the direction of Washington. Their constant nightmare throughout the period after the Syrian intervention must have been that of massive Israeli counteraction.

Israel

The Lebanese Civil War was political "manna to the Israelites." In addition to the considerations listed above which made it attractive in Washington's eyes, there were added bonuses for the Israelis: the deepening Christian-Moslem cleavage within Arab society in Lebanon and the other Arab countries where Christian minorities exist; the consternation sown among Arabs in the occupied territories; and, most important of all, the likely impact of the war on the declared Palestinian aim of establishing a unitary democratic secular state to include both Jews and Arabs.

Fundamentally, though, the Lebanese Civil War was yet another chapter in the Thirty Years War between the Arabs and Israelis that has wracked the region since 1948.

Even before the 1969 Cairo Agreement, the Israelis were set on demonstrating to the Lebanese government and the civilian population the high cost of "hosting" the Palestinian commandos. However, except for their unrelenting raids and air strikes in the border area against Lebanese villages and the raid on Beirut International Airport in 1968, they at first by and large avoided inland Lebanese (though not Palestinian) civilian targets. Fundamentally the same strategy was applied to Lebanon as that applied in the Border War in the 1950s, first against Jordan, then against the Gaza Strip, and, both before and after the 1967 war, against Jordan again. The Israelis hoped that as they themselves confidently climbed the rungs of retaliatory escalation, the "host" government (in this case the Lebanese), unable to take the cumulative punishment any longer, would take their courage in both hands to turn against the commandos in a repeat performance of the Jordanian liquidation of 1970/71. But even failing that, the Israelis, aware as they were of the sectarian brittleness of Lebanese society, and the polarization that would ensue within it over the issue of commando activity, hoped that their strategy would reinforce the trend towards Maronite separatism (i.e., partition) or create such a state of chaos that several options would be open to them, from which to choose at leisure. These options could range all the way from *de facto*, if indirect, control of the border area to its outright annexation in the event of the total disintegration of the country. In the latter case the border area could be held as a new bargaining counter in future settlement talks or alternatively retained *ad infinitum.*

If partition was anathema to the superpowers and the Syrians as well as to the other Arab countries, the same did not hold true for the Israelis.[124] And one can readily see why, since partition would be a powerful vindication of the establishment of the state of Israel and an ironically gratuitous debunking of the Palestinian concept of a secular democratic state. Given the circumstances, it would be surprising indeed if long before the overt Israeli aid to Maronite militiamen on the border the Israelis had not secretly extended substantial aid to the Maronites farther north and if the Israeli Military Intelligence had been able to resist the temptation of infiltrating *agents provocateurs* to fan the Lebanese embers. Recent Western reports quoting Israeli sources indicate that overall Israeli aid to the Maronites before the cessation of hostilities in October 1976 amounted to as much as $100 million. This included $35 million in direct aid and the cost of such services as naval blockade and air patrols along the Lebanese coast. According to the same reports, Israeli military aid included the provision of 12,000 rifles, 5000 machine guns, and 110 tanks. Clearly, a radicalized or unitary Lebanon was not Israel's utopian vision of the country.[125]

The Israelis were wary of Syrian intervention, but the Syrians, by dragging it out, allowed the Israelis time to reach the correct conclusion that it did not constitute a military threat to themselves. The Israelis were quick to perceive that it rather entailed a dispersion of Syrian military energies and logistical resources in a potential "Vietnamese" situation. Such a situation absolved the Israelis from the task of making blatant moves that could create unwanted international repercussions. At the same time, Syrian intervention was pounding the Palestinian commandos and setting the Arabs against one another. No wonder that Tel Aviv was not shedding too many tears at the sight of the traditional anti-Israeli hard-line core of the Arab world (the Syrians and the Palestinians) tearing each other to pieces.[126]

4

THE INTERPLAY BETWEEN EXTERNAL AND INTERNAL FACTORS

1. Looking Outside the Lebanese Box

It is perhaps clear from the foregoing that one cannot look exclusively or even mainly inside the Lebanese box for an explanation of the course of events leading to the Civil War, or for its intensity and duration once it broke out. No such explanation could be satisfactory without taking into account the impact of the external political environment—and particularly its regional dimension—on the Lebanese scene or the degree to which it influenced the pace and direction of events.

Two components of the regional environment are relevant: the Arab-Israeli component, and the Pan-Arab component. The Arab-Israeli conflict influenced events through: a) the general radicalization of opinion among the Moslem Lebanese intelligentsia (particularly the students) and masses—especially since Israel's diversion of the Jordan waters in the mid-1960s, and in the aftermath of the 1967 War; b) the emergence of the Palestinian Resistance on Lebanese soil in the late 1960s and the shifting of the center of their activity and physical presence from Jordan to Lebanon after 1970/71; c) Israel's retaliatory strategy against Palestinians in Lebanon; and d) the political fallout of Sinai II.

The radicalization of the Moslem Lebanese intelligentsia and masses had three major consequences. First, it strengthened their disposition to challenge the Lebanese *status quo* with regard to both the authority of the Moslem and Maronite establishments and the confessional premises of the system. Secondly, it enhanced their receptivity to the Palestinian doctrine of revolutionary armed struggle. Thirdly, it put the Maronites increasingly on the defensive, reinforcing their suspicions and fears of Moslem restlessness. Simultaneously, it put the Moslem establishment itself on the defensive vis-à-vis its own constituency, thus heightening intra-Moslem outbidding tendencies which in turn struck at the very roots of the strategic alliance between the Maronite and Moslem establishments.

The appearance of the Palestinian Resistance on Lebanese soil had many consequences. Objectively, it upset the Christian-Moslem balance of power in favor of the Moslems. It offered not only a model to the radicalized Moslems but also a protective umbrella against Maronite high-handedness. It initiated a period of unprecedented tension between Lebanon and Israel. It mobilized the Palestinian refugee camp populations, exacerbating friction with their Maronite neighbors and the Lebanese authorities. It created a new area of explosive discord inside Lebanese society on such issues as the legitimacy of the 1969 Cairo Agreement and the control of commando activity.

Israel's retaliatory strategy had the following major consequences. It aroused general consternation concerning the territorial integrity of Lebanon. It created yet another area of explosive discord within Lebanese society regarding the army's role in response to Israeli raids. It generated feelings of impotence and frustration within the ranks of the Lebanese army and security forces, paving the way for the polarization between their Christian and Moslem components. It produced havoc in the border areas largely inhabited by Shiites. This in turn hastened the exodus of the Shiite peasantry towards the shantytowns of Beirut, where these refugees provided a new source of friction with their Maronite neighbors as well as fertile soil for radicalization directed against their own establishment and the system as a whole.

Sinai II exacerbated relations between Egypt on the one hand, and Jordan, Syria, Iraq, Libya, the Palestinians, and the radicalized Lebanese on the other. The resultant tensions sought and found an outlet in the open society of Lebanon, where the Maronites as a pro-Western and conservative, pro-status quo community were cast in the role of villains, irrespective of their motivations or the grounds of their grievances against the Pan-Arabists and the Palestinians.

Concurrently with these pressures on the Lebanese domestic scene generated by the Arab-Israeli component of the regional environment, cumulative pressures bore upon it from the Pan-Arab component. The Pan-Arab doctrine postulates the existence of a single Arab Nation as a present (and, indeed, a past) reality in respect to which the various Arab States are transient, even deviant, manifestations. It denies by definition the sovereign impenetrability of the frontiers of the Arab states. The proponents of Pan-Arabism, always self-appointed (be they a dynasty, party, or charismatic leader), derive their putative legitimacy from the same fountainhead as those who claim to represent *vox populi* within a single state. In the case of the Pan-Arabists, however, their supra-national legitimacy overrides that of established *states*. Even if one concedes genuine missionary zeal to this or that exponent of Pan-Arabism and a greater or lesser degree of reciprocity between him and the intelligentsia and masses in this or that Arab country, the actual division of the Arab world into states, the conflicting interests and priorities of these states, the social, political, and economic differences between them, including their rivalry for prestige and for the very leadership of the Pan-Arab movement, inevitably turn—as we have observed—this Pan-Arab doctrine into a potent manipulative instrument of Arab *realpolitik*.

2. Looking Inside the Lebanon Box

To this instrument, as well as to the pressures from the Arab-Israeli area, Lebanon was especially vulnerable. Perhaps the foremost reason for this is Lebanon's "anonymity" as a nation. The irony is that the very confessional system which was supposed to propel the Christians and Moslems on Rupert Emerson's road from Empire to Nation[127] militated against arrival at their consensual "rendezvous." And if the Moslem Lebanese was at a loss as to which identity card to pick up—the Islamic, Arab, or Lebanese,—the Maronite was equally ambivalent with regard to the Lebanese identity that he openly urged on his Moslem compatriots but secretly did not dare look fully in the face himself. The reason for this was that in spite of the political and socio-economic advantages accruing to the Maronites from the expanded frontiers of the 1920 Grand Liban,[128] they had by no means persuaded themselves that to step out of their Maronite armor was anything but an adventure into the unknown. There was a sense in which the Moslem provinces added to Mount Lebanon in 1920 were perceived as frontier areas inhabited by Moslem political helots and constituting, in Maronite consciousness, a buffer zone against the universe of Arabdom and Islam. Hence the stubborn Maronite attachment to the 1943 National Pact (weighted as it was in their favor) while simultaneously preserving a mental line of retreat into the womb of Mount Lebanon proper. This was ideal ground for the Pan-Arab pull on the capricious loyalties of the Moslem Lebanese.

This brittleness of the Lebanese system was heightened by four domestic factors. *First*, the liberal openness of the regime which afforded anarchic leeway to "non-Lebanese" political organizations and expression. The government's rationale in tolerating this state of affairs seemed to have derived from the hope that the diverse Pan-Arab and radical groups allowed to operate on Lebanese soil would somehow cancel each other out. It also reflected a desire to keep lines of communication open with as many Arab countries as possible. But, fundamentally, it was an index of the state's lack of self-confidence, itself a reflection of the delicacy of the sectarian equilibrium on which it was based.

Secondly, the radicalization of the Moslem intelligentsia and masses already noted. But this radicalization was itself partly the product of an earlier phenomenon to which Karl Deutsch's concept of social mobilization aptly applies. According to Deutsch, social mobilization can be defined "as the process in which major clusters of old social, economic and psychological commitments are eroded or broken and people become available for new patterns of socialization and behavior."[129]

Perhaps the most relevant aspect of the social mobilization experienced by Lebanon was the educational explosion the country witnessed from the mid-1960s onwards. In 1965, for example, the total number of students in both private and public schools was 418,665. In 1973-74 the number was 801,488. At the same time the number of students in universities rose from 16,000 in 1963 to 51,000 in 1973-74. An interesting detail pertaining to the latter figure is that 27,951 of the university students or 54.8 percent of the total university population were non-Lebanese, mostly Arab.[130]

Deutsch is undecided in his overall assessment of social mobilization between its "assimilationist," i.e., nation-building, potential and its disintegrative effect.[131] The Lebanese example falls in the latter category, a view now only too tragically confirmed. (It is to Michael Hudson's credit that he noted the disintegrative potential of social mobilization on Lebanon as early as he did.[132]) This disintegrative effect on Lebanon cannot, however, be viewed in isolation from the influences of the external environment noted earlier. These influences of the external environment were crucial in determining the intensity and pace of Moslem Lebanese radicalization.

Thirdly, if social mobilization was a key phenomenon at the non-elite level, the falling-out among the members of the Lebanese oligarchy (the traditional sectarian leaders) was a phenomenon of parallel importance at the elite level. It is true, of course, that conflict among the Lebanese oligarchs had always been endemic and in a sense supplied the motive power of the system. But what we witness as of the late 1960s is a new intensity in personal estrangement among these oligarchs, increasingly precluding political dialogue and more often than not leading to a total breakdown of communication between them. Although there had always been isolated instances of this breakdown (Karami and Chamoun since 1958, and Chehab and Salaam since the early 1960s), the new development was the unprecedentedly high proportion of the number of leading oligarchs who had become anathema to each other. Already *before* Ain Rummaneh (April 1975), for example, not one of the ten to twelve leading oligarchs was on speaking terms with *all* the others and certainly not on such terms with more than half their number. This is not to suggest that if they had hung together they would have saved the commonwealth. It is rather to make the point that if there is such a thing as learning the rules of the game, as has been suggested,[133] which enables leaders to acquire the knack of consensual politics in open but divided societies, there is also a process of unlearning these rules.

Fourthly, the erosion of the power of the Sunnite oligarchs. The power of the politically important Sunnite families—the Salaams and Solhs of Beirut and the Karamis of Tripoli—did not have the feudal or semi-feudal landlordism base of the Shiite and Druze leaders, nor the semi-religious aura the latter enjoyed. Sunnite power was not based on traditional tribal or clan loyalties, nor did it have the geographically concentrated rural constituencies of the Shiite, Druze, and Maronite leaders. Of all the sects, with the exception of the Greek Orthodox (though similar in this regard to the Maronites), the Sunnites were the least hierarchically organized. Like the Maronite leadership (but unlike the bipolar Druze and Shiite leadership), Sunnite leadership was multipolar. Its power derived from a tradition of public service (first, second, or third generation), supplemented by the actual assumption in the past and therefore potentially in the future of the Prime Ministerial office, as well as by personal magnetism. It was based on shifting political alliances across the Christian-Moslem cleavage line and within each community with fellow oligarchs and lesser political figures. One of its most important ingredients was access to heads of Arab states. It was perpetuated through sponsorship of "new men" in the cabinet and Parliament as well as patronage in the civil service and the private sector.

It is noteworthy that no Sunnite (nor for that matter, Shiite) oligarch ever succeeded in organizing a political party in any viable sense of the term, not even one confined to his sect (such as Pierre Gemayel's Phalanges); nor until very recently could any Sunnite oligarch be said to have a permanent if rudimentary secretariat. Likewise, no Sunnite (or Shiite) oligarch has clearly or consistently identified himself with any overall political or socio-economic program or legislative strategy. These closely interrelated failures are probably to be attributed to a fundamentally proprietary state of mind which regards leadership as a matter of ascription rather than achievement. The organizational failure is as likely as not due to an aversion to sharing decision-making with "unequals," while the programmatic one probably reflects exaggerated concern for privileged status.

What, then, is the material power base of the Sunnite oligarchs? At the core are a few close relatives and family attendants, some on a more or less full-time basis with continuous access to the leaders. Beyond that are always-shifting alliances with heads of families and extended families, some of whom may be linked by ties of blood or marriage to the leader. Beyond that is informal sponsorship of various philanthropic, professional, commercial, or sports unions, clubs, committees, and organizations. This power was translated into potential physical force by way of the traditional Moslem urban network of *qabadais* or neighborhood strongmen. This is an indigenous institution with medieval roots originally related to requirements of self-defense and local security at times of chaos or invasion. In his modern version the *qabadai* could be a quayside boss, the owner of a cinema chain, or gas station, etc. His power is based on gangs of *mini-qabadais* numbering in each case a dozen at the most, who have a flair for throwing their weight about. Through these, the *qabadai*, under the umbrella of the leader (for it is a two-way relationship), can control a neighborhood or a whole urban quarter. With fellow *qabadais* (there are coalitions and counter-coalitions in the *qabadai* world) he can organize a demonstration and enforce or break a strike. Individual services can include insulting a rival oligarch (at odds with the *qabadai's* leader) or browbeating a bothersome journalist.

Above all, the *qabadai* acts as an election agent (known as *miftah*, literally "key"), securing votes through various means of persuasion or purchase for the leader at election times. In return, the *qabadai* receives a wide range of favors and exemptions through the leader's patronage. The *qabadai* has his ear to the ground and reports every grass-roots political nuance to the leader, to whom he always has direct access. The finest hour of the *qabadai* is when *his* leader is Prime Minister, but *qabadais* are mercurial. Hence the oligarchs, whether in or out of office, expend considerable energy in consulting the daily *qabadai* political maps of their city. Beyond the *qabadais* are the Sunnite Moslem masses—the "Street." These masses are concentrated in the major coastal cities of Beirut, Tripoli, and Sidon. Relatively sophisticated and volatile, it is to them that the leader "gestures" with Pan-Arab slogans and "tough" postures vis-à-vis the Maronites.

It is perhaps not difficult to understand why this Sunnite leadership was submerged at the point of confluence of the internal and external factors noted above. Not only were the Sunnite leaders unable to satisfy the demands of the rapidly expanding new intelligentsia in terms of job opportunities, but there was a deliberate turning away from them by the latter, expecially the students, in the direction of the new radical or Marxist parties and the National Movement under the dynamic leadership of Jumblat. The Palestinian commando organizations were natural magnets for the *qabadai* network, which was ironically set adrift by Saeb Salaam himself (when Prime Minister under Franjieh) through his dismantling of the Chehabist Deuxième Bureau.[134] As already noted, an important source of strength of the traditional Sunnite Moslem oligarchs had been close links with Arab heads of state. But the new radical Arab capitals were actively engaged in undermining the authority of these oligarchs as relics of feudalism. At the same time, the conservative Arab regimes were disposed to throw their weight behind the Maronite rather than the Sunnite Moslem establishment. Finally, the fickle "Street"—the urban Sunnite Moslem masses—by now had many alternative Pied Pipers of Hamelin to choose from both inside and outside the Lebanese frontiers.

In their new insecurity the Sunnite oligarchs hit all the harder not only at the Maronites across the Moslem-Christian cleavage line but at their fellow Moslem oligarchs as well, thus eroding still further the basis of the system. For a while the premiership of Salaam under Franjieh (1970-1973) concealed the extent of the shift in the balance of the power in the Sunnite community away from the oligarchs. But Salaam's fall after the Israeli Beirut raid in April 1973 could no longer obscure the reality that there was no Sunnite leader to deliver the Sunnite community nor any Sunnite "community" to be delivered. Given the pivotal role in the system of a functioning Maronite-Sunnite working rapport at the Presidential/Prime Ministerial level, it was not surprising that with the undermining of one of its two main pillars the central Lebanese arch fell crashing to the ground.

3. The Failure of a Model

Why were the Lebanon watchers misled about the viability of the system practically until the eve of the Civil War?[135] This would seem to have been due to the ostensible credibility of a model of the Lebanese system which alone seemed to account for its continued survival in the period 1943-1970. This was the model of what might be described as a virtual or functional (as opposed to a constitutional/territorial) federation which contained and controlled the dominant Christian-Moslem cleavage. The modalities through which this control was effected seemed to be: 1) the existence on each side of the cleavage line of semi-autonomous sects constituting the principal sub-national units of the system; 2) the more or less hierarchical structure of these sects; 3) the existence of recognizable strong leaders at the top of each sectarian hierarchy; 4) the commitment of the leaders to the perpetuation of the system, since, as its ruling "federal" oligarchy, they were its chief beneficiaries through whom rewards and benefits were channeled to their respective sectarian constituencies; and 5) the acceptance by the ruling oligarchy of the consensual rules of the game.

Until the early 1970s the model seemed to retain its relevance to political realities despite the obvious strains to which the Lebanese system was increasingly being subjected. Like a convalescent recovering from a bout of fever, the country seemed to have emerged none the worse from the 1958 Civil War. As the Chehabist reforms floundered in the 1960s, even "planless planning" seemed the unique Lebanese recipe for "modernization without revolution."[136] Deeply divided as it was, Lebanon somehow managed to retain its open system while avoiding intense conflict. This seemed to qualify it alongside a small number of other pluralistic democratic states whose stability did not derive from the operation of the majoritarian principle.

In fact, the model never altogether applied. The viability of the Lebanese system in the 1940s stemmed from two factors. On the one hand, Lebanon was still in the premodernization stage; on the other, the Lebanese ruling elite belonged to the same ruling elite that held power in the other Arab capitals. This regional elite shared an essentially conservative outlook buttressed by the essentially non-interventionist commitment that was exemplified in the loose confederal formula on which the Arab League was structured. It is to this period that Arend Lijphart's and Eric Nordlinger's descriptions of Lebanese consensual politics particularly apply.[137]

Already by the mid-1950s, Lebanon began to be caught in the vise which was subsequently to crush it: on the one hand, the increasing pace of modernization in a laissez-faire economy on which mounting demands were made by the now socially mobilized Moslem have-nots of society, and on the other, an Arab world which had been radicalized in the aftermath of the Arab-Israeli wars of 1948 and 1956 and the Egyptian-Syrian union of 1958-61. The system appeared to escape the vise because Chehab's leadership (1958-1964) brought it domestic respite through an accelerated reform program and external respite through détente with Nasser. But in fact Chehab's very reforms only served to hasten the pace of "social mobilization" with the attendant multiplication and intensification of demands on the system, while the fading out of these reforms under Helou (1964-1970) magnified the sense of deprivation and disillusionment. Concurrently, beginning with the Syrian secession from union with Egypt in 1961 and climaxing in Nasser's supreme humiliation in June 1967, the Egyptian leader began to lose his grip over the radicalized and politicized Lebanese (and Palestinian) intelligentsia, which underwent a deep doctrinal reappraisal from the mid-1960s. By the late 1960s, the external factor was impinging with particular intensity on the Lebanese scene from both the Arab-Israeli and Pan-Arab areas; thus the explosion of the early 1970s.

At the risk of repetition, it must be emphasized that it is the cumulative temporal confluence of the external and internal factors that hit Lebanon with such devastating effect, taking Lebanon watchers by surprise. For the fundamental interpretive weakness of the "federal" model described above lies precisely in its concentration on the contents of the Lebanese box. Perhaps the basic lesson to be learned from all this is simply that when a deeply divided society (like Lebanon) belongs to a regional system characterized by the level of turbulence prevailing in the Arab world, and when the Pan-doctrine is actively espoused within this system, the centrifugal tendencies within this member society are likely to be maximized. In their assessment of the viability and future of the society under consideration, watchers are therefore put on notice to scrutinize the regional environment of the box no less than the contents of the box itself.

5

FROM THE END OF GENERAL HOSTILITIES TO THE ISRAELI INVASION

1. An Auspicious Beginning

Seventeen months separated the cessation of general hostilities in October 1976 from the Israeli invasion in March 1978. During this period the first faltering steps towards a return to normalcy were taken. But the psychological and physical damage inflicted on the country had been so great that the end of this period found the principal local protagonists still far apart. In the first few months after October 1976 the Arab-Israeli conflict and regional inter-Arab politics had relatively less impact on the Lebanese scene than in the previous two years. But as 1977 advanced, this external environment once again began to bear down heavily on Lebanon. When Israel struck in March 1978 the country was still in a pre-convalescent state.

In October and November 1976 several factors had seemed to augur well for an early start on the journey to normalcy. First of all, the Arab Deterrent Force (ADF) entrusted by the Riyad and Cairo summits with the task of restoring law and order possessed overwhelming strength compared to that of the local combatants. The Syrian troops, which formed the largest component of the ADF, had both the power and the will to carry out their responsibilities. This ruled out the resumption of general hostilities. It precluded any attempt by either the right-wing Maronite militias or the Leftist-Palestinian alliance to impose their terms on the other. It also precluded the possibility of a unilateral Maronite declaration of independence in a partitioned Lebanon while reducing the incentive for it. Secondly, the man in the street—whether Christian or Moslem, the real victim of the carnage—experienced an immense sense of relief at the prospect of a return to peace and of movement towards a settlement. The end of the fighting enabled him to inspect the devastated sites of the combat zones and to ponder the price of internecine war. Thirdly, President Sarkis emerged as a rallying point. His technocratic background, administrative ability, non-confrontational political style, as well as the support he received from the Arab governments, singled him out as the architect for national reconciliation and reconstruction. And finally, the apparent readiness of Arafat to disengage not only militarily but also from direct political involvement in Lebanese domestic affairs afforded a chance for the Lebanese protagonists to engage in a dialogue among themselves.

Regional and international developments pointed in the same direction. The Arab consensus behind the Riyad and Cairo summits seemed to end the "Spanish Civil War" role that Lebanon had assumed in regional Arab conflict in the years 1975-1976. In addition to the Syrians, the United Arab Emirates, the Sudan, Saudi Arabia, and Northern Yemen contributed contingents to the ADF. The interregnum caused by the American presidential elections and the change of administration in Washington produced a lull of sorts in the Arab-Israeli conflict.

The immediate tasks facing Sarkis were monumental. The toll in human lives even in the final official estimate was put at 30,000 killed (of whom some 5000 were Palestinian).[138] More than twice as many were wounded. Some 250,000 needed immediate relief. Some 600,000 had migrated internally during the fighting in panic or under compulsion. Even more had fled to the sanctuary of neighboring countries or farther abroad. Although these figures included Palestinians and Syrian residents in Lebanon, the bulk were Lebanese.[139] This was staggering for a country the size of Lebanon (3400 square miles) with a population of some 3,250,000 (excluding the Palestinians).

Lebanon's economy had been largely service-oriented. For nearly two years both air and sea communications as well as telephone, telegraph, and telex services with the outside world were virtually paralyzed. Beirut International Airport was under constant bombardment, Beirut Harbor a battle area. Tourism, transit trade, commerce, and banking services were at a standstill. Hotels, restaurants, office blocks, and commercial centers were gutted. At least 25% of industrial plant and agricultural equipment was destroyed.

Much of the infrastructure was also in shambles: roads, bridges, sewerage systems, electricity networks, and public transportation facilities. Many schools, hospitals, and university buildings were destroyed. The government apparatus, its personnel and property, were no less affected. The civil service was utterly demoralized. The internal security forces and regular army were reduced to warring bands, their weapons turned against one another. The Prime Minister's office, ministerial and government bureaus, police stations, army barracks, and courts were occupied or ransacked; their equipment and archives commandeered or burned. Prisons and even mental hospitals were broken into and their inmates "released."

A conservative estimate puts capital loss in the public sector (excluding the army and security forces) at 1.33 billion Lebanese pounds (£L) and that in the private sector at £L 6.17 billion—a total of £L 7.5 billion.[140] This is just short of the Gross Domestic Product (GDP) for 1974, the year preceding the outbreak of the civil war. Another estimate puts the drop in GDP in 1975 at about £L 2.0 billion to a level of £L 6.0 billion. The drop in 1976 is estimated at £L 3.0 billion to a GDP level of £L 3.0 billion.[141] Assuming the restoration of public order, progress towards a political settlement on the domestic and regional levels, the re-establishment of business confidence, adequate and prompt financing, and the efficient implementation of a reconstruction program, there was a chance of regaining the 1974 level by the end of 1979.

The priorities dictated themselves to Sarkis: security, the establishment of the nucleus of a central administration, the resumption of essential services, relief, and the planning of economic reconstruction.

To these ends Sarkis took several steps. On 9 December 1976 he appointed a "non-political" government of technocrats headed by the Sunnite economist and ex-professor Salim Hoss. One of Hoss's first actions was to tour the Arab countries to solicit economic assistance. On 24 December 1976 Parliament passed a bill authorizing him to rule by decree for a period of six months. A Lebanese was named commander of the Arab Deterrent Force which, according to the Riyad and Cairo summits, was to be under the command of the Lebanese President. New chiefs were appointed for the army and the internal security forces, which were both in the process of reconstruction. Special legislation was enacted to allow army officers to resign without loss of benefits as a face-saving exit from the services for those who had taken part in the internecine fighting or had become too demoralized by it. In January 1977 Sarkis established an autonomous Board of Reconstruction and Development directly responsible to himself to supervise planning and the expenditure of incoming aid. In the same month censorship was imposed on the press in an attempt to restrict inflammatory propaganda.

In keeping with its mandate, the Arab Deterrent Force (ADF) moved to separate the combatants and supervise their withdrawal "to the positions they occupied before 13 April 1975" (the date of the Ain Rummaneh Massacre) as well as to collect the heavy arms from all parties. A special four-nation committee formed by the Riyad summit and composed of representatives of Syria, Kuwait, Saudi Arabia, and Egypt was charged with the task of coordinating with Sarkis the strict implementation of the 1969 Cairo Agreement.[142]

As the ADF deployed in territories controlled respectively by the Maronites and the Leftist-Moslem-Palestinian alliance, the forces of the principal militias disappeared from the streets. The PLO sent the bulk of its local troops to the south. Regular Palestine Liberation Army units that had come from Syria and Egypt, as well as the volunteers from Iraq, were sent back to these countries. The ADF occupied the army barracks and police stations seized by the rebel Lebanese Arab Army or the Leftist-Moslem militias. Some heavy equipment was collected from all sides. The rest disappeared into the depots of the various militias, Lebanese and Palestinian, or was taken south by PLO units and the hard-core remnants of the rebel Lebanese Arab Army. Enough was collected, however, to enable Beirut Radio to announce on 13 January 1977 that the collection of heavy arms had been completed. Units of the ADF manned hundreds of checkpoints along the main roads throughout the country (except in the south). These developments did not take place without incident. There were scores of instances during these early months when the Syrian units of the ADF, often aided by the Syrian-sponsored Palestinian *Saiqa* militia, engaged dissident leftist and Palestinian elements. But these incidents served only to emphasize the ADF's seriousness of purpose.

In these circumstances the slow return to normalcy began. The roads linking the principal cities and regions were reopened, allowing for freedom of travel and transport across sectarian lines. The police reappeared in the streets. By 15 December 1976 both the airport and the harbor of Beirut were in operation. Essential communication and municipal services were gradually restored. Ministerial offices and governmental agencies came to life with skeleton staffs. So did state and private educational institutions. Business began picking up even amidst the rubble of the commercial centers. Most national and some foreign banks reopened. Many of those who had fled the country, including foreign corporations and international organizations, began to return. Cinemas, hotels, and restaurants resumed business.

2. The Harvest of War

But appearances belied the underlying reality. It found violent expression not only in the intermittent clashes between the ADF and dissident leftist and Palestinian elements but also in incidents between the ADF and dissident right-wing Maronites. There were bomb outrages, mysterious kidnappings and killings, and attempted assassinations of public figures.

The most serious incident in the early months involved the assassination by unknown assailants on 16 March 1977 of Kamal Jumblat and the massacre of scores of Christians in spontaneous retaliation by his enraged followers. Meanwhile the rapidly deteriorating situation in the south cast a dark shadow over the whole country. Here right-wing Maronites in border villages backed by Israel ranged themselves against the local as well as the redeploying militias of the Leftist-Moslem-Palestinian alliance.

The reality underlying the facade of the return to normalcy had several ominous features. Foremost was what might be termed the psychological harvest of the Civil War. At best, communal traumas are conducive to collective irrationalities, and both Christians and Moslems (not to mention the Palestinians) had been traumatized by the brutalities they had visited upon each other. The result had been a degree of inter-sectarian alienation the likes of which can be found only in the aftermath of the Lebanese communal massacres of 1860.[143] Poignantly illustrating this had been the internal migration that had accompanied the fighting during 1975-76, involving some 600,000 out of a total of 3,250,000 Lebanese. With the end of hostilities it was expected that the refugees would return to their pre-civil war abodes. This did happen to a certain extent, but it was counterbalanced by a second migration which took place after the end of general hostilities, and under the stresses of the inter-sectarian psychological alienation. This is not to say that Lebanon was breaking up into geographic areas of sectarian exclusivity. For centuries there had been areas characterized by distinctive sectarian densities. And even today as many Lebanese live as "hostage" communities as those who reside in areas predominantly inhabited by their own faith or sect. It is nevertheless true that the areas of sectarian exclusivity had significantly expanded during the war and continued to do so even after the cessation of general hostilities.

Another feature of the reality underlying the facade of normalcy was the nature of the post-civil war "political map" of Lebanon. The central institutions revived by Sarkis were still in an embryonic state, their further development depending upon the achievement of national reconciliation. This particularly affected the reorganization of the armed forces whose future leadership, command structure, and composition were issues which, *inter alia*, lay at the center of inter-sectarian controversy. Sarkis had to make do with the developing nucleus of a future army some 3000 strong—a mere palace guard. Meanwhile, he depended on borrowed security—the ADF. But this created its own problems. Thus while *de jure* Sarkis' writ extended throughout the country, *de facto* it was confined within narrow geographical limits.

These were set by the presence of the other protagonists who, for all intents and purposes, divided the country into the following zones of influence:

1) A narrow strip along the border with Israel some five to six miles wide. This included five or six Maronite villages close to the border as well as twice that number of Shiite villages. Maronite units of the disintegrated Lebanese army, as well as Maronite right-wing militiamen, dominated the Maronite villages and their environs and made themselves felt throughout this zone. The Maronites were in alliance with the Israelis whose aid had begun to assume an increasingly military character as of the summer of 1976. Units of the rebel Lebanese Arab army, as well as Lebanese leftist and PLO militiamen, disputed control of this zone with the forces of the Maronite-Israeli alliance. The ADF was barred from entry to this zone by an Israeli veto. Sarkis' administration had no presence here.

2) A zone lying to the north of this all the way to the Litani River and some 10 miles beyond it. Israel had postulated a Red Line north of its own borders which it warned the ADF not to cross. Although it was generally assumed that the Litani was the Red Line, Israel had not made this explicit and had shown ostensible restlessness when ADF units had tried to approach the *northern* bank of the Litani. The ADF had therefore kept well away from the river.[144] This zone was overwhelmingly Shiite and dominated by the Leftist-Moslem-Palestinian alliance. Here the Sarkis administration existed on tolerance.

3) A zone extending between this and the Damascus-Beirut highway. The ADF was present here in force and the Sarkis administration had, as a result, a greater presence in it. But this was also the Shuf, the heartland of the Leftist-Moslem alliance.

4) Beirut and its suburbs, constituting a zone by itself. It was the seat of the Sarkis administration and the ADF was present in force. But Western Beirut was virtually the headquarters of the PLO as well as of the National Movement, while Eastern Beirut was the Maronite "capital."

5) The coastal and central mountain area north of the Damascus-Beirut highway and extending to the environs of Tripoli. This was Mt. Lebanon proper—the Maronite heartland. The ADF was present but not conspicuous here and the Sarkis administration existed strictly on tolerance.

6) A zone constituting a wide arc which stretched from Tripoli and its hinterland in the north and skirted the above-mentioned zones in the east all the way down the Bekaa Valley towards the Israeli border and the Golan. The ADF was present here in force and so was the Sarkis administration.

The most obvious danger posed by the continuation of these conditions was that of their routinization. This danger was particularly evident in the areas under Maronite control. Here the political leadership was still in the hands of the Lebanese Front, the coalition composed of the principal Maronite leaders: ex-Presidents Suleiman Franjieh and Camille Chamoun, Pierre Gemayel of the Phalanges, and Father Sharbel Kassis of the Maronite monastic orders. The Front supervised both political and administrative matters in the territories under its control. The United Forces of the Maronite militias under the command of Basheer Gemayel, son of Pierre, were responsible to it. The Front controlled an airport and a radio station. It was in direct contact with Major Saad Haddad, an ex-Lebanese Army officer who now emerged as the commander of the Maronite militias on the border with Israel.[145] It levied its own taxes.[146] Internal security was in the hands of its United Forces rather than in those of Sarkis or the ADF. It insisted on the establishment in Maronite territory of branches of the Lebanese State and American universities whose main campuses were in the "Moslem" half of Beirut. It was a shadow government in all but word. (By the same token, of course, the continued presence of the PLO on Lebanese soil appeared to the Maronites as tantamount to a state within a state.) But in practice, the Sarkis administration tended to prevail in the zones where the ADF was not prevented from operation by an Israeli veto. The threat of the routinization of the *de facto* partition just described was therefore greatest (outside the south) in Maronite-controlled territory.

3. The Mood of the Protagonists

It was against this background that Sarkis tried, with Syrian help, to prod and probe in the direction of national reconciliation. But the political mood of the principal protagonists was not conducive to this end.

Because of the military outcome of the war the Maronites were exultant and defiant. But they were haunted by the caveat: Never Again. Any future settlement, if one were desirable, would have to include built-in guarantees to prevent the recurrence of the events of 1975-76. It would therefore have to be established on completely different bases from those of the 1943 National Pact.[147] The issue of the Palestinians on Lebanese soil would have to be tackled root and branch. Many Maronites took heart from their growing alliance with Israel. In their eyes the principal task of the ADF was to disarm the "rebel" Palestinian and National Movement militias. The Maronite militias represented "Lebanese" legitimacy.

Conversely, the Moslem-Leftist side felt battered and betrayed. The euphoric Maronite mood compounded their sense of frustration and humiliation. So did the continued presence of the ADF. At best, the Maronite "conditions" for national reconciliation seemed designed to consolidate Maronite predominance in a unitary state. At worst, they were formulated to be rejected by the Leftist-Moslem alliance to justify subsequent Maronite secession. The growing Israeli-Maronite alliance seemed to confirm the darkest fears of the Leftist-Moslem alliance. It further inhibited them from exploring with the Maronites the new bases for national reconciliation, and even more from adopting a joint position on the Palestinians. The assassination of Kamal Jumblat left the National Movement leaderless, increasing its general disorientation. These characterizations describe the more extreme attitudes on each side, neither of which, needless to say, was monolithic.

The positions of the non-Lebanese protagonists further complicated the picture. The PLO's general attitude could perhaps be summed up in the words, "My head is bloody but unbowed." The events of 1975-1976 had only shown how mortal was the threat posed by the "Conspiracy" against them. But the course of the fighting had vindicated their strategic alliance with the Lebanese National Movement. They were not against Lebanese national reconciliation. But they were not about to denude themselves of arms and so liquidate their liberation movement and their struggle against Israel. They would respect Lebanese sovereignty and abide by the resolutions of the Riyad and Cairo summits, but at the same time they would insist on their rights under the 1969 Cairo Agreement[148] which both Damascus and Sarkis had endorsed. The continued Maronite-Israeli alliance was an attempt to prolong the civil war to somehow engineer their destruction. They would cooperate with both the Sarkis administration and the ADF. They would "politically" disengage from the Lebanese scene but would not drop their "strategic" alliance with the Lebanese National Movement. If necessary, they would fight their Massada on Lebanese soil, whatever the identity of the attacker.

Syria's main objective was to promote national reconciliation under Sarkis while preventing the resumption of hostilities and denying Israel a pretext for massive intervention. The Syrians were interested in putting restraints on PLO actions which might provide such a pretext. At the same time they were anxious to refurbish their Pan-Arab image which had suffered from their earlier high-handedness against the PLO. They were all the more inclined to put some distance between themselves and the more extreme Maronites because of the latter's growing alliance with Israel. The Riyad and Cairo summits had legitimized their role in

Lebanon in Arab eyes. But they did not interpret this role to be that of the executioner of the PLO, which was urged upon them by Maronite hawks. If these Maronites were shifting their alliance from Damascus to Tel Aviv they could not count on the same cooperation that Syria had extended to them in 1976. And if Israel drew Red Lines on the map for the ADF, the ADF's role outside the Red Line could not as easily be dictated by Israel.[149]

Israel's declared objective was to prevent the "reactivation" of the south of Lebanon by the PLO. During 1976, Palestinian units stationed in the border area, in keeping with the 1969 Cairo Agreement, had been drawn into the fighting in and around Beirut. The Riyad and Cairo summits had ordered the disengagement of the Palestinians from central Lebanon and their return to the south. The ADF was charged with the implementation of these provisions, to be supervised by the four-nation committee comprising the representatives of Egypt, Syria, Kuwait and Saudi Arabia.[150] Palestinian presence in the south was to be regulated by strict adherence to the 1969 Cairo Agreement. There was an understanding that operations against Israel, theoretically permissible under the Cairo Agreement, would be put in moratorium. The PLO units would deploy in the south at a distance of some six to nine miles from the border.[151] This process was complicated by two developments. 1) The Israelis vetoed the entry of ADF units (including non-Syrian components such as the Sudanese and Saudi Arabians) beyond the putative Red Line generally believed to be congruent with the Litani River.[152] Given the collapse of Lebanon's central administration, and the fact that the reconstruction of the new Lebanese armed forces was dependent on the progress of national reconciliation (which was bound to take time to gather momentum), Israel's policy was tantamount to creating and perpetuating a power vacuum between the Litani River and its own border. 2) Simultaneously, the Israelis escalated their military aid to the Maronite villages on their border. This encouraged the Maronites to try to expand their control beyond their villages in the area south of the Litani. This area was predominantly inhabited by Moslem Shiites (the Maronites constituting some 5% of the population). One result was increased Shiite-Maronite friction. Another was spiraling conflict between the Israeli-backed Maronites on the one hand, and the redeploying PLO units, on the other.[153] Accompanying the PLO units to the south were National Movement militias and remnants of the Lebanese Arab Army. These were increasingly involved in the fighting. A repeat performance of the 1975-76 Civil War was in the making. The new inter-sectarian tensions generated by the developing situation cut across Sarkis' efforts at national reconciliation, and like a gangrened limb the south spread its poison throughout the country. This gave rise to speculation as to Israeli motives. From the perspective of Damascus, for example, Israel seemed bent on keeping Lebanon, and therefore Syria, off balance. The object could be to force Syria to quit Lebanon or alternatively to nudge it into a showdown with either the Maronites or the Palestinians. The general Israeli hope seemed to be that its strategy in Lebanon would somehow compel Syria to soften its position in any negotiations for an overall Middle East settlement.

4. National Reconciliation and the Palestinians

Presently two issues began to dominate the political "discourse" in Beirut. These were: a) How to effect the national reconciliation, and b) How to "solve" the problem of the Palestinian armed and civilian presence on Lebanese soil.

With regard to national reconciliation several questions arose. *First:* The question of the desirability of the principle itself. Should the Lebanese Humpty-Dumpty be put together again, and a unitary Lebanese state preserved within the international frontiers of 1920?[154] Or, alternatively, should Maronite predilection for a territorial sanctuary be institutionalized within some new federal or confederal formula? Even if a unitary state were to be opted for, how could Maronite territorial susceptibilities be accommodated without violence to the principle of unity or the encouragement of centrifugal forces?

Second: The question of the bases for the new settlement. Were the 1943 National Pact and the February 1976 Constitutional Document of President Suleiman Franjieh still relevant?[155] If only partly relevant, what modifications in them were desirable and possible? And was deconfessionalism still a precondition of the National Movement for its political participation?

Third: The question of who was to be party to the settlement. This question acquired particular relevance with regard to the Moslem-Leftist side. Here the military outcome of the Civil War, the assassination of Kamal Jumblat, as well as the presence of the ADF, had weakened the National Movement's position and, by the same token, allowed the Moslem oligarchs to reemerge. But the National Movement, though in disarray, represented not only the Moslem-Leftist combatants, but also new grass-roots forces which challenged the authority and credibility of the reemerging Moslem oligarchs.[156] Who, then, was to represent the Moslems in the settlement and what role, if any, was the National Movement to play? The problem was further complicated by the vetoes placed by various parties on the participation of others in the settlement.

Such vetoes were traded between the Moslem oligarchs and the National Movement. The Maronite Lebanese Front placed vetoes on the participation of the National Front *per se*, though not on some of its members. Such, ironically, was also the attitude of Syria, whose veto extended, however, to some of the Moslem oligarchs acceptable to the Maronites.

Fourth: The question of the modality of the settlement. Should it be negotiated by the technocratic government of Prime Minister Salim Hoss or by a new government of politicians? Should it, in other words, precede the formation of a government of politicians or should such a government be entrusted with the task? If the latter, who was to take part in the government, and, in particular, who was to represent the Moslems?

A parallel running debate occurred with regard to the issue of the Palestinians. This centered on the 1969 Cairo Agreement. Both Sarkis and Syria considered the Agreement still valid. So did the Riyad and Cairo summits to which both were party. So also did the National Movement and the Moslem oligarchs. To them all, the issue was its strict implementation, which was specifically enjoined by the two summits. But even its strict implementation ran up against the situation in the south created by Israel's military alliance with the Maronites as well as its Red Line policy. Meanwhile, as far as the Lebanese Front was concerned, the Cairo Agreement was null and void. This it formally declared to be the case on 27 May 1977. It therefore expected the ADF to remove all Palestinian armed forces from Lebanon. Unless this were done, the Maronite militias would remain under arms, and, presumably, the Maronite-Israeli alliance in the border area and elsewhere would continue. The patent reluctance of the Syrians to comply served only to exacerbate Maronite-Syrian relations. At the same time, the Lebanese Front raised the issue of civilian Palestinian presence. This amounted to some 350,000, which was about 200,000 in excess of the number of Palestinian refugees accepted in 1948 after the creation of Israel.[157] The Lebanese Front demanded the dispersion of these additional Palestinians among the Arab countries. In their outraged postwar consciousness the Maronites were seized by an obsessive desire to be "rid" of the Palestinians once and for all. From their perspective, the Palestinians were not only the root cause of the Civil War, but the major obstruction in the path of a new national entente. To see eye to eye on this issue with the Maronites became the touchstone of loyalty to Lebanon, the passport for admission to a dialogue leading to national reconciliation. Complex as the issues facing reconciliation were in themselves, the right-wing Maronite insistence on the prior "solution" of the issue of the Palestinians made the task of reconciliation even more problematic.

The resulting impact of this deadlock made itself felt in three key areas that absorbed the energies of Sarkis after his first tentative steps on the journey to normalcy.

First: The area of political participation. A technocratic government such as that led by Prime Minister Hoss overburdened Sarkis himself. It left untapped and unharnessed the real centers of power in the country, both those that had been created by the Civil War, and the older ones that had survived it. But the transition from a technocratic to a political government was ineluctably contingent upon progress in the dialogue towards a new national entente. Similarly, at the legislative level, Sarkis had to make do with the Parliament elected in 1972 whose four-year mandate had ended in May 1976. This mandate had already been extended for two years, until May 1978. In January 1978 Sarkis had wisely extended the parliamentary mandate for another two years in a desperate attempt to maintain the semblance of legislative legitimacy, however specious. *Second:* The rebuilding of the armed forces. Perhaps the most crucial institution to feel the effect of this continued political immobilism was Sarkis' fledgling army. Without a strong expanded national army Sarkis could not assert his authority, maintain the unity of the country, ask the ADF to leave, or move to fill the vacuum in the south. Before such an army could be created, the Maronite and National Movement militias had to be dissolved or an agreement reached to absorb them in it. Whatever the solution, it would not only cut across vested interests that were getting more entrenched by the day, but it would also be caught up in the whole tangle of issues with regard to national reconciliation and the Palestinian presence underlying the continued political immobilism. *Third:* The economic recovery of the country. Given the scale of the country's devastation, Sarkis was in need of large infusions of aid. This was to some extent forthcoming from the United States, the E.E.C., the World Bank, and the U.N.[158] But Sarkis' chief reliance was on Arab aid. He did receive some from Saudi Arabia, Kuwait, and the United Arab Emirates.[159] But this aid was not on the scale expected, in spite of Sarkis' plausible plea that more assistance could go a long way in lubricating the political process. Arab diffidence was largely a product of the political deadlock. The growing Maronite-Israeli alliance was another inhibiting factor.

5. Centripetal Forces Gather Momentum

Nevertheless, as 1977 advanced, a set of new factors and developments both domestic and international tended to increase the pull of centripetal forces. Domestically, and at the general level, there was the very fear of continued immobilism. No great clairvoyance was needed to realize that the more drawn-out the postponement of national reconciliation, the more irreversible the translation into hard realities of the existing chaos would become. The man in the street craved for peace and normalcy. The business community was growing increasingly restless.[160] So were the Arab donor countries and participants in the ADF. In spite of their inexhaustible willfulness, the old oligarchs were not immune to nostalgia for governmental office. The political forces that had emerged on both sides during the fighting were anxious to take possession of their share in the new political system.

More specifically, there were four factors in this centripetal development. First, a general softening of attitudes within the Moslem and leftist ranks. There were fewer and fewer references by the National Movement to deconfessionalism. Emphasis was not laid on *tawazun*, or balance and co-equality between Christians and Moslems in any new settlement. There was growing disenchantment among more and more Moslems (particularly among the propertied Shiites) with the Palestinians. This was partly due to high-handedness and misconduct by certain Palestinian factions and their Lebanese allies in the south. But largely it was the result of the terrible punishment in lives and property taken by the Shiites who constituted the vast majority of the inhabitants in the south. Not only were the Shiites there caught in the cross-fire between the Maronite-Israeli alliance on the one hand and the National Movement-Palestinian alliance on the other: it was they who were at the receiving end of Israel's devastating retaliatory blows. These had been raining on them continually since 1968 and had resulted in expediting their exodus from their towns and villages to the metropolis.[161] The outbreak of communal fighting in 1975-1976 had engulfed the suburban shantytowns of Beirut into which the Shiite poor had crowded. The conquest of these shantytowns by the Maronite militias in 1976 had resulted in a second mass exodus of Shiites back to their villages in the south.[162] Now, as a result of the deteriorating situation in the south, the Shiites were once again treking to the north. By October 1977 it was calculated that the total number of refugees, mostly Shiites, was about 300,000.[163] Under these circumstances several Shiite oligarchs were emboldened to demand a reassessment of Arab strategy. They argued that unless all the other front-line Arab states endorsed and participated in a joint endeavor involving Palestinian action against Israel so that the "cost" was shared by all alike, it was unfair to expect that the Shiite south alone should remain a battleground.

But it was not only the Shiites who were showing such signs of restlessness. Some Sunnite oligarchs who traditionally gave unqualified support to the Palestinians voiced sympathy with the demands of the Shiite leaders. And even in Sidon, traditional Sunnite and pro-Palestinian stronghold, the infringements and transgressions of certain dissident Palestinian and National Movement militias produced a reaction. In January 1978 a popular demonstration against these transgressions prompted the PLO to take strong measures against its dissident elements. This did not necessarily mean that Moslem Lebanese support for the Palestinians was being withdrawn but rather that many Moslem Lebanese were becoming more critical of Palestinian conduct and were saying so publicly. This had the effect of somewhat bridging the gap between the Maronites and the Moslems and thus strengthening the centripetal forces pulling in the direction of national reconciliation. The "strategic" alliance between the PLO and the National Movement remained, however, unaffected by these developments.

The second centripetal development constituting an additional common denominator between the Maronites and the Lebanese Moslems was a growing disenchantment with the ADF and particularly its principal component, the Syrians. The presence of any "foreign" force, however friendly and legitimate, is bound to generate over time cumulative tensions between the members of this force and the host country. But the Syrians in addition faced a number of specific problems with the principal local protagonists. The mere juxtaposition of the Sarkis administration and the ADF forces in the same territory created problems which were compounded by the inevitable confusions and misunderstandings arising from parallel or interlocking prerogatives and chains of command. Syrian attitudes toward the PLO could not remain identical with Sarkis' in all details. To the Maronites, the Syrians had at first seemed saviors, which indeed they had been. But from the beginning, the Maronites had been allergic to Syrian deployment in their own territories.[164] As the Maronites saw it, the principal, if not exclusive, task of the Syrians was to tame and disarm the PLO and the National Movement. The Syrians, by their very presence, acted also as a deterrent to extreme Maronite adventurism. They had a stake in the future national reconciliation, and strong views on who was to be party to it, particularly on the Moslem-leftist side. If they saw eye to eye with the Maronites on the exclusion from the reconciliation process of the more radical members of the National Movement, their anxiety to include some of their own Lebanese protégés was considered unwarrantable by some Maronite leaders, though not by Sarkis himself.[165] Disenchantment with the Syrians was also felt by some Moslem oligarchs and by some members of the National Movement. The Moslem oligarchs concerned were those whose participation in the national reconciliation had tacitly been vetoed by the Syrians, either because of their "hostility" to Damascus or because they were considered obsolete. Some of these Moslem oligarchs yearned for the good old days when they could politick with their Maronite counterparts—as did the latter—without outside interference. Although the Syrians had mended their relations with Walid Jumblat, Kamal's son and successor, as leader of the National Movement, many members of the Movement were at odds with them. Indeed, the Syrians had leaned on the National Movement more heavily than they had on the more extremist Maronites. They had tacitly vetoed their participation in the national re-conciliation and, therefore, in any future government. They had bypassed them in favor of their own protégés who had pulled out of the fighting against the Maronite militias during the Civil War.[166]

This growing general disenchantment with the Syrians did not affect the central alliance between Sarkis and Asad. Nor did it affect Palestinian-Syrian relations, which, if anything (and partly as a result of this disenchantment), were characterized by growing detente. But it did tend to push most of the Lebanese protagonists closer together. It also created a dangerously volatile and trigger-happy state of affairs between the Syrian components of the ADF and the Maronite militias. This burst into the open on 8 February 1978 in the most serious security incident—apart from Kamal Jumblat's assassination—since the cessation of general hostilities. The incident involved a fierce clash between Syrian troops and Maronite units belonging to Sarkis' new army. Whether the clash was a spontaneous explosion of frayed nerves on both sides or specifically timed by some *agent provocateur* to mar President Asad's reelection the same day, is uncertain. The fighting threatened to spill over into Maronite neighborhoods, but was brought under control by the joint efforts of Sarkis and Asad. The ominous implications of a repetition of such an incident gave another push to the centripetal forces.

A third development that indirectly exerted a centripetal effect involved certain structural tendencies with regard to the communal organization of the country as well as the leadership of the Maronites. In the course of 1977 a general phenomenon was observable. This was the greater assertion of sectarian affiliation characteristic of pre-Civil War days. It was as if the Civil War and its debris had shocked people into greater awareness of their respective sectarian roots. This was not as significant for the Maronites as for some of the other sects because Maronite self-consciousness had been consistently high (some would argue too high) throughout, though increased Maronite self-assertiveness as a result of the war almost certainly contributed to the phenomenon being described here. But there were other causes. One of them, perhaps, was the prevailing chaos and insecurity which forced people to seek sanctuary in their traditional identities. Another, as far as the Moslems were concerned, was possibly the military defeat of the National Movement, the ostensible champion of the cause of deconfessionalism, and the Movement's own acknowledgement that its cause had been defeated, at least for the foreseeable future. The assassination of Kamal Jumblat had the same effect. In addition, the Druzes may have felt that Jumblat's dynamic trans-sectarian leadership had over-extended them, the Sunnites and Shiites that it had blurred their "boundaries." With the Shiites, the feeling that they had been uniquely both underdog and scapegoat must have fed on their singular agonies and tribulations. Whatever the reasons (including, to be sure, encouragement from the conservative Arab countries), the general re-emergence of sectarian consciousness cannot be denied. It found expression not only in the return to the stage of some sectarian oligarchs but also in the tendency of leaders and opinion makers outside the hard-core members of the National Movement to form strictly sectarian caucuses. At first glance one would assume this was a centrifugal phenomenon, which indeed it potentially could be, particularly with regard to the Maronites. But under the circumstances it seemed to signify a retreat from the apocalyptic to the mundane, and a return to familiar grounds, where tried, if hackneyed, modalities for conciliation were at hand.

Equally significant were the new alignments within the Maronite leadership. Here the quadripartite Lebanese Front of septuagenarians maintained overall political power underpinned by a ready second-tier of militant heirs-apparent whose legitimacy was confirmed by the unwritten laws of Lebanese political primogeniture.[167] But the tensions generated by the situation described above were having their effect on the solidarity of the Front, which though impressive, had never been monolithic. The Maronite Church represented by Kassis (and behind him by the Maronite Patriarch)[168] tended, once the issue of Maronite survival was not at stake, to put their eggs in the basket of Sarkis and to shy away from a liaison with Israel or a confrontation with Syria. Ex-President Franjieh, true to his mountain chieftain's word, stuck by Syria and, therefore, Sarkis, and while adamant about the PLO, was no less adamant about no alliance with Israel and no partition. Ex-President Chamoun, a perennial and masterful tactician growing more unrelenting with the years, restlessly kept all confrontational options open whether actual or hypothetical. Hemmed in on his flanks by Chamoun's charismatic appeal, as well as by his own son's strident militancy (Basheer Gemayel was commander of the United Forces of the Maronite militias), Pierre Gemayel of the Phalanges, a fundamentally commonsensical, if excitable leader, half-heartedly followed in the footsteps of Franjieh. This state of affairs was reflected in Maronite activity outside the Lebanese Front. For the first time since the Front's formation, concerned groups of Maronite parliamentarians and opinion leaders met, in the late autumn of 1977, *outside* its aegis to discuss the prevailing situation and the prospects of reconciliation. To be sure, the Front continued to set the pace for the Maronites, but its members were not marching in lockstep. Somewhere within the folds of these developments the nucleus of a Maronite Presidential Party was in diffident formation. Its general, if oblique, message seemed to be that it was perhaps time to give the long-suffering Sarkis the benefit of the doubt and some freedom of action.

The quickening pace of regional and international developments during 1977 subtly contributed in their net effect to the same end, notwithstanding appearances to the contrary. President Carter's initial positive statements about the Palestinians encouraged the PLO doves and raised hopes for an early overall settlement of the Arab-Israeli conflict. The resultant Palestinian moderation in Lebanon was evident in the agreement reached in July 1977 between the PLO, the Sarkis Administration, and the Syrians on a timetable for the implementation of the 1969 Cairo Agreement within the framework of the Riyad and Cairo summits. The new accord, known as the Shtaura Agreement (after the Lebanese town where it was concluded), envisaged the collection of heavy arms from the Palestinian camps and depots, the surveillance of these camps, and the restriction of Palestinian armed presence to specified areas in the south away from the border. It also confirmed the moratorium on Palestinian operations across the border. Menachem Begin's electoral victory and his explicit and ostensibly fervid espousal of the Christian cause in Lebanon raised the expectations of many Maronites. But the more intimate the Israeli-Maronite military alliance on the border, the greater the embarrassment of Sarkis and his supporters, both Maronite and non-Maronite. As the prospects for the convening of an early Geneva conference including Palestinian representation began to wane, and Washington's policy on the Palestinians wavered,[169] tension mounted in the south to reach a peak in the autumn of 1977.[170]

But a brief respite was won as a result of Sadat's visit to Jerusalem, even though the PLO and its Lebanese allies gravitated towards the anti-Sadat Rejectionist Arab camp in reaction to the Sadat visit. The most significant political impact on Lebanon of the Sadat initiative was, however, that it elicited from Begin a detailed plan with regard to Israeli policy on the West Bank and the Gaza Strip. The plan, announced in

December 1977, served only to underline how remote were the prospects for an overall settlement of the Arab-Israeli conflict. This had the effect of alerting the Lebanese to the need for setting their house in order rather than waiting indefinitely for such a settlement to "solve" the question of the Palestinians on Lebanese soil. It created a greater incentive to step out of the chicken and egg quandary of whether national reconciliation should precede or follow the "solution" of the Palestinian presence in Lebanon. The veto envisaged in the Begin Plan on the return of the Diaspora Palestinians to the West Bank and the Gaza Strip was a further eye-opener to some Maronites.[171] Its implication that the bulk of the Diaspora Palestinians should be permanently settled in their Arab host countries, including Lebanon, was anathema to the Maronites, as it was, for different reasons, to the Moslem Lebanese. Not only did this bring Maronite and non-Maronite Lebanese closer together, but it also underlined the flimsiness of the "strategic" alliance between Israel and at least the moderate Maronites.

Paradoxically, the erosion of the Arab consensus as a result of the failure to reconvene the Geneva Conference, and in the wake of the Sadat visit to Jerusalem, also had an overall centripetal effect on the Lebanese scene. A case in point here was the future of the ADF. The mandate of this force was initially for a six-month period. This had already been extended twice by the Arab League (in April and October 1977, respectively.) The last mandate of the force was, at the time of writing, due to expire in April 1978. Given the deep cleavage in Arab ranks after the Sadat Jerusalem visit, a number of questions arose: Would the Arab League be able to meet to extend the mandate of the force? Would the pro-Sadat participants in the force (e.g., the Sudan) pull out their contingents as a reprisal for the anti-Sadat posture of Syria? Would the other (non-Syrian military or financial) participants in the force decide themselves to pull out rather than persevere in the absence of an Arab consensus? And, finally, in the event of the failure of the Arab League to meet and renew the mandate of the force, would a wholly Syrian force be possible or desirable?[172]

It was not so much the legalistic, procedural, or even financial problem connected with the Arab peacekeeping force and the Arab consensus, or lack of it, that came to the fore. Sarkis, in the last analysis, could exercise his sovereign power to conclude bilateral agreements with Syria and other willing Arab countries to reconstitute the force. What the erosion of the Arab consensus highlighted were the uncertainties and vicissitudes of continued reliance on a security deriving from others.

The proposition being advanced here is that the interplay between the internal tensions and external influences throughout 1977 and the first months of 1978 before the fateful Ides of March had given an edge to the centripetal over the centrifugal forces within Lebanon.

The proposition is not that just before Menachem Begin struck, the ripe apple of Lebanese national entente was about to drop into the ample lap of Elias Sarkis or that of anybody else. It is rather that because of the very hideousness of their wounds, with the promise of still more to come, some collective survival instinct seemed to be stirring among the Lebanese and beckoning them away from their lemming race. It was a matter of a mood, or the setting of a dispositional mold within the framework of which entente was seen both as an imperative and a process. Progress would be incremental, starting with the areas of greatest consensus and reaching probingly beyond: not much, perhaps, to go by, but a prerequisite condition, necessary if not sufficient, and hitherto missing since Sarajevo at Ain Rummaneh in April 1975.[173] Now, however, it seemed to be anchored to a deeper awareness of the fact that, if one can be the worst enemy of oneself, there is no divine ordinance that this should be so.

It was upon this climate of opinion that Menachem Begin intruded on 15 March 1978.

6

THE ISRAELI INVASION AND
ITS AFTERMATH

1. Israel's Motives and Objectives

A main theme in the foregoing chapters has been the interplay between developments inside the Lebanese "box" and external factors.[174] The external factors that have impinged most heavily on Lebanon have been the Arab-Israeli problem and inter-Arab conflict, itself largely exacerbated by this problem. The Israeli invasion of March 1978 was a climax in this interplay, pulling Lebanon more directly than ever before into the vortex of the Arab-Israeli problem.

As stated earlier, it is possible to view the Lebanese Civil War of 1975-76 as fundamentally another phase in the unfolding tragedy of Palestine since 1948. The Palestinians were not in Lebanon by choice: most inhabitants of the Palestinian camps in the country were refugees or children of refugees from their towns and villages in Galilee across the border with Israel, whence they had fled or been expelled in the 1948 Palestine War.

The occasion for the Israeli invasion was the terrible Palestinian bus raid on the road between Haifa and Tel Aviv in which 34 Israelis lost their lives and 78 were wounded. A massive Israeli response was inevitable: Israel's policy of super-retaliation had become established practice. The raid in itself was a challenge to Begin. It was doubly so because it exposed the weaknesses in his security system.[175] It came in the wake of a marked increase since his electoral victory in violent acts of Palestinian resistance in the occupied territories and in Israel.[176] The challenge was all the greater because of the drop in his popularity ratings from 78.3% in December 1977 to 59.4% in mid-March 1978 on the eve of his visit to Washington.[177]

But a massive response was also inevitable for more general

considerations. Begin's political posture on the PLO and the occupied territories in the West Bank and in the Gaza Strip was bound to generate a military counterpart. The vacuum in South Lebanon was a standing invitation. The continued presence in the country of the Syrian forces was increasingly intolerable. Syria's isolation from Egypt and Iraq and the disenchantment of many Lebanese with Damascus and with the Palestinians created seemingly favorable conditions. There was need to demonstrate toughness before calling on Carter again. But given Begin's self image as the ex-Irgun chief, as well as general Israeli (and non-Israeli) "expectations" of him, his response would not only be massive but qualitatively different from that of his predecessors.

It may be pertinent at this point to mention that provocative as the Palestinians had often been on the Lebanese border, it was Israel that had, as it were, called the shots there since the border became a "hot" one in 1968.[178] According to the tally of the Lebanese army (before its disintegration in 1976),[179] Israeli violations of Lebanese territory in the period 1968-1974 occurred at the rate of 1.4 violations per day. This increased to 7 violations per day during 1974-75. In the eight months' period between 1 January 1975 and 21 August 1975 (when the Lebanese army's tally ended), the following Israeli violations were recorded: air space 1,101; territorial waters 215; artillery shellings 2,180; machine-gun firing 303; air and naval raids 40; temporary installation inside Lebanese territory 193; road building 3; land incursions 151. This averages out to 17 violations per day.

Already before Begin, the Israeli government had initiated the strategy of pitting the Maronite border villages against their Shiite neighbors and the Palestinians. What Begin did was to escalate this strategy into continuous warfare by proxy on Lebanese soil. When the proxy faltered, Israeli fire power and reinforcements were ready at hand.

Opinions are divided as to whether or not Begin's response to the bus raid was justified by the character and extent of Palestinian activity across the border itself. Many believe it was.[180] To others, pointing to the overall reduction in Palestinian operations against Israel in 1977, it appears unwarranted. According to the PLO, the number of operations mounted from all countries during that year was 156. This was the lowest total since 1967. It compared, for example, with 244 operations (1976), 411 (1975), 2,256 (1970), and 145 (1967).[181] A Western source puts the number of Israelis killed by Palestinian action since the 1973 war at 143 and that of Arabs (Palestinians and Lebanese) killed in "retaliation" before the invasion of Lebanon at 2,000.[182] As far as the Lebanese border itself is concerned, there is no record of a single Israeli casualty there during the first six months of 1977.[183] In the second half of the year the first Israeli casualty occurred on 31 August when a soldier was killed in undisclosed circumstances.[184] In the following weeks, however, three Israeli civilians were killed—victims of Palestinian shelling across the border. The shelling occurred on 6 November. But it did not occur in a total vacuum. On 14 September the Maronite militias on the border had launched—with Israeli encouragement and assistance—a large-scale offensive against the positions of the National Movement and the PLO.[185] Tension had mounted dangerously as a result.

On 5 November the Israelis sank a Lebanese boat, killing three Lebanese fishermen. On 6 November a rocket fired by Palestinian rejectionist elements hit Nahariya in Israel, killing the above mentioned three civilians. On 8 November Israel continuously shelled a total of 20 Lebanese villages, including the marketplace and residential quarters of Tyre. The casualties were 10 killed and 20 wounded—all Lebanese civilians.[186] Still more terrible vengeance was to be wreaked, as will be mentioned below,[187] for the Israeli victims of 6 November. Between this date and the Israeli invasion in March 1978 there is no record of a single Israeli casualty on the border.[188]

This relative Palestinian restraint[189] on the border in spite of the aggressiveness of the Maronite-Israeli alliance was due to two reasons. The first one was the understandings and constraints agreed upon between the PLO, the Syrians, and the Sarkis administration at Shtaura in July 1977 for the implementation of the Cairo Agreement in the spirit of the Riyad and Cairo summits. The most important of these was the suspension of operations against Israel across the border and the deployment of the PLO away from it. The second was the decision taken by the PLO in 1973—and reconfirmed in the light of their assessment of the Civil War—to change their strategy from reliance on action across the Lebanese border to operations inside Israel and the occupied territories.[190]

Under the circumstances, the events on the border prior to March 1978 would not seem to justify the scale of the invasion or of the punishment inflicted on Lebanese civilians. Nor does it make sense from the standpoint of the declared Israeli objective of "severing the evil arm of the PLO"[191]—much less of that of "liquidating" it, as resolved at a special Knesset session soon after the bus raid.[192] The three-day interval between the raid and the invasion gave the PLO ample warning time to pull the bulk of its forces northwards across the Litani. The preliminary carpet bombing by the Israelis by land, sea, and air had had the same effect. So also had the pattern of attack from the south northwards. A "liquidation" strategy would have called for surprise seizure of the Litani by amphibian and helicopter-borne troops to cut off the PLO forces' lines of retreat. The argument that this would have pulled the Syrians into the fighting does not seem to have inhibited Israel's subsequent thrust towards the river. Also incompatible with the "liquidation" strategy was the treatment of the Tyre salient and the coastal corridor linking it to the Litani and beyond. The largest concentration of PLO and Lebanese combatants was in this area. It included three of the largest Palestinian refugee camps.[193] The city and the three camps were not spared bombardment, but there was no attempt to capture them. Concern for civilian casualties could not have been the cause, as evidenced by the carpet bombardment. In any case, most of the civilians had already fled the salient, as Israeli intelligence must have known. The most likely explanation is that Israel, aware of the desperate resistance the Palestinians would put up in the Tyre salient, was not prepared to accept the military casualties the town's capture would entail.

One specific political objective of Israeli strategy would seem to have been the disruption of the Shtaura accord of July 1977, and therefore the entire infrastructure of the Sarkis-Syrian-PLO consensus on the interpretation and implementation of the 1969 Cairo Agreement. The Shtaura accord was the only possible compromise for Sarkis, given the distribution of power inside Lebanon and the resolutions of the Riyad and Cairo summits. Its implementation under Syrian surveillance may not have been a perfect solution. But no such solution was in sight, given the political deadlock on the Palestinian issue in the Middle Eastern talks. The Shtaura accord had at least the merit of imposing a freeze on Palestinian operations across the border. Given its centrality to the slowly emerging Lebanese consensus on national reconciliation and the reconstruction of a national army, as well as its vital importance in the whole range of Lebanese-Syrian-Palestinian relations, the Israeli objective can only have been to throw everything into turmoil again.

There is evidence of such a policy long before the invasion itself. Major Haddad, Israel's Maronite ally on the border, was clearly opposed to the Shtaura accord. At a press conference on 5 August 1977, organized on Israeli territory within a few days of the signature of the accord, he violently attacked the Syrian role in Lebanon, describing the accord as "a trap."[194] In fact, even before the accord, Haddad had been encouraged to go on the offensive. On 19 February 1977, his troops, with Israeli support, fanned out from his enclave based on Marj Uyun against the neighboring Moslem villages.[195] Fighting continued until early April when Haddad was repulsed by the combined forces of the National Movement and the PLO. Meanwhile, announcing that he was "saving the Christians" from genocide,[196] Begin further escalated this war by proxy. By 30 July the first phase of the Shtaura accord (surrender by the

PLO of heavy arms in the camps near Beirut) was completed, however inadequately. By 6 August the second phase (institution of joint ADF-Lebanese-PLO checkpoints at the entrances of the Beirut refugee camps) was completed. By 26 August the PLO announced its readiness to implement the third phase of the accord.[197] This, in addition to the freeze on operations across the border, forbade the PLO forces from deploying within a six-mile belt adjacent to it. On 10 September the Sarkis administration announced that units of its reconstructed army were ready to move south to reestablish governmental authority in the area and confirm the implementation of the Shtaura accord.[198] Within a week Haddad had launched his second major offensive of the year. On 14 September he moved against the strategic Khardali bridge on the Litani under cover of heavy Israeli artillery support.[199] National Movement and PLO forces engaged and routed Haddad's troops. In the heavy fighting 40 were killed and 100 wounded. The Israelis sent in their own forces to extricate Haddad.[200] According to some observers, the Israelis had intended to seize the occasion for a massive operation in the south. This was at a time when the only announced Israeli casualty since 1 January 1977 had been the single soldier killed on 31 August. Apparently, pressure from Washington prevented an early version of the March 1978 invasion.[201] On 22 September Sarkis declared that the fighting in the south had disrupted his plans to send his army units there and that his government had reached agreement with the PLO units stationed in the area.[202] This agreement was presumably what the Haddad offensive was designed to undermine.

An uneasy truce was maintained for the next few weeks which was broken by both sides. It was during this period that the Palestinian shelling across the border on 6 November (referred to above) took place with the loss of three Israeli civilian lives. However, it was in retaliation for these casualties that on 9 November an Israeli air raid wiped out a Lebanese hamlet, Izziyeh, in the hinterland of Tyre. Sixty-five Lebanese civilians were killed and sixty-eight wounded.[203] Three guerillas were reported killed. By 10 November the civilian death toll had risen to above 100, with 150 wounded. On 11 November another air strike wounded 14 more.[204] Commenting on these developments, the Israeli Chief of Staff, General Mordechai Gur, affirmed that the raids had been "purely against terrorist bases."[205] Simultaneously, President Carter indicated that "some retaliation" by Israel was called for.[206]

This analysis of developments in the border area points to the Cairo and Shtaura accords (and through them, Lebanese national reconciliation) as major targets of Israeli strategy, both before the invasion and throughout the invasion itself. But what concerns us more specifically here is the manner in which the invasion seemed to punish the Lebanese civilians, as much, if not more than the Palestinian commandos, its ostensible target. It must surely be self-evident that non-stop bombardment for several days and nights from the land, sea, and air of densely populated areas possessed of no central government and no civil defense system can have only one outcome: a pandemonium of panic and a mass stampede of civilians, not to mention a wanton loss of innocent lives.

The Israeli brigadier generals were not novices in this regard. The argument that armed elements were intermingled with the population was only partly true. They were also known to be largely concentrated in certain localities which could have been pinpointed for reduction, given the reputation of Israeli intelligence and the precision of Israel's weapons systems. Such was the standard of performance of Israeli intelligence that we are told that the particular taxi in which a Palestinian field commander was traveling north of the Litani during the invasion was intercepted by an Israeli naval raiding party in the middle of the flood of refugee vehicles.[207]

It is difficult therefore to escape the conclusion that the punishment wreaked on the pathetically vulnerable Shiite farming and small-town people of the south was part of some policy.[208] The Israelis themselves admit that their army morticians buried 180 Lebanese civilians and estimate that a 100 more lay under the rubble or were buried by relatives.[209] But a Western source puts the total number of civilians killed at more than 2000, the bulk of whom were Lebanese.[210] The number of wounded must have been at least as high. As to how many died in the stampede, from exposure, malnutrition, or shock nobody knows. The new Lebanese refugees numbered over 250,000. In some 100 largely Shiite villages in the area south of the Litani, 2500 houses were completely destroyed, 5200 partly damaged.[211]

The sources of livelihood in southern Lebanon are fishing, tobacco, and citrus. The first was interrupted and is to this day severely curtailed. The tobacco crop had been collected but not sold before the invasion. How much of it was still there at the end of the invasion is uncertain. The citrus crop should have been picked during April. This was possible only within very narrow limits. In addition, much of the infrastructure was destroyed: bridges, electricity and telephone networks, hospitals, schools, clinics, water reservoirs. There was also the extensive looting perpetrated by all invading armies in history, as TV sets, cameras, and radios, as well as the modest if exotic furnishings of Shiite provincial life, disappeared southwards as "mementos."[212] Even if all the refugees were eventually to return to what is left of home, it will be some time before settled life in southern Lebanon could be said to have been resumed. Solitudinem faciunt, pacem apellant.

Another possible clue to Israel's strategy against the Lebanese civilian population lies in the initially declared territorial objective of the invasion: the seizure of a six-mile belt north of the border. Israel would not leave this belt, unless measures were taken to prevent its use by the PLO for attacks against Israel. Militarily, the concept of this security belt does not make much sense. The bus raiders had not come across the border but by sea. According to one of them who was captured, their point of departure had been Tyre.[213] But Tyre lay outside the six-mile belt, and in any case was not stormed even during the Israeli drive towards the Litani in the second phase of the invasion. Palestinian action on the border during 1977 had not taken the form of border crossings but of shelling with rockets whose range was some 15 miles. The shelling continued from north of the Litani even after the Israelis had reached the river. All the Palestinian camps lay outside the six-mile belt. There were countless points of departure for raids against Israel from other parts of Lebanon outside the six-mile belt, as well as from countries other than Lebanon.

To some observers, therefore, the security belt concept was a euphemism for annexation. To these observers, the operative word "security" seemed to be synonymous with additional territory on all the other frontiers of Israel. The small Maronite enclaves on the border had already been annexed de facto by Israel. Attempts had been made even before the invasion to "persuade" the Shiite border villages to accept inclusion within the Israeli "fence," i.e. annexation.[214] Because of the small number of Maronites in the border area (the security belt) and the refusal of the Shiites to accept annexation, the Israelis had organized a shuttle service via Jounieh harbor with the Maronite extremists in the north. Maronite militiamen had been brought by sea to Haifa, trained, armed, and despatched to swell the ranks of Haddad's forces.[215] In time, they could presumably be encouraged to settle on abandoned Shiite land in the security belt under the Israeli umbrella.

Already in the wake of the invasion, Haddad's militiamen had been given a free hand with their Shiite neighbors. In one village 70 Shiites, all civilians, were massacred.[216] The eventuality cannot be altogether discounted of Israeli settlers being encouraged to move in. These could be zealots acting against the Israeli government's wishes. Or they could be para-military Nahal (Israeli) units whose presence would at first be officially temporary. The policy of encouraging Haddad to resist the Shtaura accord to which his President, Sarkis, was a party, would fit into this scenario. So would the depopulation of the countryside.

That this would not solve the security problem would not necessarily be seen as a drawback. The continued inevitable turbulence of the area between the security belt and the Litani could under certain circumstances justify the expansion of the belt in the direction of the Litani. There is nothing particularly original in this strategy. It is orthodox by the standards of nineteenth century European conduct. Certainly the Litani has been a cherished Israeli objective.[217] If in the process Lebanon re-exploded, the worst that could happen would be its partition.[218] Israel's Red Line policy was already a signal of sorts to all capitals as to which part of Lebanon Israel considered its legitimate share. At any rate, the continued danger or threat of re-explosion would keep Damascus and the PLO off balance.

Something like this may have been sensed by Washington. Hence its swift move to obtain a Security Council decision to demand Israel's withdrawal from all Lebanese territory. To be sure, Washington had been consistently ambivalent about the Israeli-Maronite border alliance. It was not against the principle of the alliance—only against the publicity which it feared would complicate the task of Sarkis and make the Syrians less cooperative.[219] It welcomed the Israeli-Maronite counterweight to the PLO and its leftist allies south of the Litani. It hoped to cash in on the resultant pressure against Asad, while wary of pushing him too hard. The U.S. opposed a major Israeli offensive against the PLO in September 1977,[220] not so much to save the PLO from being bludgeoned as to maintain the sputtering momentum towards a Geneva Conference. Having meanwhile found the PLO the apparently easiest party to ditch in the Middle East,[221] it may even have encouraged Begin in March 1978 to deal it a heavy blow in the wake of the bus raid.[222] It may also have calculated—with the Sadat initiative seemingly in its death throes—that such a blow might knock some sense into Asad. But Washington was most probably against outright if "temporary" annexation by Begin of the six-mile belt because of the scenario outlined above. Hence probably Begin's misreading of just how much leeway he had. When the U.S. resolutely pushed for a Security Council resolution calling upon Israel to withdraw forthwith from all of Lebanon, Begin was not only caught off guard but must also have felt let down. His invading forces had already reached the six-mile "limit" and gone beyond it in places. But they were getting into trouble because of the nature of the terrain and the guerrilla tactics pursued by the PLO.[223] He now decided to go all out for the Litani. This would increase the area he would trade with the U.N. It would leave him maneuvering room to fall back on all the way to his security belt. It would enlarge the area of depopulation. It would set a precedent that could come in handy some day.

2. The Security Council Intervenes

The U.S. set the pace and direction of international political reaction to the Israeli invasion. Even if the explanation suggested above as to why the U.S. acted with such speed and determination is only partially true, there were many other cogent reasons for U.S. concern. It urgently needed to put some distance between itself and Israel to banish or preempt Arab charges of collusion. This was all the more necessary once (which was fairly quickly) the high toll of civilian lives became known. Any hint of American acquiescence in the occupation by Israel of yet another Arab country would deliver the coup de grace to whatever was left of Sadat's daydreams. Moreover, Begin had to be disabused of expecting to divert the forthcoming talks with Carter from an overall Middle East settlement to a discussion of the Lebanese situation. On 18 March, Syria had declared its borders open to Arab military aid to the Palestinians, and Syrian (as well as Soviet) restraint had to be encouraged.[224]

The main features of the U.S. attitude were clear enough by 16 March: a quick end to the latest cycle of violence was necessary "to keep attention focused on the basic problems which produced it." The only solution to these problems lay "in a search for a comprehensive settlement of the Arab-Israeli conflict in all its aspects." As for Lebanon, its territorial integrity was of fundamental concern to the U.S. An important objective was the extension of the authority of the Lebanese government to southern Lebanon. Arrangements to promote stability there, "including a U.N. role," were being explored.[225] Israel was expected to withdraw "fairly soon."[226]

These principles were enunciated before Israel's expansion of its invasion. They became the bases of U.N. action. The expansion of the invasion only increased the American sense of urgency. By 19 March the Security Council had taken two resolutions: Resolution 425 called *inter alia* upon Israel to "withdraw forthwith" from "all Lebanon," and provided for the establishment of a United Nations interim force for southern Lebanon—dubbed UNIFIL.[227] Resolution 426 spelled out the force's terms of reference.[228] Begin was due to arrive in New York on the following day, 20 March, and meet Carter the day after. If Begin had seized the occasion of the bus raid to invade Lebanon, the U.S. had seized the occasion of the invasion to implement an equally long-contemplated plan.

Resolution 426 constituted the Council's endorsement of Secretary General Waldheim's recommendation on the implementation of Resolution 425. Waldheim envisaged a two-stage operation. In the first, the

U.N.Force would confirm Israel's withdrawal to the international border. Once this was achieved, the force would establish "an area of operation." It would supervise the cessation of hostilities, "control movement," and take all measures to restore Lebanese sovereignty. At a preliminary estimate, the force was to be 4000 strong; its initial mandate would be for six months.[229]

The reactions of the principal protagonists were, of course, varied. Israel was probably the most discomfited of all. The U.N. resolutions had not condemned the invasion, but they cut across the plans that, it has been argued here, were entertained by Israel. Instead of strengthening his hand in the coming talks with Carter, Begin had been outflanked by Washington through the U.N. Instead of the almost total freedom of action that Israel had heretofore enjoyed on the border with Lebanon, Begin found himself face to face with the Security Council. A successful U.N. regime in southern Lebanon, whatever its short-range security benefits, carried the long-range political danger of serving as a model for other occupied areas.

The only option left Begin for the immediate future was to extract as many concessions as possible for withdrawal at his own pace. But U.S. pressure on him in the following few weeks was continuous. On 5 April, Secretary of State Vance stated that "a violation of the 1952 [Mutual Defence Assistance] Agreement may have occurred by reason of the Israeli operations in Lebanon."[230] On 7 April, Washington confirmed that Israel had used cluster-bombs during the fighting.[231] On 15 May, Israeli-American relations reached their nadir since Eisenhower's stand during the 1956 Suez War, when the Senate approved the package sale of planes to Israel, Saudi Arabia, and Egypt.

Nor was the establishment of UNIFIL at first acceptable to Syria. The idea of the introduction of U.N. forces in southern Lebanon was by no means a new one. It had last been suggested by Vance to Asad in August 1977.[232] Asad's response had been negative. The reason was fundamentally that a U.N.Force was seen as a derogation of the role of the ADF, and therefore of Syria. It would raise the issue of its compatibility with the Cairo and Shtaura accords. This would complicate an already over-complex Lebanese situation. It would cut across Syria's laborious efforts to sponsor the implementation of these accords. This could retard such progress as had been achieved towards Lebanese national reconciliation.

But lurking behind Syria's attitude toward a U.S. sponsored U.N. force was the suspicion that the whole series of recent events (the Israeli invasion and the creation of UNIFIL) was somehow orchestrated between Tel-Aviv and Washington with a view to embarrass and humiliate

Damascus. Syria would have preferred a U.N. action calling unconditionally for Israeli withdrawal with no linkage to a U.N. force. Presently it realized that such a resolution would not have U.S. backing. It also realized that in the absence of a resolution calling on Israel to withdraw (albeit coupled to a U.N. force) there could be an indefinite Israeli occupation of Lebanon up to the Litani. This could usher in a phase of uncontrollable conflict and increase the possibility of a major confrontation with Israel. Hence Syria's acquiescence in the Security Council resolutions. Hence also the re-closing of its own borders which had earlier been declared open to Arab military aid to the Palestinians.

Sarkis was torn in two directions—a chronic stance by now. His principal ally was Syria, whom he could not afford to alienate. At the same time, the UNIFIL formula could constitute a breakthrough in the resolution of the situation in southern Lebanon. Hence Lebanon's initial reluctance even to call for a meeting of the Security Council to discuss the Israeli invasion.

The PLO's first reaction was that the Security Council resolutions had not mentioned them by name and therefore did not concern them. They would cooperate with the U.N. but fight the Israelis so long as they were in southern Lebanon. An ideal scenario for Maoist guerrilla warfare could develop there.

3. UNIFIL Deploys South of the Litani

Secretary General Waldheim briskly set about his business. The area Israel had finished occupying by the time it accepted on 21 March the Security Council's call for a cease-fire was several times larger than the one it had said it would occupy. Some 425 square miles were now under Israeli occupation, about one tenth of the total area of Lebanon.[233] The front line extended in an arc from the Mediterranean near Tyre in the west to the foothills of Mount Hermon in the east—a distance of more than 60 miles.

The U.N. forces in Lebanon faced a different situation from that in the Golan or Sinai. In the latter two cases the U.N. forces were interposed between regular armies with the consent of their governments. The Lebanese government had no control over southern Lebanon and only the shaky nucleus of a national army. A host of questions faced Waldheim. Would the 4000 troops of UNIFIL suffice in the vastly enlarged area of Israeli occupation? Would the Israelis withdraw at all? And if so, at what rate and on what conditions? Would the Maronite militia, the PLO, and the National Movement cooperate with UNIFIL? Would the PLO and the National Movement continue fighting the

Israelis or infiltrate areas vacated by them, thus giving Israel an excuse for not withdrawing or for halting its withdrawal? Would Sarkis be able to put together a coherent force in time to take over from UNIFIL and so reassert the authority of his central government? What would the attitudes of Damascus and the ADF be to all this? In the event of prolonged clashes between UNIFIL and the combatants, would UNIFIL itself hold together?

Undaunted, Waldheim initiated immediate contacts with all parties. On 22 March the vanguard of UNIFIL arrived on the scene. On 27 March Waldheim issued a general appeal for the observance of the cease-fire. The following day he elicited a favorable response from Arafat. By 2 April he had dispatched to Lebanon a force of 1280, composed of contingents from Canada, France, Iran, Norway, and Sweden. The French deployed inside and around the Tyre salient in the western sector, the Swedes outside the Haddad salient at Marj Uyun in the eastern sector. The other UNIFIL contingents took up positions along the southern bank of the Litani.[234]

Although the PLO had accepted Waldheim's appeal for the cease-fire, they had not specifically accepted the Security Council resolutions. Neither had the Maronite hawks and their representative, Haddad, or the National Movement. There were other complications, too. The PLO and the National Movement resented UNIFIL's entry into the Tyre salient on the grounds that it had not been occupied by Israel in the first place. Their resentment was all the greater in that UNIFIL units were not stationed in the Haddad-controlled salient in the eastern sector. From Haddad's point of view, reflecting as it did that of the Maronite hawks in Beirut, UNIFIL was no ally in comparison with the Israelis. The buffer it constituted between the Israelis on the one hand, and the National Movement and PLO forces on the other, was tantamount to a rescue operation for the latter. Moreover, UNIFIL could not be counted on to prevent the re-infiltration of these forces in the wake of the Israeli withdrawal. To Haddad in person a UNIFIL regime was the prelude to the reassertion of Lebanese sovereignty. This would mean not only the end of his "autonomous" rule but his possible discharge from the Lebanese army (in which technically he still held the rank of Major). To the Maronite hawks in general the reassertion of Lebanese sovereignty in the south would mean the sealing off of the international frontier with Israel. This would restrict their operational access to Israel. It would eliminate a major point of pressure against both Damascus and the National Movement-PLO alliance.

Tension ran high in both the western sector (Tyre) and the eastern sector (Marj Uyun). In the former, several clashes occurred between the

National Movement-PLO forces and the UNIFIL French contingent, which was already suspect because of France's historical association with the Maronites.[235] In the latter, Haddad's militia pursued obstructionist tactics against UNIFIL.[236] There were also continued artillery exchanges between Haddad's forces on the one hand, and the National Movement and PLO militias deployed outside UNIFIL's area of operation on the other.[237]

The first concrete indication of Israeli intentions came on 6 April when Tel-Aviv announced a two-stage plan for limited withdrawal to take place on 11 and 14 April. On 7 April, Waldheim pronounced the intended withdrawals "inadequate," since the Security Council had called for "total withdrawal forthwith."[238] The same day, Begin informed Waldheim that Israel's intention to withdraw was related "to the deployment of the U.N. in the area"[239]—a hint that Israel considered UNIFIL's 4000 troops inadequate for the task. (By 17 April, UNIFIL was 2502 strong, including the addition of a Nepalese battalion.)[240]

Waldheim toured the area from 17-19 April. On 17 April he met Arafat in Beirut, who reiterated his acceptance of Waldheim's appeal for a cease-fire. He understood the Security Council resolutions to mean the supervision of the complete withdrawal of the Israeli forces and the assistance of the Lebanese government to reestablish its authority over the area under Israeli occupation. On this basis the PLO would continue to facilitate UNIFIL's task. Its forces would hold their fire and not play into the hands of Israel by responding to the provocations of Haddad's militia. Arafat reminded Waldheim that the Cairo and Shtaura agreements were not bilateral (i.e., solely between Lebanon and the PLO), but inter-Arab, since they had been endorsed by the Riyad and Cairo summits. Waldheim informed Arafat of the need to expand UNIFIL by about 2000 troops because the area occupied by Israel was much larger than had been originally anticipated. He urged continued observance of the cease-fire.[241]

On 18 April Waldheim met Begin. He later indicated that the Israeli Prime Minister had reaffirmed the Israeli intention to withdraw but that "a vacuum had to be avoided."[242] On his return to New York Waldheim advised the Security Council of the need to increase the Force to a level of 6000. Meanwhile, UNIFIL was scheduled to reach a total strength of 3500 (including the addition of a Senegalese battalion) by the end of April, and shortly thereafter its originally authorized strength of 4000 through the addition of a Nigerian battalion.

On 30 April Israel evacuated a further 213 square miles, which were taken over without incident by UNIFIL. Total Israeli withdrawals to date comprised 65% of the territory occupied. The area remaining in Israeli hands approximated the six-mile belt (including the Maronite enclaves)—the area Israel had originally declared its intention to confine itself to. On 3 May the Security Council authorized UNIFIL's increase to 6000, the additional contingents to be provided by Fiji, Iran, and Ireland.

Meanwhile, restlessness was growing among the radical Lebanese and Palestinian forces. Its principal cause was fear that Israel would not leave the six-mile strip. These dissidents chafed at the controls imposed on them by Arafat. On 1-2 May their activities resulted in the most serious clashes to date with UNIFIL and particularly its French contingent in the western sector near Tyre. In a meeting on 5 May with UNIFIL commander Major-General Emmanuel Erskine, Arafat renewed his pledge of cooperation with the U.N. but warned of possible continued attempts at infiltration by Rejectionist Lebanese and Palestinian elements. On 15 May, Erskine somewhat indiscreetly declared the Cairo and Shtaura agreements to be irreconcilable with the Security Council resolutions.[243] This declaration was seized upon by the Maronite hawks who had meanwhile been conducting an escalating campaign against the agreements in Beirut.

It was against this background that Israel announced on 21 May that it would pull out on 13 June from the six-mile belt still under occupation. This focused the "debate" in Beirut even more sharply on the future role of the Haddad militia. Would Israel hand over the six-mile belt to UNIFIL or Haddad? If it handed it over to Haddad (as the Maronite hawks urged), would it be possible before a national reconciliation was achieved to send units of the reconstituted army to replace, control, or absorb the Haddad militia? Assuming the Israelis handed the six-mile belt over to Haddad, how could Lebanese army units be dispatched to the south in these circumstances? These units would have to cross the territory north of the Litani. This area—a "no man's land"—was outside UNIFIL's mandate. The ADF was barred from entering it by Israel's Red Line policy. Would the National Movement and PLO militias, who controlled the area, facilitate the passage of the Lebanese army units to the south? And what would the effect be on the safety of their supply routes in the event of an Israeli hand-over to Haddad?

As the date set for Israel's final pull-out approached, these and other issues were at the center of intensive discussions in Beirut between Sarkis, Syria, and the PLO. A crucial question was whether Israel would "allow" ADF units to approach the northern bank of the Litani across the "no man's land" and what precisely was "expected" of the ADF there. Behind the scenes, Washington acted as a liaison between Israel on the one hand, and Beirut and Damascus on the other. On 31 May a meeting was held betweeen Sarkis and Asad.

On 12 June, the day before the Israelis were scheduled to leave, Begin faced the world with a fait accompli. He handed over the bulk of the six-mile belt to Haddad, who found himself the recipient of a whole complex of bunkers and fortifications constructed by Israeli engineers.[244] He also inherited from Israel "large quantities" of arms, including tanks and artillery.[245] The force under his command was now believed to be 3000 strong. The bulk of it must have been transported via Israel from central Lebanon and probably included a stiffening of Israelis masquerading as "Maronites."[246] This was Begin's real if delayed response to Waldheim.

Paradoxically, Washington, the ardent author of the Security Council resolutions, seems to have acquiesced in the new Israeli-Haddad deal. There are several possible explanations for this. The less charitable one is that Washington continued to see advantage in the retention by Israel of a fulcrum of pressure inside Lebanon against Asad and Arafat. A more charitable explanation is that it hoped by making amends for the earlier vigor with which it sponsored the Security Council resolutions to coax Begin into greater flexibility on the Middle Eastern talks. Hence the Israeli-Haddad deal—probably viewed by Washington as a compromise solution between Begin's original plan for indefinite retention of the six-mile belt and its take-over by UNIFIL. Whatever the reason, Washington will not be altogether blameless if the Haddad time-bomb explodes with a louder bang than in March 1978.[247]

4. The Impact on the PLO

A closer look is in order at the overall impact on the PLO of the Israeli invasion of Lebanon. Generally speaking, the PLO had fared better than either Israel or the U.S. (or the PLO itself) had probably anticipated.

There was a certain historic irony in the manner the two primary protagonists in the Arab-Israeli conflict had at last met face to face. For decades now the Israelis and their predecessors in Palestine had appeared from the Western perspective as a David tilting against an Arab Goliath. There was no doubt as to who was who in March 1978 on the bloody plateaus of southern Lebanon. Also, when the PLO had first taken up the armed struggle in earnest against Israel after the rout and emasculation of the Arab regular armies in June 1967, Israel had sent a couple of thousand men with armor across the river into eastern Jordan against the Palestinian stronghold of Karameh and the adjacent Jordanian position.[248] Eleven years later (notwithstanding all the Israeli retaliatory blows, the killing, and the destruction), that act of symbolic acknowledgement at Karameh of the PLO's existence was unwittingly if tragically magnified many times over in the unmistakable mobilization of Israel's formidable arsenal in March 1978.

The PLO had no illusions about its ability to withstand the full fury of Israel's frontal assault. Its forces therefore dispersed, resorting simultaneously to harassing attacks by small groups and dogged rear-guard resistance in selected strongholds, making full use of the terrain and other favorable local factors. The Tyre salient had held out. Partly because of Palestinian resistance, Israel had to modify and perhaps even abandon its original invasion plans. The loss in Palestinian civilian lives was high—some 500. The new Palestinian refugees numbered 60,000. But the loss in combatants was relatively low while that in material was both tolerable and replaceable.[249] Militarily, the structure of the PLO emerged intact. Its ranks were swollen with new recruits and volunteers.[250] But it was on the psychological level that the military outcome was most deeply felt. For seven to eight days and nights the PLO had fought against numerical odds of approximately 1:15, not to mention the overwhelming Israeli superiority in equipment and firepower.[251] To the Arab world, and certainly to the Palestinians in the Diaspora and the occupied territories, this compared favorably with the performance of the regular Arab armies of the three Arab states in the Six-Day War of June 1967. The fact that most Arab states had confined themselves to moral support and half-hearted gestures during the Israeli invasion of Lebanon strengthened Arab popular sympathy for the Palestinian plight, while the Palestinians' own sense of solidarity and martyrdom was further enhanced.[252]

These considerations redounded to the political advantage of Arafat and the PLO. So did the salience the PLO acquired as a "de facto partner" (in the words of the Israeli General Mordechai Gur) in the implementation of the Security Council resolutions.[253] Also to Arafat's political credit was the skill with which he conducted his complex tergiversations to prevent an all-out confrontation between his Rejectionists and UNIFIL, thus denying Israel both the excuse for postponing its withdrawal and the satisfaction of witnessing a showdown between the PLO and its principal potential international ally, the U.N. Even while the Israelis were still in occupation of the six-mile belt, the PLO organized two operations deep inside Israel: the first in Jerusalem on 2 June, the second in the Jordan valley on 12 June.[254] These seemed to be reminders to Israel of the fundamental irrelevance of its military operation in Lebanon as a means of curbing Palestinian action. If the earlier Palestinian bus raid in March near Tel Aviv had been a cynical assertion of the PLO's presence in the Middle Eastern scene, Israel's invasion of southern Lebanon massively if inadvertently drove the same message home.

Nevertheless, there was also a debit side for the PLO. The tension between Fath and the radical elements in the PLO rose sharply because of Arafat's strategy of cooperation with UNIFIL. In April, the disaffection involved even some Fath veteran members, though it was swiftly brought under control.[255] On 24 May the radical elements openly complained of Fath's monopoly of decision-making and demanded a return to the collegial process.[256] The Israeli invasion had once again propelled the issue of the Palestinians in Lebanon into the center of the Lebanese dialogue for national reconciliation. Indeed, the occasion for the 24 May Palestinian complaint about the PLO's decision-making process was Arafat's negotiation of a new understanding with Lebanese Prime Minister Hoss on the future operational status of the Cairo and Shtaura accords.[257] The pressure on Sarkis and Hoss from the Maronite hawks (coordinated as it may have been with the Israelis) to bring the Palestinians under control was reaching dangerous proportions. But so was the pressure from an increasing number of Shiites whose toleration for suffering was understandably exhausted. Sarkis was determined to effect qualitative progress in regard to the political reconstruction of the country, using UNIFIL's presence and mandate to the full. The very presence of UNIFIL had created constraints on the PLO's freedom of action and on the implementation of the Cairo and Shtaura accords. To be sure, the Syrians did not relish acting as the gendarme of Israel or the U.N. against the PLO. But the scale of the Israeli invasion foreshadowed the gathering of darker clouds on the horizon (Israel's surprise attack in June 1967 had been preceded by heavy raids against Syria and Jordan, just as the occupation of Sinai since 1967 had been preceded by its invasion in 1956). Conditions had to be speedily created to limit the further development of the Israeli-Maronite alliance. The Sarkis-Asad meeting on 31 May reflected the need felt by Beirut and Damascus for tighter coordination between them. The alienation of the U.N. by the PLO could do irreparable harm to the Palestinian cause. All this demanded a new look by PLO leaders on their entire Lebanese strategy in the days ahead.

5. The Impact on the Lebanese

The first immediate effect of the Israeli invasion was to put the Palestinian item back at the top of the Lebanese political agenda. This instantly re-polarized the country into two groups.

The first group considered that the overriding priority was to get the Israelis out of the country. UNIFIL was welcome if it secured Israeli withdrawal, but if this were delayed the Israelis should be fought, UNIFIL notwithstanding. This group maintained that there was no con-

tradiction between Security Council resolutions 425 and 426 and the
Cairo and Shtaura agreements. To raise the issue of these agreements
while Israel was in occupation of the country was to do Israel's bidding.
Israel's invasion revealed its territorial ambitions in Lebanon. Therefore
all Lebanese should unite to defend their country against Israel rather
than seize the occasion to betray the Palestinians and annul official
agreements with them. This group included the National Movement, the
pro-Syrian Baathist and Shiite parties and organizations, and some
Sunnite oligarchs, especially ex-Prime Minister Rashid Karami.

The second group held diametrically opposite views. The Israeli invasion was the direct result of PLO activities and transgressions behind the
transparent cover of the Cairo and Shtaura accords. These accords were
contrary to the Security Council resolutions which in any case had
superseded them. The main flaw in the Security Council resolutions was
that they did not call for Palestinian withdrawal from Lebanon. The
government should forthwith declare the Cairo and Shtaura accords null
and void. Only this would ensure Israeli withdrawal and preclude
another invasion. This group included a wide spectrum of Maronite
opinion led by the hawks Camille Chamoun and Basheer Gemayel, as
well as several Shiite oligarchs.

Sarkis' problem was how to avoid alienating either group by word or
deed while at the same time addressing himself to the task at hand. He
performed this tour de force with a benignly Delphic statement on 24
May to the effect that the Cairo Agreement was one thing, the Security
Council resolutions another![258] Simultaneously, his Prime Minister Hoss
reached an understanding with Arafat, according to which the PLO
would inter alia cooperate with UNIFIL, prevent transgressions by
dissidents in the south, help in the restoration of Lebanese sovereignty in
the area, and pursue discussions for the regulation of Lebanese-Palestin-
ian relations.[259] By avoiding a frontal assault on the Cairo and Shtaura
accords, Sarkis and Hoss secured PLO cooperation for the immediate
future, while leaving open the possibility of renegotiating these accords
with the help of Damascus after the complete Israeli withdrawal.

Another effect of the Israeli invasion was that it strained to the limit
relations between the Maronite hawks and Syria. The opinions of the
Maronite group outlined above were in fact directed most of all at Asad.
The Maronite hawks hoped to exploit the Israeli invasion to panic
Damascus into drastic action against the PLO. Some, including Basheer
Gemayel, openly if unrealistically declared the moment opportune for a
general Maronite offensive "to liberate" the country from both
Palestinians and Syrians. Others equally unrealistically hoped that
UNIFIL's role could be expanded to cover the whole of Lebanon as a
substitute for the ADF.

Presently, these tensions were translated into exchanges of fire in Beirut suburbs between the militias of the National Movement and the Maronites. The ADF intervened massively to prevent them from spreading. Fighting continued between 9 April and 12 April, leaving some 33 killed and 240 wounded, mostly on the Maronite side. The country teetered on the brink of renewed civil war. The situation was saved by the resignation of Premier Hoss on 19 April. This seemed to administer the equivalent of an electric shock to the Lebanese protagonists as they now contemplated the likely consequences of a continued constitutional vacuum in the Sunnite premiership. The truth of the matter was that there was no alternative to the Syrians and the ADF except all-out chaos. Sarkis realized this, as did the majority of the Lebanese except for the Maronite hawks.

The rising tension between the Maronite hawks and the Syrians had two interesting effects. In the first place, it checked the growing general disenchantment with Syria described in the previous chapter. Thus, for example, the National Movement, which had grown increasingly alienated from the Syrians and the pro-Syrian parties and organizations in Lebanon, drew closer to the latter. Secondly, and more significantly, it accelerated the drifting away of ex-President Suleiman Franjieh from his Maronite colleagues on the Lebanese Front, already alluded to in the previous chapter. Franjieh, though in favor of strong measures against the PLO, was staunchly pro-ADF and pro-Asad and categorically opposed to either partition or a Maronite-Israeli alliance. On 13 May Franjieh was reconciled under Syrian auspices to his old rival and colleague, ex-Premier Rashid Karami.[260] This was tantamount to withdrawal from the Lebanese Front. The significance of this reconciliation lay of course in its trans-sectarian character. Already in northern Lebanon (Franjieh's center of power), the Maronites, and their next-door neighbors, the Sunnites of Tripoli (Karami's center of power), had achieved under the aegis of the ADF an entente at the level of the man in the street. This viable model of Pax Syriana was not altogether palatable to some Maronite hawks. Hence the increasing friction during May between Franjieh's Maronite militia and those under the central command of Basheer Gemayel. The Maronite hawks notwithstanding, Sarkis' incentives for closer coordination with Damascus were, however, overwhelming. Hence the meeting between him and Asad on 31 May.

Meanwhile, the pressures generated by Hoss's resignation on 19 April underlined two contradictory facts (a commonplace phenomenon of the Lebanon scene): On the one hand, new manifestations of the survival instinct among the Lebanese political practitioners; on the other, the enormous difficulties still obstructing national reconciliation, given the extraordinary tangle in the parallelogram of Lebanese, Palestinian,

Syrian, and Israeli (not to mention Arab and international) forces interacting with one another. Hoss's resignation prompted 13 politicians (including Chamoun, Pierre Gemayel, Sunnite ex-Premier Saeb Salaam, and the Shiite Speaker of the Parliament Kamel As'ad) to draw up a program for a new entente which Parliament unanimously endorsed on 27 May with the 74 votes of those present.

The program was to serve as the basis of a new government of national reconciliation. The immediate effect of this move was to defuse the looming crisis produced by the fighting in the suburbs of Beirut between 9-13 April. It also allowed Sarkis to entrust Hoss with the formation of the new government. So much for the positive side. However, when deliberations were initiated for choosing the members of the government, all the old contradictions and enduring animosities resurfaced. For one thing, the program drawn up by the veteran oligarchs was a vague compromise and therefore subject to differing interpretations. Its central provisions were that "all Palestinian and other armed action . . . must be halted" and that "any armed presence except that of the Lebanese legitimate authority must be prevented." This implied the disbandment of both PLO and other (including Maronite) militias, which was patently impracticable. For another, the veteran oligarchs, still true to form, had not taken counsel with the new Moslem-leftist extra-Parliamentary forces in the field—a telling if characteristic purblindness considering the changes in the political map and the balance of forces produced by the Civil War.

Another obstacle reflecting this same purblindness was the insistence by some of the program's signatories that the new government be formed exclusively of members of Parliament—a politically superannuated body.[261] But the stratagem was in fact deftly aimed at the new leftist leaders of the National Movement and, more specifically, the Lebanese "ideological" (Baathist) protégés of Syria. Because of the ensuing deadlock, Sarkis had no alternative but to reinstate Hoss's technocratic government. The episode was not altogether futile. For several days the Lebanese public concentrated its attention on increasingly abstruse compromise formulas for the composition of the new government. This served to take their minds if not their fingers off their triggers. It was a rehearsal of sorts of a possible new venture in the same direction in better days—if any—ahead.

Meanwhile, on 13 June, with the attention of Sarkis and Damascus riveted on Israeli withdrawal tactics in the farthest south, an ugly turn of events occurred in the opposite end of the country in the Maronite north, the territory of the Franjiehs. A Phalangist force of 800 militiamen stormed Ehden, the mountain stronghold of ex-President Suleiman

Franjieh. The attack was in retaliation for the alleged murder of some five Phalangist members by Franjieh followers. Some 35 people were killed in the fighting including Suleiman's eldest son and heir-apparent, Tony, his wife, and two-year old daughter. The Maronite hawks had thrown the gauntlet to ex-President Franjieh and through him to Damascus. The timing of the attack in conjunction with the Israeli hand-over to Haddad did not augur well for the future. It is too early, however, to predict its long-term impact on intra-Maronite relations and the Lebanese scene in general. With luck it might yet tap some heretofore dormant streak of pragmatism in the hearts of other Lebanese leaders who have their own heirs-apparent and grandchildren.

7

THE OUTLOOK

1. Lebanon and Palestine

In the aftermath of the Israeli invasion the resolution of the Lebanese Problem has become more closely linked than ever before to that of the Palestine Problem. But a distinction can and must be made between the two, both analytically and practically. The Lebanese Problem was brewing long before the armed presence of the PLO became a factor in Lebanon's delicate sectarian equilibrium. There was no Palestinian armed presence in 1958, for example, when the first Lebanese Civil War after independence broke out.[262] Given the pace of development and of "social mobilization" inside Lebanon,[263] as well as the revolutionary changes that were taking place in the Arab world and globally, it was inevitable that the socio-political status quo built on the 1943 National Pact[264] (and on Maronite political and economic predominance) should come under increasing strain. Already before the impact of the PLO's armed presence in the late 1960s the multi-level crisscrossing tensions within Lebanese society had become abundantly evident. In addition to the Christian-Moslem polarization, the individual sects were themselves becoming increasingly polarized from within. What the armed presence of the PLO did was to accelerate an already existing process and bring it to explosion point earlier than would otherwise have been the case. But given the general turbulence of the region, Lebanon was heading towards explosion with or without the Palestinians.

It cannot, however, be denied that an honorable overall solution of the Palestine Problem would bring immense relief to the Lebanese scene. No such solution is in the offing. Therefore it is unrealistic to suspend all progress towards Lebanese national reconciliation pending the fulfillment of a condition that is unrealizable in the foreseeable future. It is equally unrealistic to hope in the meantime to solve all aspects of the Palestinian presence in Lebanon. The best that can be expected in the circumstances is to try to soften the impact of the Palestine Problem and the Arab-Israeli conflict. This task falls equally on the shoulders of the Maronite leadership, the U.S. (Israel's principal sponsor), the PLO (and its Arab sponsors), and Syria. The presence of UNIFIL in the south affords an opportunity to all parties that is potentially less limited than might appear at first sight. It would be tragic to miss it.

2. The Crisis of Identity

What formula for Lebanese national reconciliation is desirable and possible given the existing realities? To paraphrase the late T. D. Weldon, the British philosopher, what we are dealing with is a many-faceted problem that needs to be worked around, rather than a "puzzle" susceptible to one or more recognizable "solutions."

At the base of intra-Lebanese violence and conflict is a crisis of identity and loyalty. This is most acutely felt by the Maronite community of Lebanon. The Maronites by and large think of themselves as constituting a distinctive cultural, religious, and even ethnic group.[265] They are obsessed by the fear of submersion in or assimilation by the oceans of Arabdom and Islam. To them Lebanon is meaningless if it is so constituted as to entail the loss of this distinctive identity. They have therefore tended to equate Lebanism with Maronitism, and both with a paramount Maronite political and economic status in the country. If Lebanon were to remain within the international frontiers of 1920,[266] i.e., unpartitioned, it can only do so on the basis of the recognition by all other Lebanese (and the Arab countries) that Lebanon is a pluralistic composite of sub-national groups—the sects—each with its own special heritage. Hence the adamant Maronite opposition to the concept of political deconfessionalism. This, as they see it, entails the by-passing of the sects as the constituent political units of the Lebanese system. It is the prelude to the application of the principle of majoritarian rule. In the event of the development of a Moslem majority, the application of this principle would mean Moslem hegemony.[267] In the short run this would entail Maronite subordination to the Moslems; eventually it could pose the threat of cultural "annihilation."

Conversely, the Moslem sects by and large think of themselves as constituting an integral part of the worlds of Arabdom and Islam. Lebanon is meaningless to them in any other context. They tend to equate Lebanism with Arabism. Maronite opposition to political deconfessionalism is designed to prevent them from exercising their full political rights as the actual or potential majority. It perpetuates Maronite political and economic hegemony in the name of maintaining the sectarian equilibrium of the country. Both parties, Maronites as well as Moslems, are in effect equally guilty of attempting to dictate cultural identities to one another. And it is clear that these twin crises of identity and loyalty are inextricably linked to the question of who is to be top dog in the country politically and economically.

There are three different paths for the Lebanese to follow: a) to agree on a modus vivendi, as they did in 1943 and 1958; b) to agree to disagree; and c) to disagree on a modus vivendi without agreeing to disagree. The last of these options is to perpetuate the present state of affairs. It is to invite more chaos. The second is the path of partition. A partition solution, even when agreed to by the leadership on both sides, can be a disastrous experience, as evidenced by the partition of India in 1947. It is likely to be even more horrendous when no such agreement can be expected, as in the case of Palestine in 1947-1948 and Cyprus in 1974. All forms of partition are opposed by the Lebanese Moslems. The Syrians will forcibly prevent it. All Arab states are against it. Neither of the superpowers favors it. It is opposed by the major countries, including France, as well as by the Vatican. Its only sponsor is Israel. But even if it were feasible, it would not be to the benefit of the Maronites, the non-Maronite Christians of Lebanon, or the Christian communities in the Arab world. Apart from the additional suffering it would bring to many Maronites and other Lebanese Christians (not to mention Moslems) in the process of its implementation, it would seal off the state from all contact with the Arab world. In one stroke it would deprive the Maronites from reaping any advantages from the entrepôt role of Lebanon and Beirut in the Middle East. Achievement of national reconciliation is bound to revive this role of which the Maronites have traditionally been the chief beneficiaries. Partition would preclude Arab financial aid to the Maronite state. It would block access for the Maronite entrepreneurial talent to the oil-rich Arab states. It would impose an intolerable strain on the Christian communities throughout the Arab world. It would start the Maronite state on a *via dolorosa* of endless strife with its Arab hinterland. For these reasons it is highly doubtful whether there is in fact enough popular Maronite, let alone non-Maronite Christian, support for partition. To be sure, Maronite hawks have advocated partition under various guises and still do.[268] But the attractiveness of such a solution has varied with the sense of the imminence of a threat to Maronite survival. Such a perception has prevailed at certain critical moments since the beginning of the Civil War in the spring of 1975. To most Maronites, however, partition is a counsel

of despair. The growing strains among the Maronite leaders in the
Lebanese Front were in themselves an indication of the lessening sense of
imminent danger. So were the multiplying instances of clashes between
the militiamen of the various Maronite political groupings. The
Phalangist massacre of members of the Franjieh family at Ehden may yet
have shattered Maronite unity for many years. It is unlikely to have enhanced the image of the Phalanges as defenders of the faith. It is likely to
provide some food for thought to Maronites and non-Maronite Christians alike in regard to the conditions of life in a Maronite state
dominated by militants. It would be surprising if it did not strengthen
general Christian yearning for a return to legitimacy. Under the circumstances, partition would seem to be undesirable and impracticable.

3. Grounds for Optimism

The bases for a *modus vivendi* are not altogether absent. Around the
central core issue of identity and loyalty, there exist two other closely
related ones: a) the "nature" of the Lebanese system, and b) the division
of power between Christians and Moslems.

On the issue of identity and loyalty, the bulk of the Maronites even
today would opt against rather than in favor of partition. Conversely,
not even the most radical of the Pan-Arab parties in Lebanon are
prepared explicitly to renounce their allegiance to Lebanon or to
advocate its merger into a larger (and non-existent) Arab unity. The
realization by the Moslems and the radical Lebanese parties that the
Maronite predisposition to partition is not merely bluff has had a
sobering effect on them. The changing attitudes of many Moslems to the
sacrifices that Lebanon (in the absence of an all-Arab strategy towards
Israel) continues to suffer on behalf of the Palestinians have further nar-
rowed the gap between Christians and Moslems. The gap is of course still
there. The Moslems, and particularly the radical and leftist National
Movement, are not prepared to ditch the Palestinians. But, except for
their extremist fringes, they are more disposed than before to draw the
line of their support short of the total disintegration of their country.
Moslem and National Movement leaders are more aware than before of
their own responsibility to wean the Maronites from their partitionist
tendencies. There will be continuous debate on just how "Arab" Lebanon
is. Neither side will succeed in converting the other to its point of view,
nor need it. In the prevailing mood, the issue could be skirted by a practical formulation. Such a formulation was foreshadowed in Franjieh's
Constitutional Document of 14 February 1976, as well as by Sarkis in his
inaugural speech.[269]

On the issue of the nature of the Lebanese system there is implicit if not explicit agreement that the division of the country into distinctive sects is a fact of life. There will be continuous disagreement between the bulk of the Maronites and radical Moslems and Christians as to whether this is desirable or not, and whether it is a transitory or permanent state of affairs. There will also be disagreement in regard to the "cultural" significance of these sects and their relationship to Pan-Arabism. But to all intents and purposes, the National Movement has abandoned its earlier call for overall political deconfessionalism, i.e., the dismantling of the sects as the constituent political units of the Lebanese system. This amounts to acquiescence in the Maronite premise of the composite pluralistic nature of Lebanese society, though not in the metaphysical connotations with which the Maronites endow it. Indeed, the Maronites in this regard have themselves called the bluff of the National Movement. To the latter's earlier call for political deconfessionalism they had opposed a demand for total secularization.[270] Such secularization would not only affect the political role of the sects but their inner structure. It would entail, for example, the abrogation of the laws of personal status observed by each sect, and thus universalize civil marriage and civil laws of inheritance to replace those based on religious law and custom. Such secularization is abhorred not only by the Moslem religious hierarchy but by Moslem mass opinion. The return by the Moslems, however grudging, to the acknowledgement of the composite pluralistic multi-sectarian structure of Lebanese society banishes from the Maronite point of view the threat of majoritarian (and therefore Moslem) rule which would have replaced it through political deconfessionalism.

With the sects reinstated for the foreseeable future as the political constituent units, the focus shifts to the overall division of power between Christian and Moslem. This was the main subject of Franjieh's Constitutional Document of February 1976. Here again there is growing consensus on balance and co-equality (*tawazun*)—the increasing orientation of the National Movement.

The easiest application of this principle is to the Legislature where the seats would be divided on a 50:50 basis as between Christians and Moslems as opposed to the pre-Civil War 6:5 distribution in favor of the Christians. Franjieh's Constitutional Document has already provided for this. The Moslems and the National Movement itself would now accept this new ratio. So would the Maronites. But the latter are likely to demand, as a safeguard, the introduction of the principle of concurrent majorities (i.e., the requirement for a majority vote within each half—Moslem and Christian) on a selected range of vital issues.[271] The Moslems would balk at this, but might accept it as part of a package.

The package would entail two other crucial areas for the application of the principle of co-equality (*tawazun*). One is the Executive, and the other the Army. The Moslems and the National Movement would accept the perpetuation of the status quo with regard to the distribution of the three highest posts of the state: a Maronite President, a Shiite Speaker, and a Sunnite Prime Minister. This too was provided for by Franjieh's Constitutional Document. More specifically, the issue of *tawazun* in the Executive hinges on the prerogatives of President and Prime Minister. The Constitutional Document maintained presidential primacy although it took away some of the President's prerogatives.[272] The Maronites would insist on presidential primacy and are unhappy with the way in which the Constitutional Document had whittled it down.[273] It is not clear whether the two sides would settle for the provisions of the Constitutional Document in this regard—themselves a compromise—or would renegotiate a new compromise on the issue.

The control of the reconstructed army is likely to be one of the thorniest problems. Before the civil war the army was fundamentally Maronite-dominated.[274] The Maronites would, of course, want this to continue, but this is altogether unacceptable to the Moslem side. A more structured system of Christian-Moslem checks and balances is likely to emerge for the control of the new army. This might make political sense but could also lead to the operational immobilization of the new national army. But in a post-reconciliation era the "coercive" role of the army is in any case likely to be minimized.

Looming over all this is the "territorial" issue. Given the de facto partition of the country, the psychological harvest of the Civil War, and the predisposition of some Maronite hawks toward partition, no political formula would be viable if it did not take into account the territorial imperative of the Maronites. The problem is how to do this without giving momentum to centrifugal forces all around. A possible compromise is a formula for extensive administrative rather than political decentralization which would both satisfy Maronite susceptibilities while not arousing Moslem suspicion and fears of partition. Both sides could yet come around to seeing the mutual benefits of such a formula.

4. Syria's Role

The task of national reconciliation is monumental but not hopeless. The *sine qua non* for its achievement is the continued presence of both the ADF and UNIFIL. Both face the most exacting challenges and constraints.

Syria, the backbone of the ADF, has swung from support of the PLO to that of the Maronites and now back to the support of the PLO. But there is an inner logic to these fluctuations of policy. The immediate objective has consistently been to effect a balance of power between the combatants and to prevent the extremist forces, whether on the Maronite side or that of the PLO-leftist alliance, from dominating the country. Syria is categorically opposed to partition, decisively in favor of national reconciliation on the bases outlined above, and staunchly pro-Sarkis. But it operates within several concentric circles of constraints. One circle is that of the Israeli veto on the movement of its troops in the direction of or across the Red Line. Another is that of the constraints imposed on its freedom of action by the Arab members and financial sponsors of the ADF. Yet a third circle is imposed by the fact that its forces in Lebanon are technically under the command of Sarkis. This means that Sarkis can actively employ them only in limited roles for fear of eroding his fragile political credibility. Except in moments of extreme crisis or provocation, Syria's operational leeway in Lebanon against both the Maronite and PLO militias has become circumscribed.

Syria is the direct or indirect target of all parties interested in retarding and subverting any progress towards national reconciliation. At the same time its stake in Lebanon has become vital for the very survival of its own regime. Hence perhaps the temptation for all anti-Syrian parties (local, regional, and international) to compound the difficulties for Syria in Lebanon. The Israeli invasion of Lebanon was directed as much at Syria as at the PLO. It has enhanced Syria's sense (always present) of the vulnerability of its soft Lebanese flank. Militarily, Syria must seriously consider the possibility of a rapid Israeli thrust from Marj Uyun (Haddad's base) and up the Bekaa Valley. From there the Israelis could swing eastwards along the main Damascus-Beirut highway attacking Damascus from the *west*. Alternatively, or simultaneously, they could move northwards to reach Syria's entrails in the Homs-Hama area and thence swing southwards attacking Damascus from the *north*. This would obviate the need for Israel to slog it from the Golan to Damascus past the heavy Syrian defence complexes along the foothills of the Mt. Hermon range. With these perceptions and apprehensions Syria has a compelling interest in the return of Lebanon to normalcy. It also has little obvious incentive to gratuitously take on the principal Maronite force, the Phalanges. This is why Syria has bent over backwards to coordinate its actions with the Phalanges.[275] And this is why the Phalanges attack on the Franjieh stronghold at Ehden and the Phalanges-Israeli pre-emption of UNIFIL in the border area (both took place on the same day) acquire special military and political significance for the future.

Under no circumstance would Syria volunteer to serve as the anvil to the hammer of Israel, UNIFIL, or the Maronite militias on which the PLO would be crushed. But it would be prepared to be forthcoming in the surveillance of the PLO-Lebanese-leftist-controlled "no man's land" north of the Litani in certain circumstances. These would include the transfer of the six-mile border belt to UNIFIL and the new Lebanese army, the sealing off of the Lebanese border with Israel, and the dispersal or transfer of the Haddad and other Maronite militias sponsored by Israel there. But even in the most favorable circumstances there is a limit to what Syria could do vis-à-vis the PLO, given continued Israeli intransigence on the Palestinian problem.

The PLO can greatly simplify Syria's task in Lebanon. The paramount need is for a new look at the role and function of Palestinian armed presence in Lebanon in the PLO's overall strategy. Long before the Israeli invasion, the PLO had stopped operations across the border. It would do well to persevere in this policy. The preemption of UNIFIL by the Maronites on the border should not provoke the PLO into parallel defiance of UNIFIL. It has so far resisted the temptation. It would do well to continue to do so. The negative light in which the Cairo and Shtaura Agreements appears to their enemies far outweighs their usefulness to the PLO. There is no reason why they should not be renegotiated. This need not entail Palestinian disarmament. Such a course would be tantamount to surrender and the abandonment of the struggle for Palestinian legitimate aims. It would render the Palestinians defenseless not only against the Israelis but also against the Maronite militias. A renegotiated agreement with the Lebanese government that maintains the spirit and substance of the earlier ones while taking into account the new political realities on the Lebanese scene might constitute an important gesture towards Lebanese, and particularly Maronite opinion. The PLO morally owes it to all the Lebanese to make some such gesture.

5. UNIFIL's Role

The flashpoint in Lebanon and in the Middle East the six-mile border belt. The Sadat initiative has reached its crossroads. It could sputter on, come to an end, or produce an anemic Palestinian dressing for a bilateral Egyptian-Israeli deal. Any of the three outcomes can instantly reactivate the border area. The continued presence of the Israeli-sponsored Maronite militias there is in itself a perpetual challenge to the Lebanese leftist and radical Palestinian elements. A deliberate policy of provocation inspired by the Israelis or the Maronite hawkish leadership, or both, would start a new cycle of uncontrollable violence. Even without such a policy, the mere presence of the Israeli-sponsored Maronite militias maximizes the chances for actions by individuals on either the Maronite or Palestinian-leftist side to start such a cycle. Where this cycle would end is anybody's guess. This is why the presence of UNIFIL is an opportunity that should not be missed. It has already proved its usefulness in getting the Israelis out of the greater part of the Lebanese occupied territory as well as in policing (with PLO cooperation) this area south of the Litani. Not to extend its writ to the entire border area is to negate its raison d'être. With UNIFIL installed in the whole border area the incentive for the PLO to continue in its policy of cooperation would be increased. So would its control over the radical Palestinian forces and its influence over the Lebanese leftist extremists.

The presence of UNIFIL would be not only a physical buffer between Israel and the PLO. It would also be a time buffer affording the central Lebanese government the breathing space to send in units of its army to begin the restoration of Lebanese sovereignty in the south. The more Lebanese sovereignty is restored, the more favorable the political climate for parallel progress in national reconciliation. This is one reason why UNIFIL's mandate should be prolonged indefinitely. The incentive for the countries who have contributed contingents to it to keep them in the field would vary with their perception of the degree of success achieved by UNIFIL in restoring a measure of peace to the area. The greater the friction by any party with UNIFIL, the less its credibility and the willingness of the countries participating in it to extend its mandate. With UNIFIL withdrawn before the restoration of Lebanese sovereignty in the south and before the expected parallel start of progress on national reconciliation, the situation in Lebanon would be utterly open-ended. Except that with no U.N. deus-ex-machina in the wings, the stage would be set for a tragedy that could extend well beyond the frontiers of Lebanon.

The responsibility for continuing UNIFIL's task rests primarily on Washington, the force's progenitor. It would be shortsighted for Washington to believe that developments in the border area in southern Lebanon have been reduced to parochial dimensions and are therefore unworthy of the attention of a superpower. It is self-evident that Maronite military power in the border area is a direct manifestation of Israeli might. The less the Israeli support to the Maronite border militias, the easier the task of UNIFIL, the quicker the restoration of Lebanese sovereignty, and the calmer the entire area south of the Litani. It does not make sense for Washington on the one hand to finance the reconstruction of the Lebanese army, and on the other to increase, however inadvertently, the difficulties, already overwhelming, it faces.

There is no ambiguity in the Security Council's resolutions 425 and 426 in regard to the total withdrawal of Israeli forces from Lebanon. The U.S. itself is the author of the phraseology of these resolutions. It should not abdicate its responsibility in the implementation process. The statesmanship it displayed immediately after the Israeli invasion would have been displayed in vain if it does not bring matters to a natural consummation. What is specifically required is the effective resurrection of the Mixed Lebanese-Israeli Armistice regime.[276] Buttressed by UNIFIL and restored Lebanese sovereignty, this regime could credibly regulate relations between Lebanon and Israel pending an overall Middle East settlement. To do less than this, and worse, to try to derive political mileage against the PLO and Syria from the *de facto*, if indirect, "presence" of Israel inside the Lebanese border is simply irresponsible. It is to miss a golden opportunity to bring substantial relief to a tiny and fundamentally pacific country, Lebanon, that has had more than its share of tribulations. It is to bury one's head in the sands and with it the prospects of defusing the flashpoint of the Fifth Arab-Israeli War.

6. Prudence is Compassion

The strength of sub-national group identities is a universal phenomenon. It is observable across the globe from Canada to Spain, to Switzerland and Yugoslavia, and across the Soviet bloc and the USSR, all the way to Malaysia and the Philippines. It is a challenge to the values of humanism and compassion as well as those of prudence of the local dominant system, ideology, or group. The same phenomenon is observable in the Arab World: from the Berbers in the Maghreb to the Azanian movement in southern Sudan, to the Kurds in Iraq, and the Maronites in Lebanon. Here too the dominant ideology, Arabism or Pan-Arabism, is on trial. Here too compassion and prudence are called for; here indeed prudence is compassion.

The future of the Middle East, including that of Israel, hinges on the achievement of an honorable overall settlement of the Arab-Israeli conflict. The balance of power almost by definition is a mercurial thing. The region is dotted with the debris of fallen empires. Many of these had resorted to the stratagem of *divide et impera*. A perpetually destabilized and turbulent Middle East is no lasting asset to the Israelis or the world. Today, behind the militant rhetoric, wherever it exists, a fundamentally pragmatic mood vis-à-vis the Arab-Israeli conflict reigns simultaneously in more Arab capitals than ever before since the creation of Israel in 1948. The Arab-Israeli conflict is derivative from the Palestine Problem. Every Israeli knows in his heart of hearts what injustice to the Palestinians the establishment of Israel has involved. Jewish genius has amply manifested itself on the field of battle. Its impact is yet to be felt at the conference table on the core issue of the Palestinians. Complete justice is unattainable for the Palestinians. But the mockery of justice is no infrastructure for self-sustaining peace. There is room for pragmatic justice. Pragmatic justice takes cognizance of the imperatives of both equity and reality. It embraces both the changes brought about by the evolution of time and the historical context in which the changes took place. It is instrumental, addressing itself to the practicable. An honorable overall solution of the Palestine Problem is realizable within such a framework.[277] This will not usher in the millennium. It will make life more civilized and tolerable for all concerned.

NOTES
APPENDIXES

1. In the spring of 1916 a secret trilateral agreement was entered into by Great Britain, France, and Russia for the division of the Ottoman Empire into spheres of influence among themselves. That part of the agreement affecting the Arab provinces of the Empire is known as the Sykes-Picot Agreement after Sir Mark Sykes and F. Georges-Picot, the British and French delegates, respectively. See George Antonius, *The Arab Awakening* (London, 1938), p. 244 ff.

2. On June 28, 1919, the Treaty of Versailles and the Covenant of the League of Nations were signed. According to Article 22 of the Covenant, the general principle to be applied to the peoples in territories that formerly belonged to the vanquished powers was that their "well-being and development" constituted "a sacred trust of civilization." But the best method of giving effect to this principle was that "tutelage" of these people should be undertaken by "advanced nations" in their capacity as mandatories on behalf of the League. Certain communities formerly belonging to the Ottoman Empire had, however, "reached a stage of development where their existence as independent nations can be provisionally recognized subject to the rendering of administrative advice and assistance of the Mandatory." But the wishes of these communities should be "a principal consideration in the selection of the Mandatory." Acting on this last provision, President Wilson pressed for the dispatch of an inter-Allied commission to the Near East to ascertain the wishes of their peoples. When Great Britain and France balked at this suggestion, Wilson sent an American commission composed of Henry C. King and Charles R. Crane. The King-Crane Commission reported in August 1919 that 80.4 percent of petitions received specifically called for a united Syria, 73.5 percent for independence. A French mandate was rejected outright if it were "obligatory" and was favored by only 14.5 percent of the petitions if it came about by consent. On 22 April 1920, the Supreme Council of the Peace Conference at San Remo allotted the mandate for Lebanon and Syria to France. For the full text of the King-Crane Report, see Department of State, *Foreign Relations of the United States, The Peace Conference, 1919* (Washington, 1947), Volume XII, p. 758 ff.

3. For the text of the resolutions of the General Syrian Congress announced on 2 July 1919, see Antonius, *op. cit.*, p. 440.

4. For the administrative divisions of the Arab provinces under the Ottomans, see Map I.

5. The Sunnites are so called because they claim adherence to the *sunna* or life-style and rules of conduct of the Prophet Muhammad. They are the "orthodox" sect in Islam, and most Arab Moslems are Sunnites. The Shiites are so called because they originally were *shiah* or partisans of Ali (d. 661 A.D.), first cousin of Muhammad and husband of his only surviving daughter, Fatimah. The Shiites insist that Ali was divinely designated to succeed Muhammad and that his descendants were entitled to the caliphate by hereditary right. To most Shiites, Ali is an exemplar; to the extremists among them he is the incarnation of the deity.

6. The Druzes derive their name from their eponymous founder, al Darazi, "the tailor," a Persian who lived in Egypt during the reign of the eccentric Shiite Caliph al Hakim (996-1021 A.D.). Darazi carried his ultra-Shiite teachings to Lebanon where he died in 1019. These teachings and those of his successors included *inter alia* the concepts of the divinity of al Hakim, predestination, and the transmigration of souls.

7. The Maronites are named after their eponymous patron saint, Marun, an anchorite who died about 410 A.D., although Yuhanna Marun (d. 707 A.D.) was the founder of the community. Originally the Maronites were probably monothelites, i.e., they emphasized the "one will" of Christ in the face of the controversy as to whether the divine and the human in Christ constituted one or two natures. In addition to the Maronites and the Greek Orthodox, there are several other Christian sects in present-day Lebanon. These, in the order of their numerical strength are the Greek Catholics, the Armenian Orthodox, the Armenian Catholics, the Protestants, the Syrian Catholics, the Syrian Orthodox, the Chaldaeans, and the Latins. The Greek Catholics by and large identified themselves politically with the Maronites. The Armenians generally maintained their neutrality. The other Christian sects were too small to have a significant political impact. See R. B. Betts, *Christians in the Arab East* (Athens, 1975).

8. In 1861, the total population of Mount Lebanon was estimated at 296,000. Of this number, 264,000 were Christian and 32,000 Moslem. Of the Christian total, 225,000 were Maronites, while 25,000 of the Moslem total were Druzes. In 1913, the Christian population of Mount Lebanon was 329,415 (242,308 Maronites), while the Moslem population was 85,232 (47,290 Druzes). P. Rondot, *Les Institutions Politiques du Liban* (Paris, 1947), p. 28.

9. See Philip Hitti, *Lebanon in History* (London, 1957), Chaps. XXIX and XXX, and Kamal Salibi, *The Modern History of Lebanon* (New York, 1965), p. 80ff.

10. Compare Maps I and II for the frontiers of Mount Lebanon and Grand Liban.

11. Full union between the Maronites and Rome was effected in 1736, though a Maronite College for the training of Maronite clergy was established in Rome

as early as 1584. The French connection could be traced back to 1204 when Louis IV of France is said to have given the Maronites his protection. See Hitti, *op. cit.*, p. 247ff. and Salibi, *op. cit.*, pp. 12-13, 118-119, and 121ff.

12. See Hitti, *op. cit.*, p. 244ff.

13. For the Maronite contribution to Arabic Letters and the modern Arab cultural and political renaissance, see Hitti, op. cit., Chap. XXXI, and Salibi, op. cit., pp. 121ff. and 151ff.

14. See Antonius, op. cit. p. 243ff.

15. For centuries, until the nationalist awakening at the turn of the nineteenth century, the Moslem Arabs in the Ottoman Empire had not regarded themselves as subjects of Constantinople. This was particularly true of the Sunnites, since the Ottoman Turks were Sunnites. The underlying theory of the Ottoman Empire was that it constituted the single *ummah*, or community of Islam, headed by the caliph, who was the Turkish Sultan.

16. The 1932 census put the total number of Christians "present or temporarily absent" at 396,746, and that of Moslems at 386,499. To the Christian total the census added 55,335 "emigrants possessing the Lebanese nationality," and 160,509 "who no longer retained the Lebanese nationality." This brought the Christian grand total to 612,590. To the above Moslem total the census added 11,580 and 25,285 in the latter two categories, bringing the Moslem grand total to 423,364. P. Rondot, *op. cit.*, p. 29.

17. See Hitti, *op. cit.*, p. 254ff., and Salibi, *op. cit.*, p. 151ff.

18. As Sunnites, the Ottomans tended to discriminate against non-Sunnite Moslems. See note 15 above.

19. In the early days of the French Mandate, Emile Eddé became Prime Minister once (1929-1930), Bishara Khoury three times (1927-1929). Subsequently, Eddé became President of Lebanon (1937-39). Each led a political grouping: Eddé's was called the National Bloc, Khoury's, the Constitutional Bloc. The competition between the two leaders reached its climax during World War II in anticipation of the post-war settlement of Lebanon. See Albert Hourani, *Syria and Lebanon* (London, 1954), p. 257ff. and p. 279ff.

20. After the collapse of metropolitan France, British forces together with small Free French forces occupied Syria and Lebanon to forestall a link-up between the Vichy-oriented "mandatory" administration and the Axis powers. The British were in little hurry to leave the two countries ahead of the French. See General Sir Edward Spears, *Fulfilment of a Mission* (Leo Cooper, London, 1977). General Spears was appointed by Churchill in 1941 to head a mission in Syria and Lebanon. See also Albert Hourani, op. cit., p. 230ff.

21. Solh belonged to a prestigious Sunnite family from Sidon, his father having been a member of the Ottoman Parliament. Riyad Solh had been resolutely opposed to the French and an advocate of union with Syria. He became the first Sunnite Prime Minister in the post-independence Khoury administration (see p. 13ff. below). He died by assassination in 1951.

22. The principles of the National Pact were enunciated in a speech delivered

by Riyad Solh (see note 21) in the Lebanese Parliament on 7 October 1943. It was on the basis of this speech that Solh won the Parliament's vote of confidence in his cabinet. See Note 27 below.

23. According to statistics compiled in 1942-43 (which were, however, not based on a census), the total population of Lebanon was put at 1,104,669, of whom 585,443 were Christian and 507,547 were Moslem. P. Rondot, *op. cit.*, p. 29.

24. For the Christian minorities in the Arab World, see A. H. Hourani, *Minorities in the Arab World* (London, 1947), and Betts, *op. cit.*

25. In the Alexandria Protocol of 1944 preceding the formation of the Arab League the following year, the Arab countries collectively recognized the independence of Lebanon. See Albert H. Hourani, *Syria and Lebanon* (London, 1954), p. 303.

26. For the Covenant of the Arab League see *Ibid.*

27. The use of the word "face" was a compromise formulation between the outright description of Lebanon as "an Arab country" and the denuding of Lebanon of any Arab characteristics. The formulation occurs in Riyad Solh's speech to Parliament in 1943, viz., "Lebanon is a homeland with an Arab face seeking the beneficial good from the culture of the West," Jean Malha (ed.), *Majmu'at al Bayanat al Wazariyah al Lubnaniyah* (Beirut, 1965), p. 22. See also Note 22 above.

28. There had been precedents for this distribution of the three highest posts under the French Mandate, particularly in the period 1934-1942, but the arrangement now virtually became part of the National Pact of 1943.

29. Presidential powers are extensive. Executive authority is in effect vested in the President, although he is not accountable to Parliament except for constitutional violations and crimes. The President appoints the members of the cabinet, including the Prime Minister, and dismisses them. The cabinet submits legislative and budgetary proposals to Parliament and conducts foreign policy subject to his approval. With cabinet approval he may dissolve Parliament before the end of its term and implement legislative proposals deemed urgent on which Parliament has not acted within 40 days. On his own initiative he may summon Parliament to special session. He enjoys limited powers of veto over legislative and constitutional amendments. The President is elected for six years and may not be eligible for re-election until after a period of six years.

30. The relationship between Bishara Khoury, as President, and Riyad Solh, as Prime Minister, is generally considered to have approximated most closely to the model of the rapport needed to be established between Maronite President and Sunnite Prime Minister.

31. For Lebanon's involvement in the Palestine War of 1948, see N. Lorch, *The Edge of the Sword* (New York, 1961), pp. 154, 371.

32. The 1932 census had put the total population of Lebanon at 793,426, excluding emigrants who had either retained or given up Lebanese nationality (see note 16 above; also, Rondot, *op. cit.*, p. 29). By 1956, the total population of Lebanon was estimated at 1,411,000. F. I. Qubain, *Crisis in Lebanon* (Washington, 1961), p. 8.

33. Chamoun appointed Dr. Charles Malik as Foreign Minister in the new cabinet formed just after the Suez War of 1956. Malik held strong pro-Western and conservative convictions and was the proponent of an activist foreign policy role for Lebanon in regional and world affairs. See L. Meo, *Lebanon: Improbable Nation* (Bloomington, 1965), and F. I. Qubain, *op. cit.*

34. Chamoun was on close terms with Jordan, Iraq, Turkey, and Iran in an *ad hoc* coalition against Nasser.

35. The most important Christian personage antagonzied by Chamoun was Msgr. Paul Meouchy, the Maronite Patriarch (see p. 72ff.).

36. President Chehab was a descendant of a princely family that had ruled Mount Lebanon in the 18th and 19th centuries. Its heyday was under Bashir II (1788-1840). The Chehabs were originally Sunnites (as some of them still are today).

37. For the Phalanges (Phalanges Libanaises) see M. Suleiman, *Political Parties in Lebanon*, New York 1966), p. 232 ff.

38. For the reforms under Chehab and Helou see E. Salem, *Modernization Without Revolution* (Bloomington, 1973).

39. For the intra-Maronite conflicts and coalitions during this period see K. Salibi, *Crossroads to Civil War: Lebanon 1958-1976* (Delmar, N.Y., 1976), *passim*.

40. On 12 May 1968, for the first time in two and a half years, Israeli and Lebanese forces exchanged fire across the border. This was the result of Israeli shelling of the village of Houleh in retaliation for Palestinian shelling of Kibbutz Margaliot (*Arab Report and Record*, 12 May 1968). On 20 May 1968, Lebanon complained to the Security Council that Israel had suspended the work of the Armistice Commission and threatened "to occupy the southern part of Lebanon" (*Ibid.*, 20 May 1968). Lebanese villages came under Israeli artillery fire in June (e.g., Meis-el-Jabal—see *Ibid.*, 15 June 1968) and in October (e.g., Majidiyeh, Hounine, and Malkiyeh—see *International Herald Tribune*, 28 October 1968). In these and the later incidents there were Lebanese civilian casualties as well as extensive destruction of houses and burning of crops and orchards. Already by mid-July the flight of the Lebanese peasants from the border area was under way. The Israelis justified their actions as retaliation against Palestinian operations from Lebanon. On 27 December 1968, Palestinian commandos attacked an El Al plane in Athens. On 28 December 1968, an Israeli helicopter-borne commando force attacked Beirut International Airport destroying 13 Lebanese civilian aircraft on the ground "in retaliation" for the Athens incident. On 31 December 1968, the Security Council unanimously condemned the Israeli operation. On 7 January 1969, the Israeli newspaper *Haaretz* warned the Lebanese that Israeli retaliation would devastate southern Lebanon as it had devastated the Jordan Valley in the aftermath of Palestinian activity against Israel. Israeli retaliation took several forms during 1969. In addition to the shelling of villages, the first aerial bombardment of Lebanon took place in this year, while commando raids were carried out both by helicopter-borne and mechanized units. The first air raid experienced by Lebanon occurred on 11 August 1969, against the villages of Hasbaya, Jouwaya, and Ain Qanya (*The Guardian*, and *L'Orient*, 12 August

1969). The Security Council unanimously condemned the raid, but Israel described it as an act of self-defense. On 3 September 1969 an air raid was carried out against the villages of Kfar Shouba, Kfar Hamam, Rashaya al Foukhkhar, al Habariya, Freidis, Mimas, and Snaifer (*Nahar*, 4 September 1969); while on 6 September 1969 another air raid took place against Khraibeh, Tell Mari, Bhassa, and Wadi Halta (*Ibid.*, 5 September 1969). Raids by mechanized infantry started as early as 16 March 1969 (e.g., against the village of Blida—see *L'Orient*, 17 March 1969) while on 3 September 1969 the village of Halta was the target of a helicopter-borne commando attack. (*Nahar*, 5 and 6 September 1969). This was the background of the Shiite peasant exodus from the border villages as well as of the Lebanese ministerial crisis that led to the Cairo Agreement of 3 November 1969.

41. For the full text of the Cairo Agreement see Appendix I. The text was not officially released by Lebanon until its appearance in the government White Paper, *Le Livre Blanc Libanais: Documents Diplomatiques 1975-76* (Beirut, 1976), p. 196.

42. Both candidates were Greek Orthodox, but the majority of their constituency were Sunnites.

43. Even before the Civil War in Jordan in September 1970 and the consequent expulsion and transfer of the Palestinian commandos to Syria and Lebanon, the situation on the border between Israel and Lebanon had rapidly deteriorated (see Note 40 above). For a description of conditions on this border during 1970 and before September of this year, see *Newsweek*, 19 January, 16 March, and 8 June 1970. *The* (London) *Times* wondered on 9 March 1970 whether Israel's reactions to the border situation indicated that her aim was "to annex the headwaters of the River Jordan which are now in Lebanon." On 30 May 1970, *The Economist* estimated that some 30,000 had left southern Lebanon. On 8 June 1970, *Newsweek* reported that of the 5,000 inhabitants of the Shiite village of Bint Jubeil only 500 remained. This flight followed the Israeli shelling of the town on 22 May in retaliation for the ambush by Palestinian commandos of an Israeli schoolbus. On 7 September 1970, *The Guardian* estimated that a further 25,000 had fled from the Arkoub border region. As early as 11 May 1970, Moshe Dayan had warned that if guerrilla attacks continued from Lebanon "the same devastation that exists on the canal front and on the east bank of the River Jordan will exist on our northern border." *The Times*, London, 11 May 1970.

44. The Melkart Understanding is so called after the Beirut hotel in which it was reached on 15-17 May 1973. The Understanding dealt with such issues as the number of commandos and the level of armaments permitted inside and outside refugee camps, the location of training camps, and procedures to curb violations. Its most important provision was the suspension of operations across the border against Israel which seemed to annul the tacit understanding to allow such operations contained in the Cairo Agreement of 1969. For the text (in Arabic) of the Melkart Understanding see *Le Livre Blanc Libanais etc.*, p. 200 ff.

45. Hafiz's qualifications for the job included a doctorate in Political Economy, membership of Parliament, chairmanship of the Parliamentary Foreign Relations Committee, as well as experience as a university lecturer and journalist.

46. See p. 80 ff. and pp. 85-86.

47. Since 1943, there had been instances of intra-sectarian political proscription as well as of political proscription between individual leaders across sectarian lines (see p. 96 ff.). What was ominous about the proscription of the Phalanges was that it was aimed across the sectarian lines by one broadly based grouping (the predominantly Moslem National Movement) against another (the exclusively Maronite Phalanges).

48. For the full text of Arafat's statement, see *Journal of Palestine Studies*, Vol V, Nos. 17/18, Autumn 1975, p. 279 ff.

49. For the full text of the National Movement's Reform Program see *ibid*, p. 283 ff.

50. Raymond Eddé was the son of Emile Eddé (see note 19 above). Several times a member of Parliament and cabinet minister since independence in 1943, he was outstanding among Lebanese political figures for his commitment to parliamentary democracy as well as for the irrepressible forthrightness, if not the political timing, of his pronouncements.

51. See p. 71 ff.

52. The Committee for National Dialogue held nine meetings in all between 25 September and 11 November 1975. For the minutes (in Arabic) of these meetings and of the various subcommittees that it formed, see *al Tariq* (Beirut), Nos. 1-8, January-August, 1976.

53. In an interview with the author in Paris in January 1977, M. Couve de Murville indicated that France's intervention in Lebanon had been motivated by "sentiment." During his visit to the country he had concentrated on bridging the gap between Karami and Franjieh. He did not seem overly impressed by the Lebanese leaders he had met.

54. The Unforeseen had developed quite a habit of intervention in the Lebanese Civil War. Compare the mysterious murders of Maaruf Saad and Gemayel's bodyguard, pp. 44-45 above, respectively. These and subsequent similar incidents gave rise to persistent speculation about the role of a hidden "Third Party"—the favorite hypothesis of Conspiracy Theory addicts in Lebanon.

55. See C. Chamoun, *Crise au Liban* (Beirut, 1947) p. 13 ff.

56. The author was one of two people present during the telephone conversation in which Karami submitted his resignation to Franjieh at the height of the Maronite onslaught against Karantina.

57. Although the customary allocation of the three highest posts (point 3 in Khaddam's proposed program) was to remain the same, in contrast to the former state of affairs this custom was now to be put in writing, though not in a constitutional amendment. The account of this meeting at the Mufti's house is based on a copy of the verbatim minutes of the meeting, now in the author's possession, taken by someone present at the meeting.

58. See notes 22 and 27 above. For the full text of the Constitutional Document, see Appendix II.

59. Based on a copy of the verbatim minutes of a meeting in Damascus on 18 July 1976 between a Lebanese Sunnite delegation and Syrian Foreign Minister A.H. Khaddam.

60. Interview in Beirut, August 1977, between the author and a former member of the Lebanese High Command.

61. The constitutional article in question that required amendment was Article 73. This article (as amended by the Constitutional Law promulgated on 17 October 1927) read as follows: "At the request of the Speaker, the Parliament shall meet for the election of the new President, at least one month and at the most two months before the end of the Presidential term. Should the Parliament not be called to meet for this purpose, it shall necessarily meet on the tenth day preceding the end of the Presidential term."

62. See *Al Nida*, Beirut, 21 March 1976.

63. On the day of the attack on the palace, a shell burst in Franjieh's study seconds after he had left it. The newly built Presidential palace had, inexplicably, no air raid shelters. Interview of author with daughter of Franjieh in January 1977.

64. For the Syrian version, see speech by President Asad of Syria (in Arabic) in *Le Livre Blanc Libanais*, p. 114 ff.

65. Based on experiences as told to the author in May 1976 in Beirut by a Lebanese member of Parliament who had been at the receiving end of Syrian "persuasion."

66. Some P.L.A. units stationed in Egypt started arriving in Lebanon as early as January-February 1976.

67. For President Giscard d'Estaing's statement see the *New York Times*, 22 May, 1:8, 3:2. For reactions of various French political factions to this statement, see *ibid.*, 23 May, 12:3, 3:3; 24 May, 1:1; and 27 May, 3:1. In his interview with the author, M. Couve de Murville (see note 53 above) observed that he was against foreign military intervention in Lebanon and believed that only an expeditionary force of 100,000 men could restore law and order.

68. As reported to author by an eyewitness.

69. Eyewitnesses deny any Syrian prisoners were publicly displayed.

70. For the text of Franjieh's letter to the Secretary-General of the Arab League (in Arabic) dated 9 June 1976, see *Le Livre Blanc Libanais*, p. 57.

71. *New York Times*, 17 June, 1:8.

72. Most of the inhabitants of Jisr al Basha camp were impoverished *Maronite* Palestinians. (Ali Khalaf, *al Nuhud Marra Ukhra*, Beirut, p. 180). The Palestinians in Tel Zaatar camp numbered some 17,000. The rest of the inhabitants in the camp were Shiite refugees from the area bordering Israel. The eastern suburbs of Beirut where these two camps were located contained the largest concentration of light industries in the country—hence their "attractiveness" to refugees and the unemployed. Conditions in the camp were appalling: 6-7 persons per 1-2 rooms, 86% of dwellings without baths, 20% without lavatories, 60% without running water and 40% without heating. (*Ibid.*, p. 42).

73. See Map II, for the Greek Orthodox population of North Lebanon. Many of the Greek Orthodox belonged to the Syrian Social Nationalist Party, for which see p. 77.

74. Most of those killed at Tel Zaatar were non-combatants. The casualties of the various Palestinian commando organizations have been given as follows:

Fath, 106, PDFLP, 128, PFLP, 39. (For these organizations see p. 79 ff.). In addition, the Lebanese Communist Party lost 8. *Al Nuhud Marra Ukhra*, p. 165 ff.

75. Interview of author with Salah Khalaf (Abu Iyad) in Beirut, August 1976.

76. For the text of Sarkis' address, see Appendix III.

77. For the resolutions of the Riyad summit, see Appendix IV.

78. For the resolutions of the Cairo summit, see Appendix V.

79. See statement by ex-Prime Minister Rashid Karami in *al Anwar*, Beirut, 22 November 1976.

80. Interview of author in Beirut in August 1977 with former senior member of Lebanese High Command. Also see *The Military Balance 1976* (IISS, London, 1976).

81. Statement by former Army Commander General Iskandar Ghanem in *al Nahar*, Beirut, 25 November 1976.

82. F. Lahhoud, in *Maisat Jaish Lubnan* (Beirut, 1976), p. 229, gives the following breakdown of these 24 battalions: 9 infantry, 5 armored, 6 artillery, 1 engineering, 1 intelligence, 1 transport, and 1 military police.

83. Interview of author with former member of High Command mentioned in note 80 above. For a more critical view of Franjieh's handling of the army and of the conduct of former Army Commander General Iskandar Ghanem, see F. Lahhoud, *op. cit.*, p. 58ff. See also the Karami statement (note 79 above) in which Ghanem is accused of involving the army in the transfer and smuggling of arms to the Maronite militias.

84. According to *The Military Balance 1976* (p.35), the tanks were mostly Charioteers, the armored cars, M-706s, M-6s, the personnel carriers, M-113s, M-59s and M-3s. The artillery included 75mm and 122mm guns, as well as 155mm howitzers and 120mm mortars. The self-propelled anti-aircraft guns were mostly 20mms. The anti-tank guided weapons were ENTACs, SS-11s, and TOWs.

85. Most of the barracks fell into the hands of Khatib's rebel forces because of their location in predominantly Moslem areas. F. Lahhoud, *op. cit.*, p. 204.

86. *The Military Balance 1976*, p. 36.

87. Michael Hudson believes that the most persuasive estimate of the annual rate of increase of Lebanese "residents" is 2.6%, which is the one arrived at by the Lebanese Ministry of Planning for the period 1945-1962. M. Hudson, *The Precarious Republic* (New York, 1968), p. 57.

88. For the text of the Constitutional Document, see Appendix II.

89. For these tensions, see C. Chamoun, *op. cit.*, p. 22, 26-32, 34, 58, 103, 121, 129.

90. Estimates privately arrived at after comparison of estimates by several observers. See also Joseph G. Chami and Gérard Castoriades, *Days of Tragedy, Lebanon 1975-76* (Beirut, 1976), p. 387.

91. The automatic rifles were FN FALs, Kalachnikov AK 47s, and M16s, the machine guns, FN MAGs, Browning 1919 A4s, M2s and Degturyev and 12.7mm (Dushkas), the anti-tank guns, M40A2s, the anti-tank rockets, RPG-2s, RPG-7s, and SS-11s, the mortars of all calibres (60, 81, 82, 120, 160mm, the last Soviet-made), the field artillery, USM101s, Al 105mm, and French M-50 155mm, the

rockets, BM-21s, the personnel carriers, M3/VTTs, M-113s, and BTR-152s and the armored cars, AML 90s.

92. Betts, *op. cit.*, p. 140.

93. See pp. 38, 39.

94. See pp. 34, 35.

95. Cf. Joseph Frankel, *The Making of Foreign Policy* (London, 1967), p. 112 ff., and 123 ff.

96. The figure of 4% for the "upper crust of society" occurs in an income distribution table in *Besoins et Possibilités du Liban*, Volume I, p. 93. This was the report published in Beirut in 1960-61 by a survey team of the French Institut International de Recherches et de Formation en vue de Developpement (I.R.F.E.D.). The team had been invited to Lebanon by President Chehab. The following is the table in which the 4% figure occurs:

	% of Families	Below £ L p.a.	Average Annual Income (£ L)	% Gross National Product
Wretches	8.8	1,200	1,000	1.8
Poor	41.2	2,500	2,000	16.5
Medium	32.0	5,000	3,500	22.4
Well Off	14.0	15,000	10,000	28.0
Rich	4.0	above 15,000	40,000	32.0

As was to be expected, this 4% figure became the rallying cry for the leftist radical political forces and the critics of Lebanon's free enterprise system.

97. For the Progressive Socialist and the Lebanese Communist Parties see Suleiman, *op. cit.*, p. 213-227, p. 57ff., respectively; also Hudson, *op. cit.*, p. 183ff., p. 168ff., respectively.

98. For the Syrian Social Nationalist Party see L. B. Yamak, *The Syrian Social Nationalist Party, an Ideological Analysis* (Cambridge, 1966), Suleiman, *op. cit.*, p. 91 ff.and Hudson, *op. cit.*, p. 178 ff. For the Baath Party see Suleiman, *op. cit.*, p. 121 ff.and Hudson, *op. cit.*, p. 178 ff.

99. After the death of Nasser in September 1970, the Lebanese Nasserist organizations were subject to the conflicting pulls of Nasser's would-be successors in Lebanon: Asad of Syria, Sadat of Egypt, Kaddafi of Libya and the Baath Party of Iraq. Hence the tendendy to splinter in the cause of "Correction" (i.e. "anti-revisionism") while retaining the original organizational name.

100. Interview of author with close friend of Jumblat's who accompanied him on a visit to Britain at end of World War II.

101. For the post-1948 Palestinian nationalist movement and the development

of the PLO and the commando organizations, see W. Quandt, F. Jabber, A. Mosley Lesch, *The Politics of Palestinian Nationalism* (Berkeley, 1973).

102. The PLA forces were organized around three "regiments" or "brigades":

1) Qadisiya forces - raised and based in Iraq; moved to Syria during October war; units were moved into refugee camps in Lebanon in 1974 as part of an air defense scheme against Israeli bombing raids worked out with the Syrian army (with knowledge of the Lebanese authorities)—approximately one platoon per camp, plus AA units. During the civil war, further units—bringing the total in Lebanon to approximately 1½ battalions—were moved into the country in January 1976. Virtually all these forces came over to the PLO.

2) Ain Jalout forces - raised and based in Egypt; fought in Gaza 1956, 1967, on the Canal 1968-70, and in the October 1973 war. Small units began to arrive in Lebanon, via Syria, where they arrived by air, in January 1976, although officers of Ain Jalout were seconded to Lebanon as early as 1970-71—most politically reliable—i.e., vis-à-vis the PLO—of all PLA forces. Over the period from January - June, approximately 2½ battalions of Ain Jalout were brought to Lebanon, mainly by sea, from Egypt.

3) Hittin forces - raised and based in Syria; fought in the October War. These were the largest, but the least politically motivated of the PLA forces (raised by conscription among Palestinians in Syria). They were brought in initially to police cease-fires in the fall of 1975 in Tripoli and Beirut—approximately 2 battalions; approximately another 2 battalions were brought in in the winter to increase Syrian strength in the country. In June 1976 perhaps 40% of the men and officers came over to the PLO.

103. For the official Iraqi government position that these were "volunteers," see *Le Livre Blanc Libanais*, p. 188.

104. Syrian regulars often masqueraded as *Saiqa*.

105. Syrian regular-*"Saiqa"* units remained consistently loyal to Damascus (see note 104).

106. It is a moot point whether irrespective of Syrian military presence, the Maronite-Palestinian balance of power remained in favor of the Palestinians in the autumn of 1976, particularly after the Israeli aid extended to the Maronites—see pp. 91-92.

107. See above note 5. The Alawites, more accurately known as Nusayris, were an esoteric sect founded in the ninth century. Like other extreme Shiites they deified Ali (d. 661), first cousin of the Prophet Muhammad and husband of his only surviving daughter Fatimah—hence their name, Alawites. This name became current when the French Mandatory incorporated the Syrian region around Lattakia, in which the Alawites predominated, in a separate state under that name. (See P. Hitti, *Syria, A Short History* (New York, 1959), p. 172ff.) It is to be noted, however, that President Asad of Syria had announced his adherence to Sunnite Islam.

108. In addition to Iran, both the U.S. and Israel had supported the Kurdish rebellion. Early in 1974 Baghdad launched a major military offensive against the Kurds when a new plan for regional autonomy that it had offered was turned down by them. On 7 March 1975, agreement was reached by Iraq and Iran on a

long-standing dispute which included territorial issues. As a result of this agreement Iran withdrew its support from the Kurds and by mid-March 1975 the Kurdish rebellion had altogether collapsed. For the end of the rebellion see *New York Times* 7, 12, 14, 23, 30, 31 March and 6 April 1975. For U.S. aid to the Kurds see *Ibid.* 2, 4, and 30 November 1975.

109. See Suleiman, *op. cit.*, p. 121 ff., also Kamal Abu Jaber, *The Arab Baath Socialist Party,* (Syracuse, 1966) *passim* and John F. Devlin, *The Baath Party,* (Stanford, 1976) *passim.*

110. The Palestinian population in the countries of the Arabian Gulf and Saudi Arabia is estimated at 300,000. *New York Times,* February 19, 1978, p. 16.

111. King Faisal was assassinated by a member of the Saudi royal family on 25 March 1975.

112. For Kissinger's reaction to the Rabat summit's recognition of the PLO "as the sole legitimate representative of the Palestinians," see Edward R. F. Sheehan, *The Arabs, Israelis, and Kissinger* (New York, 1976), pp. 148-149.

113. On 6 November 1975, Kissinger sent a letter of support to the Lebanese government "conspicuously" addressed to Karami. See *New York Times,* 28 November 1975, 2:4.

114. According to Kissinger, Ambassador Brown was sent to Lebanon "with something like 24 hours' notice." (*Department of State Bulletin,* 17 May 1976, p. 627). According to Brown, in an interview with the author in December 1976, it was at a chance encounter with Kissinger at an airport in the U.S. that Kissinger sprang on him his decision to send him to Lebanon.

115. The author's impression of the diffuseness of Brown's mission is based *inter alia* on the study of minutes of meetings held between Brown and a key Lebanese official.

116. For U.S. support of the principles of the Constitutional Document, see statements by Kissinger on 22 April (*Department of State Bulletin,* 17 May 1976, p. 622), 5 June *ibid.,* 28 June 1976, p. 814), 22 July (*ibid.,* 16 August 1976, p. 237), 11 September (*ibid.,* 4 October 1976, p. 414) and Department Statement of 23 September (*ibid.,* 11 October 1976, p. 460). On the specifically anti-partition stand of the U.S., see Kissinger's statements of 2 September (*ibid.,* 27 September, - p. 401) 29 September (*ibid.,* 1 November 1976, p. 563) and 30 September (*ibid.,* 25 October, p. 502). But see also Chamoun, *op. cit.,* p. 99, where Ambassador Brown allegedly urges that serious Maronite consideration of partition or a confederation be deferred for two years to try out a new coexistence formula.

117. Initial U.S. reactions to possible Syrian intervention were distinctly hostile. Cf. statements by Kissinger on January 14 (*Department of State Bulletin,* 2 February, p. 132) and 20 January (*ibid.,* 16 February, p. 162). Cf. also President Asad's version of his exchanges with the U.S. on the subject, *Le Livre Blanc Libanais,* pp. 141 ff. The tone of U.S. warnings to Syria, however, changes from early March onwards. Thus Kissinger describes Syria on 23 March as playing a "moderating role in Lebanon", (*Department of State Bulletin,* 12 April 1976, p. 466).

118. Minutes of meeting on 9 April 1976 between Brown and a key Lebanese official.

119. Interview of author with President Franjieh in December 1975. See also memorandum from Camille Chamoun as Foreign Minister to the Lebanese ambassador in Moscow, complaining about activities and contacts of the U.S.S.R. Ambassador in Beirut. *Le Livre Blanc Libanais,* p. 161.

120. See above, p. 77.

121. See the *New York Times* 5 June, 3:2 for the Russian-Syrian communiqué.

122. For the Russian attitude towards the fighting in Lebanon, see *Current Digest of Soviet Press* Volume XXVII, Nos. 21, 22, 38, 40, 41, 43, 44, 45, 46, and 50, pp. 16, 20, 22, 23, 10, 21, 20, 21 and 29, respectively; also Volume XXVIII, No. 2, p. 7.

123. For a report concerning the curtailment of Soviet arms supplies to Syria during the Lebanese crisis in 1976, see Robert E. Harkavy, *The New Geopolitics: Arms Transfers and the Major Powers' Overseas Basing Networks,* paper prepared for the Conference at Cornell University on the Middle East, Ithaca, N.Y. 21-23 April 1977, p. 36. Harkavy quotes a report on the subject in *Defense and Foreign Affairs Daily,* 14 January 1977.

124. An interesting discussion and exchange of letters occurred between Israeli leaders early in 1954 on the feasibility and desirability of encouraging a Maronite separatist movement in Lebanon with the objective of partitioning the country and establishing a sovereign Maronite state. The issue was apparently first raised by Ben Gurion, then in political retirement, at his Tel Aviv home in the presence of Prime Minister Moshe Sharett, Pinhas Lavon, the Defense Minister, and Moshe Dayan. Ben Gurion followed up the discussion with a letter dated 28 February 1954 to Moshe Sharett. Sharett replied at length to Ben Gurion's letter on 18 March. Eliahu Sassoon, the leading Israeli Arabist, contributed a long commentary on Sharett's letter to Ben Gurion. Sassoon's reactions were given in a letter to Sharett of 25 March 1954. The texts of the three letters were published by the Israeli daily *Davar* in its issue of 29 October 1971 (p. 14).

In his letter to Sharett, Ben Gurion insisted on bringing up the subject of the partition of Lebanon which he had raised earlier at the Tel Aviv meeting between himself, Sharett, Lavon, and Dayan. Ben Gurion's thesis could be summed up as follows: Lebanon was the weakest link in the chain of the Arab League. The Christians (i.e., Maronites) were a majority within the frontiers of historic Lebanon (i.e., Mount Lebanon). The establishment of a Christian state within these frontiers was a natural thing. It would win the support of both Catholics and Protestants the world over. If such an objective appeared impracticable in normal times, it was eminently practicable at times of "confusion, disturbance, revolution and civil war." The time was now propitious. But a Christian state in Lebanon could not be established "without our initiative and effective assistance." This was the "principal task, or at least one of the principal tasks of our foreign policy." No effort, time, or resource should be spared. All means conducive "to a radical change in Lebanon" should be resorted to. Israeli Arabists, including Sassoon, should be mobilized for the job. Financial considerations, even if they meant "throwing dollars away," should not stand in the way. A historic opportunity beckoned to Israel and time was of the essence.

In his reply to Ben Gurion, Sharett made the following main points:

Interference in the domestic affairs of another country for the purpose of achieving a certain aim was futile unless there already existed an autonomous movement inside the country in question which also strove towards that aim. There was no movement in Lebanon which systematically sought to convert the country into "a Christian state under the absolute rule of the Maronites." To try to stimulate such expectations from the outside was like trying to resuscitate a lifeless body. This was not to preclude an effort at such stimulation "in the wake of some tempestuous disturbance that might sweep the Near East." Moreover, the Christians in Lebanon were not a unified group. The Greek Orthodox would rather see Lebanon and Syria unified than fall victim of a war for the establishment of a smaller Christian Lebanon that had seceded from the Arab League. Even the majority of the Maronites had become reconciled to the "lesser evil" of Christian-Moslem coexistence inside Lebanon at the expense of their dreams for the revival of former Christian glories. The Maronite assumption was that this course was likely to wean the Moslems from their nostalgia for union with Syria and so activate in them an attachment to Lebanese independence. The Maronites were therefore bound to regard as "fraught with catastrophe" any waving of "the flag of Maronite glorification," since it would lead to the annexation of the country by Syria. The secession of a Maronite Lebanon from the Arab League would be resisted by the League members and the "bloody war" that would result in the course of the secession would also lead to Syrian intervention. Nor would the Western powers stand by and wait to bless the birth of "Christian Lebanon." Economic considerations likewise decisively pointed in the same direction.

In the 30 years since World War I, Moslem Lebanon, including the Moslem areas added to Mount Lebanon in 1920, had become an organic economic unity. To attempt to put the clock back was to vivisect the country and ensure economic suicide, which no significant Maronite grouping could support. For all these reasons it was one thing to try and bring about this result in a deliberate manner, quite another "if change occurred as a result of unforeseen circumstances." Nevertheless, Sharett was prepared "to completely agree to the rendering of assistance to any agitation among the Maronites that aimed at increasing their power and tendency to secession, even though there was no probability of achieving the objective of secession." Such agitation would be a good thing in itself. It would disturb the existing stability of the country. It would cause problems for the Arab League. It would divert attention from the Arab-Israeli conflict. But, alas, no such agitation existed. And for Israel to try to stimulate it might be taken as evidence of recklessness and worse: as adventurism involving the basic security of others for ephemeral tactical advantages to Israel. Nor could Israel's role remain secret. It was bound to be discovered and to damage Israel's standing vis-à-vis the Arab countries and the Western world.

Sassoon's main points, largely in rebuttal of Sharett's arguments, were as follows: He conceded that no movement that had no base inside a country could be activated from outside. But it was wrong to assume that the Maronites were reconciled to the *status quo* and had accepted the lesser evil of coexistence with the Moslems at the expense of the revival of their dreams of glory. The Maronite attitude was based on the perception of the absence of alternatives rather than on conviction. The policy of the lesser evil was at best short-lived and bound to be jettisoned should an alternative course of action appear feasible. The Maronites were well aware that the policy of Moslem-Christian reconciliation and coexistence was also short-lived. In the long run it favored the Moslems. It guaranteed the independence of Lebanon within its present frontiers, but not the present character of Lebanon. Such a policy could not guarantee that the President of Lebanon would always be Maronite or that the Electoral Law and therefore the distribution of power would remain unchanged and in favor of the Maronites. It was true that there were no obvious signs of Maronite agitation, but it was not impossible to create it, given the "existence of very strong bases for its arousal." Nevertheless, the probability for such agitation to succeed in reaching its goal was remote. And it was remote because of a) the absence of qualified Israeli personnel for the job; b) the severance of contact between Israel and Lebanese personalities since the establishment of Israel; c) the absence of adequate funds; and d) the general temperamental unreliability of Lebanese Christians—"heroes with their tongues, weaklings in their arms." As to the discovery of the role of Israel, this would not cause much additional damage with regard to the Arab countries but was likely to embarrass Israel's standing vis-à-vis the Western world.

125. *Time*, 22 August 1977, p. 10.

126. As early as June 1975, Shimon Peres, the Israeli Defense Minister, was saying that "the Lebanon we know has gone and disappeared for ever" and that "what will take its place" should be the concern of Israel. (*Davar*, 4 June 1975, p. 2). A principal leitmotif in the early statements of Israeli leaders after the Ain Rummaneh massacre was the threat to the future of the Lebanese Christians posed by the fighting. See Shimon Peres in *Al Hamishmar*, 4 June 1975, p. 1; Yigal Allon, the Foreign Minister, *ibid.*, 21 September 1975, p. 1; Itzhak Rabin, the Prime Minister, in *Maariv*, 13 October 1975, p. 3, and *Al Hamishmar*, 29 October 1975, p. 2. Concurrently, Syria was warned against intervening militarily. See Allon *ibid.*, 21 September 1975, p. 1, and *Maariv*, 13 October 1975, p. 3; Rabin *ibid.*, 15 October 1975, p. 3. On 31 October 1975, Rabin first explicitly indicated the possibility that Israeli troops would enter Lebanon in the event of large-scale Syrian military intervention (*Haaretz*, 31 October 1975, p. 1).

127. See Rupert Emerson, *From Empire to Nation* (Cambridge, 1960).

128. See p. 34.

129. Karl W. Deutsch, "Social Mobilization and Political Development," *American Political Science Review*, Vol. 55, No. 3 (1961), pp. 493-94.

130. République Libanaise, Centre de Recherche et de Développement Pédagogique: *Statistiques Pédagogiques Année* 1973-1974, pp. 29, 330. See also *Lebanese Statistical Bulletin, 1963*, Ministry of General Planning, Beirut, p. 262.

131. See Walker Connor, "Nation-Building or Nation-Destroying," *World Politics*, Vol. XXIV, No. 3, April 1972, p. 319-355.

132. M. Hudson, *op. cit.*, pp. 53-83 and 330-331.

133. Eric Nordlinger, *Conflict Resolution in Divided Societies* (Center for International Affairs, Harvard University, 1972), p. 59.

134. See pp. 39 and 42.

135. See in particular, Leonard Binder (ed.), *Politics in Lebanon* (New York, 1966), Michael Suleiman, *Political Parties in Lebanon* (Ithaca, 1967) and Elie Salem, *Modernization Without Revolution* (Bloomington, Ind., 1973).

136. Cf. E. Salem, *op. cit.*, p. 106 ff. See also the Foreword by George J. Stolnitz.

137. See Nordlinger, *op. cit., passim,* and Arend Lijphart, "Consociational Democracy," *World Politics,* Vol. XXI, January 1969, No. 2, p. 220-225.

138. Interview of author with Prime Minister Salim Hoss in Beirut in August 1977. The original official estimate widely reported in the Western press of 60,000 killed was mercifully wide off the mark. *The Report on the Effect of the Crisis on the Manpower of Lebanon,* published by the Beirut Chamber of Commerce and Industry (see *al Safir,* 4 September 1977), puts the number of Lebanese killed at 20,000-25,000, the maimed and handicapped at 3000-5000, the orphans at 25,000. A high-ranking Phalanges official interviewed by the author in January 1978 put the total number of Christians killed at about 10,000, of whom 2000 were combatants. At least half of the combatant losses were suffered by the Phalanges. *Fiches du Monde Arabe* (4 January 1978, No. 846) estimates that 70 percent of all the Lebanese war victims were below 20 years of age and predicts that these losses "will affect the demographic structure of the Lebanese population for two decades." PLO leaders (in interviews with the author) estimate total Palestinian combatant losses at less than 1000, that of the National Movement at about 600, and that of the Maronite militias at about 3000. Civilian Palestinian losses are put at 4000 killed. These figures do not include the casualties that occurred after the cessation of general hostilities in November 1976.

139. *Fiches du Monde Arabe,* 4 January 1978, No. 846.

140. Samir A. Makdisi, "An Appraisal of Lebanon's Postwar Economic Development and a Look to the Future," *Middle East Journal,* Summer 1977, Vol. 31, No. 3, pp. 267-280. There was a depreciation of the Lebanese pound from £ L2.25/U.S. $1 in June 1975 to £ L3.20-3.40/U.S. $1 in the third quarter of 1976. In March 1977 the rate was £ L3.00/U.S. $1.

141. *Ibid.,* p. 275, Nos. 21 to 22. One of the severest losses suffered by Lebanon during the Civil War was the flight of professional and skilled labor. The estimates for some of the sectors are as follows: industry 60-70 percent, trade 15 percent, transport and communications 10 percent, public administration 7 percent, hotels 20 percent. (*Fiches du Monde Arabe,* 4 January 1978, No. 846). In the liberal professions 1680 out of 4000 engineers and architects, 500 out of 3200 doctors and 400 out of 2600 lawyers left the country. Many (probably from 30-50 percent) of all these have since returned.

142. See Appendix IV. The Cairo Agreement was subject to the so-called Melkart Understanding negotiated between the PLO and the Lebanese government in May 1973. See Note 44 above.

143. See p. 33-34.

144. On 25 January 1977, Syrian troops tried to move into the town of Nabatiyeh, north of the Litani where Palestinians had concentrated. An Israeli Foreign Ministry spokesman said that the movement of Syrian soldiers to

Nabatiyeh was a cause "of serious concern." (*New York Times*) On 15 February 1977 the Syrians withdrew from Nabatiyeh (*New York Times*). Thenceforth they kept well back, their southernmost advance posts being at the Zahrani in the western sector and at Hasbaya in the eastern sector—a distance of 10 miles from the Litani in the west. This is where they stayed throughout the Israeli invasion and withdrawal periods. (Interview by author with senior UN Secretariat official in New York in June 1978.)

145. Technically, Haddad was still a major in the Lebanese army and on its payroll like all the other members (both Christian and Moslem) of the disintegrated army. He was not, however, receiving his orders from the Beirut government. (Interview of author with Lebanese Prime Minister Salim Hoss in Beirut, August 1977.)

146. A major source of friction between the Maronite militias, and increasingly between Franjieh and his Maronite colleagues in the Lebanese Front, was disputes over "the ownership of what can be called either protection rackets or unofficial tax, depending on point of view."(*Washington Post*, 14 June 1978, p. A20).

147. See p. 35-36.

148. See Appendix V and Notes 142 and 44 above.

149. See Note 144 above.

150. See Appendix IV.

151. The moratorium on operations across the border was part of the Melkart Understanding—see No. 44 above.

152. See Note 144 above.

153. See p. 126.

154. See p. 34.

155. See Appendix II.

156. See p. 75.

157. The first provision of the 1969 Agreement guaranteed "the right to work and reside and freedom of movement for Palestinians already present in Lebanon" (see Appendix I). The right-wing Maronites maintain that at about the time of the Cairo Agreement (November 1969) the number of Palestinian refugees registered with UNRWA (The United Nations Relief and Works Agency) (in June 1968) was 166,264. They argue that the guarantee provision in the Cairo Agreement referred only to these refugees.

158. The U.S. provided $50 million in assistance, while the World Bank and the European Economic Community pledged loans of $50 million and $36 million respectively (*New York Times*, 19 June 1977, p. 3). In February 1978 a $150 million international reconstruction loan on the Eurodollar market in London was about to be finalized. (*The Christian Science Monitor*, 15 February 1978, p. 5.)

159. Saudi Arabia and Kuwait provided grants of $50 million and $30 million, respectively. The Abu Dhabi Fund was considering a $67 million loan. (*New York Times*, 19 June 1977, p. 3.) The Kuwait Fund for Economic and Social Development pledged a $167 million loan to start in May 1978 (*Christian Science Monitor*, 15 February 1978, p. 5).

160. See Note 146 above.

161. See Notes 40 and 43 above.

162. See pp. 51 and 61.

163. *New York Times*, 2 October 1977, p. 17.

164. See p. 65.

165. For the pro-Syrian groups see p. 77.

166. See p. 77.

167. The sons of three of the four principal members of the Lebanese Front were in direct line of political (and military) succession to their fathers: Tony (Franjieh), Basheer and Amin (Gemayel), Dory and Dany (Chamoun). But it could certainly be argued that they had earned their spurs in combat, though Amin Gemayel tended to be a dove. The same phenomenon, on a smaller scale, was observable on the Moslem side.

168. See p. 71.

169. The high-water mark during 1977 of the Carter Administration's positive movement towards a resolution of the Palestinian issue in the Arab-Israeli conflict was the joint U.S.-Soviet statement on 1 October. This, inter alia, declared that "the legitimate rights" of the Palestinians should be accepted in any overall settlement and that the Palestinians (though not specifically the PLO) should attend the peace conference. (See *New York Times*, 7 October 1977, p. 3, for the implications of this joint statement and the reactions of the various parties to it.) As a result of the opposition to this joint statement by Israel and pro-Israeli groups in the U.S., an Israeli-U.S. accord reached on 5 October 1977 virtually put the U.S.-Soviet statement into moratorium (see *Washington Post*, 6 October 1977). On 2 November 1977, in his address to the World Jewish Congress, President Carter stated that the U.S. does not "prefer an independent Palestinian state on the West Bank." (Text of speech as released by the White House Press Secretary, 2 November, p. 6.) Four days later C. L. Sulzberger outlined in the *New York Times* (6 November) Zbigniew Brzezinski's views on a Middle East settlement. Brzezinski allegedly held that "the Palestinians must abandon claims to total independence." On 27 December 1977 Brzezinski allegedly bid farewell to the PLO in the words "Bye Bye, PLO" to *Paris Match*, 28 December 1977. In a statement published by the London *Sunday Times* (30 April 1978, p. 8), President Carter declared categorically that a Middle Eastern settlement would not include an independent Palestinian state and that he would not change his mind on the subject. American *preference* for a certain outcome (no Palestinian state) had changed into a determination to preclude it even before negotiations with the Palestinians had started.

170. See p. 126.

171. For the Begin Plan, see the *New York Times*, 28 December 1977, particularly article 21.

172. On 2 April 1978 the Arab League Council prolonged the ADF's mandate for another 6 months.

173. See p. 45.

174. See p. 101.

175. *Time*, 27 March 1978. The security "failure" in intercepting the raiders

was the subject of considerable comment in the Hebrew press. (Y. Shimshi in *Davar*, Y. Ben Furat in *Yediot Ahronot*, and U. Dan in *Maariv*, 12 March 1978; Z. Schif in *Haaretz* and Y. Allon in *Maariv*, 13 March 1978.

176. *Fiches du Monde Arabe* (10 May 1978, No. 952) lists 22 PLO operations inside Israel and the occupied territories in the period April-March 1978. These occurred in Jerusalem, Beersheba, Tel Aviv, Nablus, and Nathanya.

177. *Time*, 10 April 1978, p. 29.

178. See Notes 40 and 43 above.

179. *Fiches du Monde Arabe*, 19 April 1978, No. 933.

180. E.g., *New York Times*, editorial of 19 March 1978.

181. *Fiches du Monde Arabe*, 17 May 1978, No. 959.

182. *Time*, 27 March 1978, p. 26.

183. *New York Times*, passim.

184. *New York Times*, 3 September, p. 3.

185. *New York Times*, 17 September, p. 3.

186. The sequence between the death of the three Lebanese fishermen (5 November) and the firing of the rocket at Nabariya (6 November) is noticed by the *New York Times* (7 November). For the names and photographs of the fishermen see *al Safir* (8 November, p. 1). The civilian nature of the casualties is referred to in the letter addressed by Lebanon to the Security Council (*al Nahar*, 11 November, p. 1).

187. See p. 127 ff.

188. *New York Times*, passim.

189. See *Economist*, 25 March 1978, p. 9; *Time*, 27 March 1978, p. 30; *Newsweek*, 27 March 1978, p. 32 attributes the almost total "elimination" of guerrilla activity across the border to Israel's construction of an electronically monitored security fence along it.

190. See p. 124.

191. *New York Times*, 15 March 1948, p. 1.

192. *Davar*, 14 March 1978, reported the unanimous Knesset resolution (with the Rakah party abstaining) which called *inter alia* for, "the need to direct blows at the terrorist organizations and their delegates with a view to their liquidation."

193. The three camps were Al Buss, Burj al Shemali, and Rashidiyeh.

194. *New York Times*, 6 August 1978, p. 3; *Fiches du Monde Arabe*, 12 April 1978, No. 927.

195. *New York Times*, 20 February 1978, p. 7.

196. For the continued Maronite offensive in April in the south with Israeli backing, see *New York Times*, 4 April 1978. For Begin's pledge to save the Christians from "genocide," see *New York Times*, 8 August and 15 August 1978.

197. *New York Times*, 27 August, p. 3.

198. *New York Times*, 11 September, p. 14.

199. *New York Times*, 15 September, p. 8 and 17 September 1978, p. 3.

200. *New York Times*, 20 September, p. 13, 21 September, p. 6, 22 September 1978, p. 22. On 20 September, UN Secretary General Waldheim appealed to all parties to show restraint. On 21 September Secretary of State Vance called for an immediate cease-fire.

201. Interview of author with high-ranking U.S. official in Cambridge, Mass., in late September 1977.

202. *New York Times*, 23 September 1978, p. 3.

203. *New York Times*, 10 November 1978, p. 5; *Fiches du Monde Arabe*, 12 April and 19 April 1978, Nos. 928 and 933, respectively.

204. *New York Times*, 10-12 November 1978.

205. *New York Times*, 10 November 1978, p. 3.

206. *New York Times*, 11 November 1978, p. 1.

207. *Newsweek*, 27 March 1978, p. 31. The raid is described as "a triumph for Israeli intelligence."

208. See *The Economist*, 25 March 1978, p. 62.

209. *Washington Post*, 30 April 1978.

210. *Time*, 3 April 1978, p. 31. According to the editorial of the *New York Times* of 17 April 1978, estimates of the civilian Lebanese and Palestinian dead "range up to several thousand."

211. The figure of over 250,000 new refugees is given in a press release (ICEF/1354) dated 23 March 1978, by the UN Press Section, New York. This press release also states that "many" of the refugees were children and "most" were Lebanese civilians "along with Palestinian refugees." The figures for the houses destroyed or damaged are given in a document entitled *Affected Villages in South Lebanon Visited by UNHC (United Nations High Commissioner for Refugees) on 26 April and 10 May 1978* (Beirut, 19 May, 1978) p. 7.

212. *Ha'aretz* (4 April 1978) reports that "over 50" Israeli soldiers, including junior officers, were court-martialed for looting. Writing in *Yediot Ahronot* (15 April 1978), Knesset member Shulamit Aloni refers to the "enormous destruction and looting" that took place as a result of the invasion.

213. *New York Times*, 20 March 1978.

214. *New York Times*, 26 February 1978, p. 11.

215. *Time*, 27 March 1978, p. 29.

216. *New York Times*, 30 March 1978.

217. For the background of Israel's interest in the Litani, see H.F. Frischwasser-Ra'anan, *The Frontiers of a Nation* (London, Batchworth Press, 1955) pp. 101-2, 107-8, 115, 117-118, 122-123, 128-129, 135, 139.

218. For Israeli views on the desirability and possibility of the partition of Lebanon, see Note 124 above.

219. For the U.S. view on the need to suppress publicity for Israeli support of Maronites, see *New York Times*, 9 August, p. 1, and 13 August, p. 5.

220. See Note 201.

221. See Note 169 above.

222. Cf., for example, the observations of Ze'ev Schiff, the senior Israeli military commentator in *Ha'aretz*, 31 March 1978: "There is no doubt that the Americans knew about the operation [the Israeli invasion] beforehand. It is not inaccurate to say that they had a general idea about the principal points that Israel intended to occupy in the area adjacent to the border. Indeed, they expressed their concern that the operation might have adverse effects on the peace negotiations. But it seems to me that they did not frankly express their

opposition to it. If they had wanted to, they would undoubtedly have been able to delay and probably to prevent the operation altogether. In September 1977, when they wanted the withdrawal of the Israeli army from the [Maronite] enclaves in South Lebanon, it was sufficient for President Carter to send a letter to that effect to Prime Minister Begin. Therefore, American silence with regard to the operation was tantamount to endorsement."

223. *Washington Post,* 30 April 1978.

224. Some 600 Palestinian volunteers, mostly from Iraq, arrived in Lebanon via Syria within 48 hours of the opening of Syria's borders.

225. *New York Times,* 17 March 1978.

226. *New York Times,* 18 March 1978, p. 1.

227. See Appendix VI.

228. See Appendix VII.

229. *Report of the Secretary-General on the Implementation of Security Council Resolution 425 (1978),* S/12611, 19 March 1978.

230. For text of letter reporting the possible Israeli violation from Mr. Vance to House Speaker Thomas O'Neill, Jr., see *New York Times,* 6 April 1978, p. 14.

231. *New York Times,* 8 April 1978, p. 1.

232. *New York Times,* 18 March 1978.

233. *Fiches du Monde Arabe,* 3 May 1978, No. 946.

234. *Progress Report of the Secretary-General on the United Nations Interim Force in Lebanon,* S/12620/Add. 1, 2 April 1978.

235. *Progress Report of the Secretary-General on the United Nations Interim Force in Lebanon,* S/12620/Add. 2, 8 April 1978, pp. 2-3.

236. *Ibid.,* p. 3.

237. *Ibid.,* p. 3.

238. *Ibid.,* p. 4.

239. *Ibid.,* p. 4.

240. *Progress Report of the Secretary-General of the United Nations on the United Nations Interim Force in Lebanon* S/12620/Add. 3, 17 April 1978, p. 1.

241. Unpublished minutes (in Arabic), in the author's possession, of the meeting between Mr. Waldheim and Mr. Arafat.

242. United Nations Press Release SG/T/847, 19 April 1978.

243. *Monday Morning,* Beirut, 15 May 1978.

244. *Boston Sunday Globe,* 11 June 1978, p. 30.

245. *The Economist,* 17 June 1978, p. 67.

246. For the estimate of Haddad's force at about 3000, see John Cooley in the *Christian Science Monitor,* 15 June 1978, p. 6. For Israel's brusqueness towards UNIFIL in the border area during the final pullout, see *The Washington Post,* 14 June 1978, p. A20.

247. According to Security Council Resolutions 425 and 426 (19 March 1978), Israel was to "withdraw forthwith its forces from all Lebanese territory," while the UN interim force UNIFIL was to confirm the withdrawal, restore international peace and security, and assist the Lebanese government in ensuring the return of its authority in the occupied territories. Israel and Haddad seem to have resorted to a stratagem to give the appearance of compliance with these

resolutions during Israel's final withdrawal scheduled for 13 June 1978: Haddad (who along with all the other rebel officers, whether Christian or Moslem, was still technically on active service, inasmuch as he was on the army payroll) "pledged" to President Sarkis to confine himself to his barracks together with his troops at Marj Uyun to permit UNIFIL units to take over the enclave he controlled. On the appointed day, however, a *"coup d'état"* was staged against Haddad by his own militiamen. This was to save Sarkis' face *vis-à-vis* Damascus and his Sunnite Prime Minister Hoss. The *coup* lasted for one day, the deadline for Israeli withdrawal from the rest of the six-mile belt. This enabled the Israelis to claim that their pullout was in conformity with the Security Council resolutions and that they had no alternative but to hand over the enclave to Haddad (who had meanwhile reappeared on the scene), particularly as in the first place they had not invaded this enclave. Since no eyebrows were raised in Washington, Sarkis (though not his Prime Minister Hoss) looked the other way, while the UN could not appear more Lebanese than Sarkis. (Interview with Prime Minister Hoss.) See also Note 145 above.

248. For the battle of Karameh and its significance, see W.B. Quandt, F. Jabber, A. Mosely Lesch, *The Politics of Palestinian Nationalism* (Los Angeles, 1973), pp. 57, 122, 179, 190, 195, 215.

249. The Israelis estimate the number of Palestinian guerrillas killed at 250. Materièl seized, according to the Israelis, included 10 tanks, 20 anti-aircraft guns, 20 recoilless rifles, 20 rocket launchers, 120 machine guns, 250-300 rifles, 35 tons of ammunition. How much of this equipment belonged to the Palestinians and how much to the rebel units of the Lebanese Arab Army is not indicated. (*Yediot Aharonot*, 27 March 1978). Palestinian sources put total guerrilla casualties for the first eight days of fighting at 71 dead and 131 wounded (*New York Times*, 1 April 1978, p. 2.).

250. Palestinian sources reported several thousand Palestinian volunteers to have come from Kuwait, Jordan, and Iraq (*New York Times*, 1 April 1978, p. 2).

251. Western sources generally put the strength of the Israeli invading force at some 25,000 (e.g., *The Economist*, 18 March 1978, p. 12). Some give a higher figure (cf., Townsend Hoopes in *The Washington Post*, 22 March 1978). General Mordechai Gur estimated Palestinian forces south of the Litani at the time of the Israeli invasion at 2000 (*Time*, 27 March 1978, p. 27).

252. A *New York Times* correspondent, writing from the West Bank, reported the conservative Palestinian mayor of Bethlehem as saying that whereas opinion on the West Bank had been 55 percent pro-PLO before the invasion, it had risen to 95 percent in favor after it (*New York Times*, 30 March 1978, p. 12). For the rise in pro-PLO sentiment among Israeli Arabs as a result of the invasion, see *Maariv* (20 March 1978), quoting Moshe Sharon, Advisor on Arab Affairs to Prime Minister Begin. For pro-PLO agitation on the West Bank and in the Gaza Strip during the invasion, see *Davar*, 16, 17, and 19 March 1978, and *Yediot Aharonot*, 21 March 1978, and particularly the commentary of Dani Rubinstein in *Davar*, 24 March 1978.

253. *New York Times*, 7 May 1978.

254. *New York Times,* 3 and 12 June 1978, respectively. The site of the attack in the Jordan Valley was Mehola, a settlement established on the West Bank.

255. First reported by *Le Monde* on 17 April 1978.

256. *New York Times,* 25 May 1978.

257. For the text of the Hoss-Arafat agreement see *al Nahar,* 25 March 1978, p. 1. Arafat agreed to a) facilitate UNIFIL's task; b) stop Palestinian transgressions in the south; c) end Palestinian armed "manifestations" in the south; d) return volunteers who had arrived in the country after the Israeli invasion; e) continue negotiations to arrive at a new arrangement compatible with Lebanese sovereignty and the interests of the Palestinian revolution. See p. 140.

258. *al Nahar,* 25 March 1978, p. 2.

259. See note 257 above.

260. See p. 47.

261. P. 113.

262. Pp. 38-39.

263. See pp. 95-96.

264. See p. 35 ff.

265. See p. 34 ff.

266. See pp. 33-34.

267. The last census to be held in Lebanon was in 1932. (See p. 35 and Notes 8, 16, 23, and 32 above). No census has been taken since that year because of the sensitivity of its political implications. The total current Lebanese population is assumed to be about 3,250,000. The Maronites assume and assert that the Christians are still in the majority. The probability is that (because of the higher Moslem birth rate) the distribution of the population is now 45-50 percent Christian and 50-55 percent Moslem; but no one really knows.

268. See *Memorandum Prepared by the Political Sub-Committee of the Conference of Lebanese Studies in regard to Four Possible Formulae for the Building of a New Lebanon* (in Arabic), Beirut, October 1976.

269. See Appendixes II and III, respectively.

270. See *Memorandum Prepared by the Political Sub-Committee,* etc. (Note 268 above), pp. 17ff.

271.*Ibid.,* pp. 12-13.

272. See p. 52.

273. For the extent of Presidential powers under the Constitution, see Note 29 above. The Constitutional Document (see AppendixII) allowed for the election of the Prime Minister by a 51 percent majority of the Parliament instead of his virtual selection and appointment by the President. For Maronite criticism of the Constitutional Document see *Texte du Document Constitutionnel* (14 *Fevrier* 1976): *La Reponse a ce Document* (1976).

274. See p. 67 ff.

275. As early as December 1975 the Syrians had tried to establish a rapport with the Phalanges. See p. 50 ff.

276. The revitalization of the debilitated Israeli-Lebanese Mixed Armistice Commission (ILMAC) was envisaged in the *Report of the Secretary General on*

the Implementation of Security Council resolution 425 (1978), S/12611, 19 March 1978, which was endorsed in toto by the Security Council—constituting Security Council resolution 426, 19 March 1978.

277. See author's article, "Thinking the Unthinkable: A Sovereign Palestinian State," in *Foreign Affairs*, July 1978.

APPENDIXES

I

THE CAIRO AGREEMENT, 3 NOVEMBER, 1969

Top Secret*

On Monday, 3rd November 1969, the Lebanese delegation, headed by Army Commander General Emile Bustani, and the Palestine Liberation Organization delegation, headed by Mr. Yasir Arafat, met in Cairo in the presence of the United Arab Republic Minister of Foreign Affairs, Mr. Mahmud Riyad, and the War Minister, General Muhammad Fawzi.

In consonance with the bonds of brotherhood and common destiny, relations between Lebanon and the Palestinian revolution must always be conducted on the bases of confidence, frankness, and positive cooperation for the benefit of Lebanon and the Palestinian revolution and within the framework of Lebanese sovereignty and security. The two delegations agreed on the following principles and measures:

The Palestinian Presence

It was agreed to reorganize the Palestinian presence in Lebanon on the basis of:

1. The right of work, residence, and movement for Palestinians currently residing in Lebanon;

2. The formation of Local Committees composed of Palestinians in the camps to care for the interests of Palestinians residing in these camps in cooperation with the local Lebanese authorities within the framework of Lebanese sovereignty;

3. The establishment of posts of the Palestinian Armed Struggle inside the camps for the purpose of cooperation with the Local Committees to

*Translated by the author from the Arabic text as published in *Le Livre Blanc Libanais: Documents Diplomatiquese 1975-1976*, Republique Libanaise, Ministre des Affaires Etrangeres et des Libanais D'Outre-Mer (Beyrouth, 1976) pp. 196-198.

ensure good relations with the Lebanese authorities. These posts shall undertake the task of regulating and determining the presence of arms in the camps within the framework of Lebanese security and the interests of the Palestinian revolution;

4. Palestinians resident in Lebanon are to be permitted to participate in the Palestinian revolution through the Palestinian Armed Struggle and in accordance with the principles of the sovereignty and security of Lebanon.

Commando Activity

It was agreed to facilitate commando activity by means of:

1. Facilitating the passage of commandos and specifying points of passage and reconnaissance in the border areas;

2. Safeguarding the road to the Arkub region;

3. The Palestinian Armed Struggle command shall undertake to control the conduct of all the members of its organizations and [to ensure] their non-interference in Lebanese affairs;

4. Establishing a joint command control of the Palestinian Armed Struggle and the Lebanese Army;

5. Ending the propaganda campaigns by both sides;

6. Conducting a census of Palestinian Armed Struggle personnel in Lebanon by their command;

7. Appointing Palestinian Armed Struggle representatives at Lebanese Army Headquarters to participate in the resolution of all emergency matters;

8. Studying the distribution of suitable points of concentration in border areas on which agreement is reached with the Lebanese Army command;

9. Regulating the entry, exit, and circulation of Palestinian Armed Struggle personnel;

10. Removal of the (commando) base at Jirun;

11. The Lebanese army shall facilitate the operation of medical, evacuation, and supply centers for commando activity;

12. Releasing detained personnel and confiscated arms;

13. It is understood that the Lebanese authorities, both civil and military, shall continue to exercise all their prerogatives and responsibilities in all areas of Lebanon in all circumstances;

14. The two delegations affirm that the Palestinian armed strugle is an activity in the interest of Lebanon as well as in that of the Palestinian revolution and all Arabs;

15. This agreement shall remain TOP SECRET and for the eyes of the commands only.

Head of the Lebanese Delegation   Head of the Palestinian
  General Emile Bustani   Delegation Yasir Arafat

II

LEBANESE PRESIDENT SULEIMAN FRANJIEH'S MESSAGE TO THE LEBANESE PEOPLE, BEIRUT, 14 FEBRUARY 1976: THE CONSTITUTIONAL DOCUMENT

(Excerpts)*

Lebanon is a sovereign, free, and independent Arab country.

It is the cradle of movements that have shed their light throughout the Arab world.

It enjoys a unique formula for coexistence between sects and religions.

It is the meeting place of the civilizations of the world and a unique human laboratory.

Its people both at home and abroad spread the views of the Arabs throughout the world.

The Arabs should realize that Lebanon must remain sovereign if it is to remain a trusty spokesman and ensure that the right continues to be made known for the benefit of our Arab brothers.

It is not necessary to remind the Palestinians that the Arab summit conference in Rabat charged Lebanon with the defence of their cause at the United Nations and that Lebanon performed this task from its belief and conviction that Jerusalem was the cradle of Christ, the first point to which the Muslims turned in prayer and their third most holy place, and that the Palestinian cause is just and right.

Nor do the Palestinians need reminding that if the Palestinian revolution was to coexist with Lebanese legitimacy in a small and compact territory like Lebanon, which is not really the territory of the revolution, there had to be consideration, precautions, and circumspection if the two were not to come into collision and explosion. [They know] that the situation today requires closer adherence to

*Al-Nahar, February 15, 1976. Translated by the Institute for Palestine Studies, Beirut.

agreements and greater punctiliousness in their implementation, especially in the case of the Cairo Agreement....

The present distribution of the three Presidential posts should be affirmed: the President of the Republic should be a Maronite, the President of the Chamber of Deputies a Shiite Muslim, and the Prime Minister a Sunnite Muslim, each of the three representing all the Lebanese.

Seats in parliament should be distributed on a fifty-fifty basis between Muslims and Christians, and proportionately within each confessional sect. In the light of this, the electoral law should be amended in such a way as to ensure that citizens are better represented.

The Prime Minister should be elected by a fifty-one percent majority of the Chamber of Deputies; then the Prime Minister should hold parliamentary consultations with a view to forming a government, and draw up the list of ministers in agreement with the President of the Republic, after which the decrees should be issued.

A majority of two-thirds of the Chamber of Deputies should be required for the passing of vital measures, and a majority of fifty-five percent for the election of the President of the Republic after the first ballot.

Provisions should be made for the President of the Republic, the Prime Minister, and the other ministers to be accountable and to this end a Supreme Council should be established to try Presidents and ministers.

The Prime Minister and the ministers should swear an oath of allegiance to the Constitution in the presence of the President of the Republic.

All decrees and draft laws should be signed by the President of the Republic and the Prime Minister together, after agreement has been reached between them. This does not apply to the decrees appointing the Prime Minister, accepting his resignation, or dismissing his government. The Prime Minister should enjoy all the powers customarily exercised by him.

A law should be promulgated to ensure that decrees and decisions are issued without delay.

The independence of the judiciary should be reinforced and a Supreme Constitutional Court should be established to decide whether laws and decrees are constitutional.

There should be greater administrative decentralization in administration.

The distribution of posts on a confessional basis should be abolished and appointments to posts should be on a basis of merit, though the principle of confessional equality should be maintained as regards senior posts.

A Supreme Council for Planning and Development should be established with the task of drawing up development plans.

Every effort should be made to ensure comprehensive social justice for all through financial, economic, and social reform.

The public educational system should be expanded so that free compulsory education may be available to all. Educational curricula should be revised in such a way as to ensure that they strengthen national unity.

A defense policy should be adopted and the army strengthened.

The press should exercise responsible freedom in accordance with the policy of achieving national unity and strengthening Lebanon's Arab and foreign relations.

The nationality law should be amended....

This program, alongside the unwritten National Pact, will constitute a further mainstay of Lebanon's national life which draws its strength from loyalty to Lebanon and from devoted service to her.

III

INAUGURAL SPEECH BY PRESIDENT ELIAS SARKIS OF LEBANON, SHTAURA, SEPTEMBER 23, 1976

(Excerpts)*

. . . The basic precondition, without which there can be no planning for future policy, is for the fighting to cease in order to pursue the road leading to dialogue . . . I am determined to play a positive role in order to arrive at political solutions resulting from the dialogue which would safeguard Lebanon's higher interests without harming the Palestinian cause. No matter what the obstacles are, I shall always act in accordance with my national duty and with consciousness toward my responsibility. Given the current situation, I feel that there is urgent need for rethinking the bases and methods of government in a more realistic manner which takes account of scientific progress. The bitter experience which Lebanon has lived through has proved that many things need to be changed in accordance with what is required. Our traditional understanding of a homeland needs to be corrected. A homeland is no longer sects, regions, and a people only but has become that historical, geographical, human, and fateful unity which guarantees to those who belong to it the opportunity for a decent life and a measure of dignity, stability, and rights in return for obligations.

. . . The institutions which make up the government of Lebanon, if we accept the foundations of the democratic parliamentary system in which I believe and of which I consider myself a guardian, these institutions contain nothing that is sacred and cannot be touched if we aim to develop them in accordance with the needs of Lebanese society. The really sacred things which cannot be touched are in my view Lebanon's

*Translated by the Institute for Palestine Studies, Beirut.

sovereignty and its territorial and national integrity. Apart from these, I am determined to initiate or champion any changes which I consider may contribute to national welfare, strengthen national solidarity, or provide the greatest measure of justice and equality among the Lebanese and in all regions of Lebanon....

The Lebanon we want is a Lebanon free of want and possessed of total social balance and full dignity. Sincere efforts were made towards this goal in the past but we still have a long way to go. Social equilibrium demands that we provide a decent living for all citizens, that we combat underdevelopment, disease, poverty, unemployment, and illiteracy, so that Lebanon would no longer have satiety at the expense of hunger, and luxury at the expense of poverty. Rather, there will be an equality of opportunity for all, where each citizen is entitled to work, education, and medical care according to his needs.

. . . The goals we seek cannot be attained all at once or by magic. Rather, this will be the result of long, hard labor and serious studies to which all Lebanese must contribute....

I take this opportunity to express my faith in individual enterprise. The importance of individual enterprise is limited only by the duty of the state to observe the private sector of the economy and control freedom of competition lest this become a means to chaos and exploitation. Society as a whole would then be threatened, especially its economically weaker groups. I further announce that it is the duty of the state to expand the area of the public sector in certain economic spheres and to intervene in order to offer guidance in a limited manner under emergency conditions, provided national interests demand such intervention. As for relations between capital and labor, which are the foundation stone of a modern society and of its stability, these are matters that require us to devote our continuous attention and efforts to arrive at just and equitable solutions which harm neither party. The prosperity of an institution is of course a precondition that should make the owners of the business invest their money and thus create jobs for labor, while labor wages should become proportionate to the contribution to production.

. . . The broad policy lines set down can only be implemented in an atmosphere of calm and security. The restoration of security to the country and to the minds of citizens is what we all seek. This will not be accomplished except by our own sincere cooperation which would allow us to rebuild the army and the internal security forces on bases that make them homogeneous forces working for a single homeland and well equipped in men and materiel to defend the homeland and safeguard its peace.

. . . At no point during its days of trouble or hope did Lebanon ever move far from its Arab reality. The nature of its belonging to that reality assigned to it a fateful role, the result both of destiny as well as free choice . . . Lebanon, that Arab country, shall faithfully be committed to every Arab cause. Its role inside its Arab family does not differ from the role of any other member regarding both rights and obligations. The problem of Palestine especially is Lebanon's problem too, as it is the problem of any Arab country . . . Lebanon will not spare any effort or sacrifice by using its own peculiar characteristics to play its role in combating the Israeli danger and helping the Palestinian people to reach their national objectives so that they may recover their homeland, and the region as a whole may then enjoy peace and security.

Relations between Lebanon and the Palestinian resistance together with the resultant fighting and incidents still taking place on the soil of this country must be properly handled and based upon a foundation of frankness and trust whereby the sovereignty of the country and the sanctity of all pacts and agreements would be respected to prevent any future violations....

For our part, as we acknowledge with gratitude the concern shown by sister Arab states over the crisis which has overtaken the country, we acknowledge also Syria's special fraternal relationship to us in the context of brotherhood, neighborliness, and common struggle, and the resultant state of mutual cooperation and coordination of effort. The presence of Syrian troops on Lebanese soil is to be understood in this context. I can declare that the future of this presence is in the hands of Lebanon's constitutional authorities which can, as regards the Syrian presence, adopt the stand that befits Lebanon's higher interests, in accordance with their responsibilities in the present circumstances.

IV

RESOLUTION ADOPTED BY THE LIMITED ARAB CONFERENCE, RIYAD, OCTOBER 18, 1976*

The limited Arab summit conference which met in Riyad, October 16-18, 1976, at the initiative of His Majesty King Khalid ibn 'Abd al-Aziz al-Saud, King of Saudi Arabia, and H. E. Sheikh Sabah al-Salim al-Sabah, Ruler of the State of Kuwait, having reviewed the resolution of the Arab League Council during the extraordinary sessions it held between June 8-10, June 23, July 1, and September 4, 1976 . . . the conference resolves the following:

1. A cease-fire and an end to all hostilities throughout Lebanese territory and by all parties in a final manner, as from 6:00 a.m. on October 21, 1976. All parties must abide by this in every respect.

2. To reinforce the present Arab peace forces so as to become a deterrent force acting inside Lebanon and under the personal command of the President of the Republic, provided their numbers are about 30,000 soldiers. Among the basic functions of this force will be the following:

a) To improve adherence to the cease-fire and the cessation of hostilities, to separate the combatants and deter all violators;

b) To implement the Cairo Agreement and its appendices;

c) To maintain internal security;

d) To supervise the withdrawal of armed elements to the places they occupied before April 13, 1975, and to remove all armed manifestations in accordance with the schedule set forth in the appendix;

e) To supervise the gathering of all heavy arms such as artillery,

*Published in *al-Nahar*, Beirut, October 18, 1976. Translated by the Institute for Palestine Studies, Beirut. This conference was attended by the heads of state of Egypt, Kuwait, Lebanon, Saudi Arabia, and Syria, as well as by Yasir Arafat, head of the PLO.

mortars, rocket launchers, armored vehicles, etc., with the various parties being held responsible for this;

f) To assist the Lebanese authorities when necessary to take over public institutions and utilities prior to reactivating them, and to protect public institutions, both civil and military.

3. To restore normal life to Lebanon to where it was before the beginning of these events, that is before April 13, 1975, as a first step and in accordance with the time schedule set forth in the appendix.

4. To implement the Cairo Agreement and its appendices and adherence to their text, in both letter and spirit, with the participating Arab states acting as guarantors. A committee shall be formed of representatives of the Kingdom of Saudi Arabia, the Arab Republic of Egypt, the Syrian Arab Republic, and the State of Kuwait, which shall undertake to coordinate its work with the President of Lebanon in all that concerns the implementation of the Cairo Agreement and its appendices. It shall function for 90 days starting from the date of the announcement of the ceasefire.

5. The Palestine Liberation Organization affirms its respect for Lebanon's sovereignty and well-being and its non-interference in its domestic affairs, all of which is based upon its total adherence to the national objectives of the Palestinian question. Lebanon's legitimate authorities, in return, guarantee the security and activities of the PLO in Lebanon within the framework of the Cairo Agreement and its appendices.

6. The participant Arab states undertake to respect Lebanon's sovereignty, security, and unity, both of its people and of its territory.

7. The participant Arab states affirm their adherence to the resolutions of the Arab summits in Algeria and Rabat and their support for Palestinian resistance represented by the PLO, as well as their respect for the right of the Palestinian people to struggle in all ways to recover its national rights.

8. Information media:

a) All media campaigns and negative psychological mobilization by all parties are to cease;

b) The media are to be directed towards the consolidation of the cease-fire, the establishment of peace, and the propagation of a spirit of cooperation and fraternity among all parties;

c) The governmental media must be reunified.

9. The schedule attached, which pertains to the implementation of these resolutions, is to be considered an inseparable part of them.

Time Schedule

1. A cease-fire and an end to hostilities is proclaimed throughout

Lebanese territory by all parties and in a final manner as from October 21, 1976 at 6:00 a.m.

2. Observation posts will be established by the deterrent force after setting up disengagement zones in areas of tension in order to consolidate the cease-fire and end the fighting.

3. Armed men are to be withdrawn, heavy weapons collected, and armed manifestations ended in accordance with the following time schedule:

a) Mount Lebanon: this is to be completed within five days;

b) The South: this is to be completed within five days;

c) Beirut and its environs: this is to be completed within seven days;

d) The North: this is to be completed within ten days.

4. Reopening of international highways:

a) The following highways are to be reopened within five days: Beirut-Masna, Beirut-Tripoli-the frontier, Beirut-Tyre, Beirut-Sidon, Marj Uyun-Masna;

b) Observation posts and patrols from the deterrent force are to be established on unsafe roads, in agreement with the relevant parties and the commander of the said force.

5. The legal Lebanese authorities shall take over all public utilities, institutions, and buildings, both military and civil:

a) They shall undertake to clear them of all armed men and non-employees and to entrust the Arab peace force with protecting them and facilitating their operation by their employees after these have taken them over. This is to take place within ten days;

b) These utilities shall be handed over to a central Lebanese governmental committee which in turn will form special subcommittees for each utility and institution, in order to make an inventory of contents and take over.

6. The forces required to reinforce the Arab peace force shall be formed with the agreement of the President of Lebanon, and these forces shall arrive within two weeks.

7. The Cairo Agreement and its appendices shall be implemented at a second stage, especially as regards the presence of arms and ammunition in the camps and the withdrawal of Palestinian armed forces that entered the country after the start of events, it being understood that this implementation shall be completed within 45 days starting from the date of the formation of the Arab deterrent force.

V

RESOLUTION ADOPTED BY THE ARAB SUMMIT CONFERENCE, CAIRO, OCTOBER 25-26, 1976*

The Kings and Presidents of member states of the Arab League at their meeting in Cairo at the headquarters of the League of Arab States on October 25 and 26, 1976, having reviewed the current situation in Lebanon, the results of the actions adopted at the six-state Arab summit conference held in Riyad on October 18, 1976, and affirming the importance of Arab solidarity, resolve the following:

1. The current situation in Lebanon:

a) To confirm the communiqué, the resolutions, and the appendices issued at the six-state Arab summit conference issued in Riyad on October 18, 1976, and attached herewith;

b) The Arab states shall contribute according to their abilities to the reconstruction of Lebanon; shall offer material aid necessary to remove all traces of armed conflict and of the damage sustained by the Lebanese and Palestinian peoples; they shall extend rapid aid to the Lebanese government and the Palestine Liberation Organization.

2. Strengthening of Arab solidarity:

To reaffirm the commitment of Arab Kings and Presidents to the resolutions of summit conferences and League council meetings in this regard, especially to the Charter of Arab solidarity promulgated at the Casablanca summit conference on September 15, 1965, and to undertake to implement all these resolutions completely and at once.

3. Financing the Arab peace force:

The Arab Summit conference, with the aim of furnishing the necessary financial resources for the expenses of the Arab peace forces in Lebanon stipulated in Resolution No. 2 of the Riyad summit conference

---

*Published in al-Nahar, Beirut, October 27, 1976. Translated by the Institute for Palestine Studies, Beirut.

resolutions, and having taken note of the report of the military secretariat of the Arab League, resolves the following:

a) To establish a special fund to take care of the expenditure and needs of the Arab peace forces in Lebanon;

b) Each member state of the Arab League shall contribute to this fund a certain percentage to be determined by each state according to its ability;

c) The President of Lebanon shall supervise this fund and shall, in consultation with the General Secretariat of the Arab League and with states contributing at least 10 percent establish general regulations for the fund outlining how the money is to be spent and the manner of its liquidation at the end of its term. The present system as regards the Arab peace forces shall remain in force until a new system is established;

d) The fund shall be established for a period of six months, renewable by resolution of the League Council which would meet at the request of the President of Lebanon.

UN SECURITY COUNCIL RESOLUTION 425, 19 MARCH 1978*

THE SECURITY COUNCIL,

TAKING NOTE of the letters of the permanent representative of Lebanon and the permanent representative of Israel, having heard the statements of the permanent representatives of Lebanon and Israel,

GRAVELY CONCERNED at the deterioration of the situation in the Middle East, and its consequences to the maintenance of international peace,

CONVINCED that the present situation impedes the achievement of a just peace in the Middle East,

1. CALLS for strict respect for the territorial integrity, sovereignty and political independence of Lebanon within its territorially recognized boundaries;

2. CALLS upon Israel immediately to cease its military action against Lebanese territorial integrity and withdraw forthwith its forces from all Lebanese territory;

3. DECIDES, in the light of the request of the government of Lebanon, to establish immediately under its authority a United Nations interim force for southern Lebanon for the purpose of confirming the withdrawal of Israeli forces, restoring international peace and security and assisting the government of Lebanon in ensuring the return of its effective authority in the area, the force to be composed of personnel drawn from state members of the United Nations;

4. REQUESTS the secretary general to report to the Council within 24 hours on the implementation of this resolution.

*New York Times, 20 March 1978.

UN SECURITY COUNCIL
RESOLUTION 426 (Excerpts)
19 MARCH, 1978*

. . . 1. The present report is submitted in pursuance of Security Council resolution 425 (1978) of 19 March 1978 in which the Council, among other things, decided to set up a United Nations Force in Lebanon under its authority and requested the Secretary General to submit a report to it on the implementation of the resolution.

Terms of reference

2. The terms of reference of the United Nations Interim Force in Lebanon (UNIFIL) are:

a) The Force will determine compliance with paragraph 2 of Security Council resolution 425 (1978).

b) The Force will confirm the withdrawal of Israeli forces, restore international peace and security, and assist the Government of Lebanon in ensuring the return of its effective authority in the area.

c) The Force will establish and maintain itself in an area of operation to be defined in the light of paragraph 2 (b) above.

d) The Force will use its best efforts to prevent the recurrence of fighting and to ensure that its area of operation is not utilized for hostile activities of any kind.

e) In the fulfillment of this task, the Force will have the cooperation of the Military Observers of UNTSO, who will continue to function on the Armistice Demarcation Line after the termination of the mandate of UNIFIL.

---

*The resolution was an endorsement of the full text of the *Report of the Secretary General on the Implementation of Security Council Resolution 425 (1978)* S/12611, 19 March 1978, from which the above is an excerpt.

BOOKS WRITTEN UNDER CENTER AUSPICES

The Soviet Bloc, Zbigniew K. Brzezinski (sponsored jointly with the Russian Research Center), 1960. Harvard University Press. Revised edition 1967.
The Necessity for Choice, by Henry A. Kissinger, 1961. Harper & Bros.
Rift and Revolt in Hungary, by Ferenc A. Váli, 1961. Harvard University Press.
Strategy and Arms Control, by Thomas C. Schelling and Morton H. Halperin, 1961. Twentieth Century Fund.
United States Manufacturing Investment in Brazil, by Lincoln Gordon and Engelbert L. Grommers, 1962. Harvard Business School.
The Economy of Cyprus, by A. J. Meyer, with Simos Vassiliou (sponsored jointly with the Center for Middle Eastern Studies), 1962. Harvard University Press.
Entrepreneurs of Lebanon, by Yusif A. Sayigh (sponsored jointly with the Center for Middle Eastern Studies), 1962. Harvard University Press.
Communist China 1955-1959: Policy Documents with Analysis, with a foreword by Robert R. Bowie and John K. Fairbank (sponsored jointly with the East Asian Research Center), 1962. Harvard University Press.
Somali Nationalism, by Saadia Touval, 1963. Harvard University Press.
The Dilemma of Mexico's Development, by Raymond Vernon, 1963. Harvard University Press.
Limited War in the Nuclear Age, by Morton H. Halperin, 1963. John Wiley & Sons. (Reprinted 1978, Greenwood Press.)
In Search of France, by Stanley Hoffmann *et al.,* 1963. Harvard University Press.
The Arms Debate, by Robert A. Levine, 1963. Harvard University Press.
Africans on the Land, by Montague Yudelman, 1964. Harvard University Press.
Counterinsurgency Warfare, by David Galula, 1964. Frederick A. Praeger, Inc.
People and Policy in the Middle East, by Max Weston Thornburg, 1964. W. W. Norton & Co.
Shaping the Future, by Robert R. Bowie, 1964. Columbia University Press.
Foreign Aid and Foreign Policy, by Edward S. Mason (sponsored jointly with the Council on Foreign Relations), 1964. Harper & Row.
How Nations Negotiate, by Fred Charles Iklé, 1964. Harper & Row.
Public Policy and Private Enterprise in Mexico, edited by Raymond Vernon, 1964. Harvard University Press.
China and the Bomb, by Morton H. Halperin (sponsored jointly with the East Asian Research Center), 1965. Frederick A. Praeger, Inc.
Democracy in Germany, by Fritz Erler (Jodidi Lectures), 1965. Harvard University Press.
The Troubled Partnership, by Henry A. Kissinger (sponsored jointly with the Council on Foreign Relations), 1965. McGraw-Hill Book Co.

The Rise of Nationalism in Central Africa, by Robert I. Rotberg, 1965. Harvard University Press.

Pan-Africanism and East African Integration, by Joseph S. Nye, Jr., 1965. Harvard University Press.

Communist China and Arms Control, by Morton H. Halperin and Dwight H. Perkins (sponsored jointly with the East Asian Research Center), 1965. Frederick A. Praeger, Inc.

Problems of National Strategy, ed. Henry Kissinger, 1965. Frederick A. Praeger, Inc.

Deterrence before Hiroshima: The Airpower Background of Modern Strategy, by George H. Quester, 1966. John Wiley & Sons.

Containing the Arms Race, by Jeremy J. Stone, 1966. M.I.T. Press.

Germany and the Atlantic Alliance: The Interaction of Strategy and Politics, by James L. Richardson, 1966. Harvard University Press.

Arms and Influence, by Thomas C. Schelling, 1966. Yale University Press.

Political Change in a West African State, by Martin Kilson, 1966. Harvard University Press.

Planning Without Facts: Lessons in Resource Allocation from Nigeria's Development, by Wolfgang F. Stolper, 1966. Harvard University Press.

Export Instability and Economic Development, by Alasdair I. MacBean, 1966. Harvard University Press.

Foreign Policy and Democratic Politics, by Kenneth N. Waltz (sponsored jointly with the Institute of War and Peace Studies, Columbia University), 1967, Little, Brown & Co.

Contemporary Military Strategy, by Morton H. Halperin, 1967. Little, Brown & Co.

Sino-Soviet Relations and Arms Control, ed. Morton H. Halperin (sponsored jointly with the East Asian Research Center), 1967. M.I.T. Press.

Africa and United States Policy, by Rupert Emerson, 1967. Prentice-Hall.

Elites in Latin America, edited by Seymour M. Lipset and Aldo Solari, 1967. Oxford University Press.

Europe's Postwar Growth, by Charles P. Kindleberger, 1967. Harvard University Press.

The Rise and Decline of the Cold War, by Paul Seabury, 1967. Basic Books.

Student Politics, ed. S. M. Lipset, 1967. Basic Books.

Pakistan's Development: Social Goals and Private Incentives, by Gustav F. Papanek, 1967. Harvard University Press.

Strike a Blow and Die: A Narrative of Race Relations in Colonial Africa, by George Simeon Mwase, ed. Robert I. Rotberg, 1967. Harvard University Press.

Party Systems and Voter Alignments, edited by Seymour M. Lipset and Stein Rokkan, 1967. Free Press.

Agrarian Socialism, by Seymour M. Lipset, revised edition, 1968. Doubleday Anchor.

Aid, Influence, and Foreign Policy, by Joan M. Nelson, 1968. The Macmillan Company.

Development Policy: Theory and Practice, edited by Gustav F. Papanek, 1968. Harvard University Press.

International Regionalism, by Joseph S. Nye, 1968. Little, Brown & Co.

Revolution and Counterrevolution, by Seymour M. Lipset, 1968. Basic Books.

Political Order in Changing Societies, by Samuel P. Huntington, 1968. Yale University Press.

The TFX Decision: McNamara and the Military, by Robert J. Art, 1968. Little, Brown & Co.

Korea: The Politics of the Vortex, by Gregory Henderson, 1968. Harvard University Press.

Political Development in Latin America, by Martin Needler, 1968. Random House.

The Precarious Republic, by Michael Hudson, 1968. Random House.

The Brazilian Capital Goods Industry, 1929-1964 (sponsored jointly with the Center for Studies in Education and Development), by Nathaniel H. Leff, 1968. Harvard University Press.

Economic Policy-Making and Development in Brazil, 1947-1964, by Nathaniel H. Leff, 1968. John Wiley & Sons.

Turmoil and Transition: Higher Education and Student Politics in India, edited by Philip G. Altbach, 1968. Lalvani Publishing House (Bombay).

German Foreign Policy in Transition, by Karl Kaiser, 1968. Oxford University Press.

Protest and Power in Black Africa, edited by Robert I. Rotberg, 1969. Oxford University Press.

Peace in Europe, by Karl E. Birnbaum, 1969. Oxford University Press.

The Process of Modernization: An Annotated Bibliography on the Sociocultural Aspects of Development, by John Brode, 1969. Harvard University Press.

Students in Revolt, edited by Seymour M. Lipset and Philip G. Altbach, 1969. Houghton Mifflin.

Agricultural Development in India's Districts: The Intensive Agricultural Districts Programme, by Dorris D. Brown, 1970. Harvard University Press.

Authoritarian Politics in Modern Society: The Dynamics of Established One-Party Systems, edited by Samuel P. Huntington and Clement H. Moore, 1970. Basic Books.

Nuclear Diplomacy, by George H. Quester, 1970. Dunellen.

The Logic of Images in International Relations, by Robert Jervis, 1970. Princeton University Press.

Europe's Would-Be Polity, by Leon Lindberg and Stuart A. Scheingold, 1970. Prentice-Hall.

Taxation and Development: Lessons from Colombian Experience, by Richard M. Bird, 1970. Harvard University Press.

Lord and Peasant in Peru: A Paradigm of Political and Social Change, by F. LaMond Tullis, 1970. Harvard University Press.

The Kennedy Round in American Trade Policy: The Twilight of the GATT? by John W. Evans, 1971. Harvard University Press.

Korean Development: The Interplay of Politics and Economics, by David C. Cole and Princeton N. Lyman, 1971. Harvard University Press.

Development Policy II—The Pakistan Experience, edited by Walter P. Falcon and Gustav F. Papanek, 1971. Harvard University Press.

Higher Education in a Transitional Society, by Philip G. Altbach, 1971. Sindhu Publications (Bombay).

Studies in Development Planning, edited by Hollis B. Chenery, 1971. Harvard University Press.

Passion and Politics, by Seymour M. Lipset with Gerald Schaflander, 1971. Little, Brown & Co.

Political Mobilization of the Venezuelan Peasant, by John D. Powell, 1971. Harvard University Press.

Higher Education in India, edited by Amrik Singh and Philip Altbach, 1971. Oxford University Press (Delhi).

The Myth of the Guerrilla, by J. Bowyer Bell, 1971. Blond (London) and Knopf (New York).

International Norms and War between States: Three Studies in International Politics, by Kjell Goldmann, 1971. Published jointly by Läromedelsförlagen (Sweden) and the Swedish Institute of International Affairs.

Peace in Parts: Integration and Conflict in Regional Organization, by Joseph S. Nye, Jr., 1971. Little, Brown & Co.

Sovereignty at Bay: The Multinational Spread of U.S. Enterprise, by Raymond Vernon, 1971. Basic Books.

Defense Strategy for the Seventies (revision of *Contemporary Military Strategy*) by Morton H. Halperin, 1971. Little, Brown & Co.

Peasants Against Politics: Rural Organization in Brittany, 1911-1967, by Suzanne Berger, 1972. Harvard University Press.

Transnational Relations and World Politics, edited by Robert O. Keohane and Joseph S. Nye, Jr., 1972. Harvard University Press.

Latin American University Students: A Six-Nation Study, by Arthur Liebman, Kenneth N. Walker, and Myron Glazer, 1972. Harvard University Press.

The Politics of Land Reform in Chile, 1950-1970: Public Policy, Political Institutions and Social Change, by Robert R. Kaufman, 1972. Harvard University Press.

The Boundary Politics of Independent Africa, by Saadia Touval, 1972. Harvard University Press.

The Politics of Nonviolent Action, by Gene E. Sharp, 1973. Porter Sargent.

System 37 Viggen: Arms, Technology, and the Domestication of Glory, by Ingemar Dörfer, 1973. Universitets forlaget (Oslo).

University Students and African Politics, by William John Hanna, 1974. Africana Publishing Company.

Organizing the Transnational: The Experience with Transnational Enterprise in Advanced Technology, by M. S. Hochmuth, 1974. Sijthoff (Leiden).

Becoming Modern, by Alex Inkeles and David H. Smith, 1974. Harvard University Press.

The United States and West Germany 1945-1973: A Study in Alliance Politics, by Roger Morgan (sponsored jointly with the Royal Institute of International Affairs), 1974. Oxford University Press.

Multinational Corporations and the Politics of Dependence: Copper in Chile, 1945-1973, by Theodore Moran, 1974. Princeton University Press.

The Andean Group: A Case Study in Economic Integration Among Developing Countries, by David Morawetz, 1974. M.I.T. Press.

Kenya: The Politics of Participation and Control, by Henry Bienen, 1974. Princeton University Press.

Land Reform and Politics: A Comparative Analysis, by Hung-chao Tai, 1974. University of California Press.

Big Business and the State: Changing Relations in Western Europe, edited by Raymond Vernon, 1974. Harvard University Press.

Economic Policymaking in a Conflict Society: The Argentine Case, by Richard D. Mallon and Juan V. Sourrouille, 1975. Harvard University Press.

New States in the Modern World, edited by Martin Kilson, 1975. Harvard University Press.

Revolutionary Civil War: The Elements of Victory and Defeat, by David Wilkinson, 1975. Page-Ficklin Publications.

Politics and the Migrant Poor in Mexico City, by Wayne A. Cornelius, 1975. Stanford University Press.

East Africa and the Orient: Cultural Syntheses in Pre-Colonial Times, ed. H. Neville Chittick and Robert I. Rotberg, 1975. Africana Publishing Company.

No Easy Choice: Political Participation in Developing Countries, by Samuel P. Huntington and Joan M. Nelson, 1976. Harvard University Press.

The Politics of International Monetary Reform—The Exchange Crisis, by Michael J. Brenner, 1976. Ballinger Publishing Co.

The International Politics of Natural Resources, by Zuhayr Mikdashi, 1976. Cornell University Press.

The Oil Crisis, edited by Raymond Vernon, 1976. W. W. Norton & Co.

Social Change and Political Participation in Turkey, by Ergun Ozbudun,

1976. Princeton University Press.

The Arabs, Israelis, and Kissinger: A Secret History of American Diplomacy in the Middle East, by Edward R. F. Sheehan, 1976. Reader's Digest Press.

Perception and Misperception in International Politics, by Robert Jervis, 1976. Princeton University Press.

Power and Interdependence, by Robert O. Keohane and Joseph S. Nye, Jr., 1977. Little, Brown & Co.

Soldiers in Politics: Military Coups and Governments, by Eric Nordlinger, 1977. Prentice-Hall.

The Military and Politics in Modern Times: On Professionals, Praetorians, and Revolutionary Soldiers, by Amos Perlmutter, 1977. Yale University Press.

Money and Power: Banks and the World Monetary System, by Jonathan David Aronson, 1977. Sage Publications.

Bankers and Borders: The Case of the American Banks in Britain, by Janet Kelly, 1977. Ballinger Publishing Co.

Shattered Peace: The Origins of the Cold War and the National Security State, by Daniel Yergin, 1977. Houghton Mifflin.

Storm Over the Multinationals: The Real Issues, by Raymond Vernon, 1977. Harvard University Press.

Political Generations and Political Development, ed. Richard J. Samuels, 1977. Lexington Books.

Cuba: Order and Revolution, by Jorge I. Dominguez, 1978. Harvard University Press.

Defending the National Interest: Raw Materials Investments and American Foreign Policy, by Stephen D. Krasner, 1978. Princeton University Press.

Commodity Conflict: The Political Economy of International Commodity Negotiations, by L. N. Rangarajan, 1978. Cornell University Press and Croom Helm (London).

Israel: Embattled Ally, by Nadav Safran, 1978. Harvard University Press.

Access to Power: Political Participation by the Urban Poor in Developing Nations, by Joan M. Nelson, 1979. Princeton University Press.

Standing Guard: The Protection of Foreign Investment, by Charles Lipson, 1979. University of California Press.

The Quest for Self-Determination, by Dov Ronen, 1979. Yale University Press.

The Rational Peasant: The Political Economy of Rural Society in Vietnam, by Samuel L. Popkin, 1979. University of California Press.

Legislative-Executive Relations and the Politics of United States Foreign Economics Policy 1929-1979, by Robert Pastor, 1980. University of California Press.

Insurrection and Loyalty: The Breakdown of the Spanish American Empire, by Jorge Dominguez, 1980. Harvard University Press.

The Collapse of Welfare Reform: Political Institutions, Policy and the Poor in Canada and the United States, by Christopher Leman, 1980. M.I.T. Press.

Palestinian Society and Politics, by Joel S. Migdal *et al.*, 1980. Princeton University Press.

Weak States in the International System, by Michael Handel, 1980. Frank Cass, London.

HARVARD STUDIES IN INTERNATIONAL AFFAIRS*

(Formerly Occasional Papers in International Affairs).

†1. *A Plan for Planning: The Need for a Better Method of Assisting Underdeveloped Countries on Their Economic Policies,* by Gustav F. Papanek, 1961.

†2. *The Flow of Resources from Rich to Poor,* by Alan D. Neale, 1961.

†3. *Limited War: An Essay on the Development of the Theory and an Annotated Bibliography,* by Morton H. Halperin, 1962.

†4. *Reflections on the Failure of the First West Indian Federation,* by Hugh W. Springer, 1962.

5. *On the Interaction of Opposing Forces under Possible Arms Agreements,* by Glenn A. Kent, 1963. 36 pp. $1.75.

†6. *Europe's Northern Cap and the Soviet Union,* by Nils Orvik, 1963.

7. *Civil Administration in the Punjab: An Analysis of a State Government in India,* by E. N. Mangat Rai, 1963. 82 pp. $2.25.

8. *On the Appropriate Size of a Development Program,* by Edward S. Mason, 1964. 24 pp. $1.50.

9. *Self-Determination Revisited in the Era of Decolonization,* by Rupert Emerson, 1964. 64 pp. $2.25.

10. *The Planning and Execution of Economic Development in Southeast Asia,* by Clair Wilcox, 1965. 37 pp. $1.75.

11. *Pan-Africanism in Action,* by Albert Tevoedjre, 1965. 88 pp. $2.95.

12. *Is China Turning In?* by Morton Halperin, 1965. 34 pp. $1.75.

†13. *Economic Development in India and Pakistan,* by Edward S. Mason, 1966.

14. *The Role of the Military in Recent Turkish Politics,* by Ergun Ozbudun, 1966. 54 pp. $1.95.

†15. *Economic Development and Individual Change: A Social Psychological Study of the Comilla Experiment in Pakistan,* by Howard Schuman, 1967.

16. *A Select Bibliography on Students, Politics, and High Education,* by Philip G. Altbach, UMHE Revised Edition, 1970. 65 pp. $3.25.

17. *Europe's Political Puzzle: A Study on the Fouchet Negotiations and the 1963 Veto,* by Alessandro Silj, 1967. 178 pp. $4.25.

18. *The Cap and the Straits: Problems of Nordic Security,* by Jan Klenberg, 1968. 19 pp. $1.50.

19. *Cyprus: The Law and Politics of Civil Strife,* by Linda B. Miller, 1968. 97 pp. $3.50.

*Available from Harvard University Center for International Affairs, 1737 Cambridge St. Cambridge, Massachusetts 02138
†Out of print. Reprints may be ordered from AMS Press, Inc., 56 East 13th Street, New York, N.Y. 10003

†20. *East and West Pakistan: A Problem in the Political Economy of Regional Planning*, by Md. Anisur Rahman, 1968.

†21. *Internal War and International Systems: Perspectives on Method*, by George A. Kelly and Linda B. Miller, 1969.

†22. *Migrants, Urban Poverty, and Instability in Developing Nations*, by Joan M. Nelson, 1969. 81 pp.

 23. *Growth and Development in Pakistan, 1955-1969*, by Joseph J. Stern and Walter P. Falcon, 1970. 94 pp. $3.50.

 24. *Higher Education in Developing Countries: A Select Bibliography*, by Philip G. Altbach, 1970. 118 pp. $4.50.

 25. *Anatomy of Political Institutionalization: The Case of Israel and Some Comparative Analyses*, by Amos Perlmutter, 1970. 60 pp. $2.95.

†26. *The German Democratic Republic from the Sixties to the Seventies*, by Peter Christian Ludz, 1970. 100 pp.

 27. *The Law in Political Integration: The Evolution and Integrative Implications of Regional Legal Processes in the European Community*, by Stuart A. Scheingold, 1971. 63 pp. $2.95.

 29. *Conflict Regulation in Divided Societies*, by Eric A. Nordlinger, 1972. 142 pp. $4.95.

 30. *Israel's Political-Military Doctrine*, by Michael I. Handel, 1973. 101 pp. $3.75.

 31. *Italy, NATO, and the European Community: The Interplay of Foreign Policy and Domestic Politics*, by Primo Vannicelli, 1974. 67 + x pp. $3.75.

 32. *The Choice of Technology in Developing Countries: Some Cautionary Tales*, by C. Peter Timmer, John W. Thomas, Louis T. Wells, Jr., and David Morawetz, 1975. 114 pp. $3.95.

 33. *The International Role of the Communist Parties of Italy and France*, by Donald L. M. Blackmer and Annie Kriegel, 1975. 67 + x pp. $3.50.

 34. *The Hazards of Peace: A European View of Detente*, by Juan Cassiers, 1976. 94 pp. $3.50.

 35. *Oil and the Middle East War: Europe in the Energy Crisis*, by Robert J. Lieber, 1976. 75 + x pp. $3.45.

 37. *Climatic Change and World Affairs*, by Crispin Tickell, 1977. 78 pp. $3.95.

 38. *Conflict and Violence in Lebanon: Confrontation in the Middle East*, by Walid Khalidi, 1979. Ca. 240 pp. $12.95, cloth; $6.95, paper.

 39. *Diplomatic Dispute: U.S. Conflict with Iran, Japan, and Mexico*, by Robert L. Paarlberg, ed., Eul. Y. Park, and Donald L. Wyman, 1979. 173 pp. $11.95, cloth; $5.95, paper.

 40. *Commandos and Politicians: Elite Military Units in Modern Democracies*, by Eliot A. Cohen, 1978. 136 pp. $8.95, cloth; $3.95, paper.

41. *Yellow Earth, Green Jade: Constants in Chinese Political Mores,* by Simon de Beaufort, 1979. 90 pp. $8.95, cloth; $3.95, paper.
42. *The Future of North America: Canada, The United States, and Quebec Nationalism,* edited by Elliot J. Feldman and Neil Nevitte, 1979. 378 pp. $13.95, cloth; $6.95, paper. (In Canada, $14.95 and $7.95, respectively.)